# Who Benefits from India's Public Services?

Published by Academic Foundation
*in collaboration with*

PUBLIC AFFAIRS CENTRE,
Bangalore

Public Affairs Centre (PAC) is a think-tank cum citizen action support group dedicated to the cause of improving the quality of governance in India. Registered as a non-profit society in Bangalore, PAC's focus is primarily on areas in which citizens can play a proactive role in improving governance. PAC undertakes and supports research on public policy and services, disseminates research findings, facilitates collective citizen action, and provides advisory services to state and non-state agencies jointly with Public Affairs Foundation, a sister organisation. It networks with other like-minded groups for linking knowledge and citizen action. The Centre is widely known for its pioneering "Citizen Report Cards" on public services, work on electoral transaparency, and its recently launched "Coalition Against Corruption." Its novel concepts and tools are being replicated in other parts of India as well as in other countries. For more details, visit PAC's website: **www.pacindia.org**.

*The Authors:*

**Samuel Paul** is founder and chairperson of Public Affairs Centre, Bangalore, India. He spearheaded the development of "Citizen Report Cards" as an accountability tool, an experience described in his book *Holding the State to Account: Citizen Monitoring in Action* (Books for Change, 2002). A former director and professor of economics at Indian Institute of Management, Ahmedabad (IIM-A), he has served as advisor to the Indian government, the United Nations, the World Bank, and the International Labour Organisation.

**Suresh Balakrishnan** is Chief Technical Advisor with UNDP in Laos, and was previously Executive Director of PAC. Dr. Balakrishnan has worked on monitoring and evaluation in the governance and development sectors, with national, provincial and city governments, as well as international agencies and NGOs, in Asia and Africa for over twenty years.

**Gopakumar Thampi** is Executive Director of Public Affairs Foundation, Bangalore and former Head of the Asia Desk at the Transparency International Secretariat in Berlin. Gopakumar holds a doctoral degree in Entrepreneurial Studies and post graduate qualifications in Economics, Journalism & Mass Communication and Conflict Resolution.

**Sita Sekhar** is Chief Research Officer at Public Affairs Centre. She holds a doctoral degree in Labour Economics and postgraduate qualification in Econometrics, and has taught at college level. Dr. Sekhar's work profile also encompasses technical and advisory support to international and national development agencies and organisations.

**M. Vivekananda** is Senior Advisor to Public Affairs Foundation, Bangalore and a former faculty member at the Institute for Social and Economic Change, Bangalore. He is an economist with an academic background in Statistics and Econometrics and has varied work experience with research, government, consultancy organisations, and also NGOs. He has authored four books and many articles in reputed professional journals.

# Who Benefits from India's Public Services?

*A People's Audit of Five Basic Services*

SAMUEL PAUL
SURESH BALAKRISHNAN
GOPAKUMAR K. THAMPI
SITA SEKHAR
M. VIVEKANANDA

**Academic Foundation**
NEW DELHI

First published in 2006
by
ACADEMIC FOUNDATION
4772-73 / 23 Bharat Ram Road, (23 Ansari Road),
Darya Ganj, New Delhi - 110 002 (India).
Phones : 23245001 / 02 / 03 / 04.
Fax : +91-11-23245005.
E-mail : academic@vsnl.com
www.academicfoundation.com

*in association with*

Public Affairs Centre (PAC)
Bangalore, India
www.pacindia.org



Photo credit (cover photograph): 1 2 3 oochappan
(http://www.pbase.com/oochappan/)

*Who Benefits from India's Public Services?*
*A People's Audit of Five Basic Services*
by
Samuel Paul, Suresh Balakrishnan
Gopakumar K. Thampi, Sita Sekhar, and M. Vivekananda

ISBN 81-7188-527-6

Typeset and designed by Italics India, New Delhi

Printed and bound in India

# CONTENTS

# List of Tables and Figures

## TABLES

## FIGURES

# List of Annexures

# Preface

In most developing countries, government is the sole provider of essential public services to the citizens as the public goods nature of many of these services does not make it attractive for the private sector to undertake their production and delivery. The state and local governments in India, for example, devote a major part of their budgets for public services and their infrastructure. But whether these huge public investments have resulted in a more efficient and equitable delivery of public services and have helped reduce inter-state and intra-population disparities is not clear. Many believe that the lack of reforms in the provider agencies and the limited 'exit' options available to the people continue to make it difficult for the weaker sections of society to access these services.

Experts have always evinced much interest in assessing governmental performance by tracking public expenditure and its long term outcomes. While public expenditure monitoring is a useful practice, it cannot shed much light on the issues of quality, effectiveness and productivity of services. A common practice is to assess the performance of a government and its development strategy by tracking outcome measures such as poverty reduction, infant mortality, longevity, and literacy levels. Comparing countries and regions in terms of these measures enables the experts to pronounce a verdict on the efficacy of governments, efficiency of public expenditure and the like. But as an approach to judging the performance of governments as service providers, it leaves much to be desired.

In reality, governments could have done much more to monitor the quality and effectiveness of the essential services for which they have invested so much. Yet all evidence points to a poor track record on their part to monitor public service delivery and its outcomes. Planning new projects and spending public funds are often higher priority for governments than monitoring performance and outcomes. There are many who believe that in the absence of external pressure by an informed public, it is unlikely that government's monitoring of services will improve.

The theme of this book is that 'user feedback' on public services can be used as an approach to correct this imbalance. We present here an assessment of five basic services across the different states of India based on user feedback gathered through a stratified random sample survey of nearly 37,000 households. The systematic information, thus, generated can be used to compare and rate the states in terms of their performance and also to explore demographic and spatial variations. It is a cost effective way to give greater visibility to this issue and to attract political attention. We believe that comparisons of services over time, using public feedback, are an efficient way to assess provider agencies and make them more accountable to the people for their performance.

The intent of this exercise is to provide public policymakers and political leaders an opportunity to bring in strategic reforms and re-orient delivery mechanisms and priorities by treating the findings as diagnostic pointers. By disseminating the key findings to the larger public, the study hopes to trigger an informed debate within the civil society to make governments more accountable and responsive. PAC's decade long experience with citizen report cards in many cities and sectors highlights the potency of user feedback to catalyse reforms.

The summary findings of this large scale user feedback study were released by Dr. Manmohan Singh in 2002 in New Delhi. Since then, seminars to discuss the findings were held in six state capitals and other centres across India. More detailed analysis of the data, especially econometric work to probe the relationships between satisfaction scores and service quality attributes, was also undertaken during the past two years. A summary of the findings was published in the *Economic and Political Weekly* (February 28, 2004).

Many persons and organisations have advised and assisted us in the course of this project. Dr. V.M. Rao, Mr. T.R. Satishchandran, Dr. G. Thimmaiah, and Dr. V.S. Vyas provided valuable guidance to the research team at different stages. Useful comments on the study were also received from Dr. K.R.S. Murthy, Dr. Kamla Chowdhry, Dr. S.L. Rao, Dr. Nirmala Murthy, Dr. S.S. Meenakshisundaram and Dr. Mark Robinson. Able research assistance was provided by Arti Pandit, Toolika Ojha, Albert Lobo, Himanshu Verma, K. Vaijayanti, Biju U. Warrier, Nischinth Keshav, T. Jayakumar, Venugopal Reddy and Verghese Kurian. Shylaja Prabhakar was responsible for timely editorial and administrative support. AC Neilson ORG-MARG provided the detailed design of the field research, execution of the survey and the preliminary data analysis. The Project was funded through the internal resources of Public Affairs Centre and a grant from the Ford Foundation. The authors are grateful to all the individuals and organisations mentioned above for their invaluable contributions. The authors alone are responsible for any errors that remain.

# Acronyms

| | |
|---|---|
| ANM | Auxiliary Nurse and Midwife. |
| CHC | Community Health Centre. |
| CSO | Central Statistical Organisation. |
| FCI | Food Corporation of India. |
| FPS | Fair Price Shop. |
| GDP | Gross Domestic Product. |
| GoI | Government of India. |
| ICD | Income Capacity Disadvantage. |
| ICDS | Integrated Child Development Scheme |
| ICMR | Indian Council for Medical Research |
| IDSMT | Integrated Development of Small and Medium Towns |
| Lpcd | Litres per capita per day |
| MNP | Minimum Need Programme |
| NABARD | National Bank for Agricultural and Rural Development |
| NCAER | National Council for Applied Economic Research |
| NCERT | National Council for Education Research and Training |

| | |
|---|---|
| NDWM | National Drinking Water Mission |
| NGOs | Non-governmental Organisations. |
| NRRDA | The National Rural Roads Development Agency |
| NFHS | National Family Health Survey |
| NSS | National Sample Survey |
| PAC | Public Affairs Centre |
| PDS | Public Distribution System |
| PHC | Primary Health Centre |
| PMGSY | Pradhan Mantri Gram Sadak Yojana (Prime Minister's Village Road Programme) |
| SC/ST | Scheduled Castes and Scheduled Tribes as per Constitution of India |
| SPSS | Statistical Product and Service Solutions |
| UNICEF | United Nations Children's Fund (formerly United Nations International Children's Emergency Fund) |

# Glossary

| | |
|---|---|
| *Antyodaya* families | Below poverty line families. |
| *Anganwadi* | Childcare centre. |
| Fair Price Shop | Public distribution outlet. |
| *Kutcha* Road | Non-metalled road. |
| Lakh | One hundred thousand. |
| *Morcha* | Protest procession. |
| *Panchayat* | Council of elected members taking decisions on issues key to the villager's social, cultural and economic life. |
| *Pucca* Road | Metalled road. |
| Ration Shop | Public distribution outlet |
| *Sarpanch* | Village council (*panchayat*) head. |
| Tarred Road | Asphalted road. |
| *Taluka* | A *taluka* or *tehsil* is an administrative sub-division. The two terms are functionally equivalent, usage preference is determined by region. As an entity of local government, *tehsils/talukas* have fiscal and administrative powers roughly equivalent to the division of counties found in many non-Asian countries. A *tehsil/taluka* is typically part of a larger District and typically contains villages and/or municipalities. |

# Overview

State governments are the major providers of basic services to the people, along with *Panchayats* (rural) and *Nagarapalika* (urban) local governments. Though State governments earmark large resources for providing services, these investments do not automatically ensure high quality of service, equity in access or adequate efficiency. Public Affairs Centre embarked on a nation-wide survey of selected public services in 2001 to assess and benchmark the effectiveness and quality of basic services from the perspective of those to whom it matters most—the users of services. The study was carried out in 24 states and this report presents the consolidated findings of the 24 state reports.

## Why Do We Need Citizen Feedback on Services?

Governments spend a significant part of our scarce resources on basic public services. The outcomes and effectiveness of this expenditure, however, are not easy to observe and measure. Governments typically monitor the progress of expenditure on schemes, and measure achievement mostly in terms of inputs. Other reports, including Human Development Reports, present information on long-term outcomes, like literacy, infant mortality and life expectancy, to name a few. But whether these services are actually delivered efficiently and meet the real needs of the people cannot be determined by expenditure monitoring or head counts alone. Services delivered may be of low quality or entail unwarranted delays. Effectiveness of public expenditure can be greatly reduced by these shortcomings.

Long term service outcomes cannot be achieved when the delivery of basic services in the short term is ineffective or inefficient. Those who manage these services should therefore begin by ensuring that proper service delivery takes place. They will be aided greatly in this endeavour if they are encouraged to benchmark their performance against realistic service standards. It is against this backdrop that the Millennial Survey was undertaken with a focus on service delivery dimensions. As will be seen from the following chapters, the Survey has generated data that will help assess service delivery in terms of dimensions that matter to the people who are the users of services, Ease of access to service facilities, aspects of the quality of service and user satisfaction are examples of these dimensions. These indicators on quality and satisfaction with services (e.g. frequency of breakdown of hand pumps, satisfaction with behaviour of doctors and display of prices at ration shops, etc.) are measures of current performance. They can provide a basis for corrective action in the short term and act as benchmarks for assessing service delivery over time.

Underlying the survey is the belief that feedback from the people who are at the receiving end of public services can effectively help fill the information gaps in assessing effectiveness of public expenditure. Citizens who interact with service providers and receive their services are not experts on the technologies and delivery systems of the services. Nevertheless, they can shed useful light on the efficiency and effectiveness of services. For example, citizens can testify whether in fact they are able to avail of a service on the conditions specified by the provider and report the level of their satisfaction with responsiveness of the service provider. Such feedback therefore is a cost effective way to articulate the 'voice' of the people. If the feedback is positive, there is a good chance that public expenditure is leading to desired outcomes and impact. If it is negative in important respects, the chances are that scarce resources may have been wasted by the government. Citizen feedback can thus provide early warning signals that could be used by governments to redesign services and make mid-course corrections so as to improve the service outcomes.

## How Did We Assess these Services?

A service is completely effective only if the user is satisfied with it in all respects. This study therefore measured effectiveness by examining public service on four key aspects:

Access – proximity of the users to the service provided.

Usage – to what extent do they use it?

Reliability – how dependable is the service.

Satisfaction – user's rating of the overall effectiveness of the service.

The survey focused on five basic public services, provided mainly by the Government. Also, these are services that matter a great deal to the poorer sections of the population:

- Drinking Water
- Health Care

- Road Transport
- Public Distribution System
- Primary Education & Child Care

The household survey covered 36,542 households selected from rural and urban areas of 24 Indian states. The rural component of the sample consists of 26,796 households selected from 2502 villages spread over 148 districts of the 24 states. The urban component of the sample consists of 9746 households selected from 107 towns spread over the 24 states.

## What are Our Findings?

The key point revealed in the study is that governments have focused on extending people's access to these public services, but they have done less about quality, reliability and effectiveness of the services. One obvious reason is that politicians feel that expanding access to a service gets them far more political mileage, whereas quality and effectiveness are more difficult to assess and much less noticed. We need a shift from spending to ensuring that people truly benefit from a service.

The study highlights not only the problems faced by the weaker sections of society in their use of public services, but also throws up inter-state comparisons on the condition of these services in terms of access to public services, the extent of corruption and quality of governance. The study has shown that the performance of public transport service and health care is better in richer states compared to poorer states. On the other hand, there is less difference between the rich and poor states in delivering services such as drinking water, PDS and primary education.

Governments have made much of their concern for ensuring that basic services reach the poor and the marginalised. These sections face problems not only because of low incomes but other factors like location in remote areas. It was found that weaker sections did not face disadvantages across all aspects of services. But there were important disadvantages they faced on ease of access to government facilities and behaviour of service providers.

**Drinking Water:** Among the public services, drinking water seems to have done better than the others, except in terms of access where it lags behind. While people depend heavily on the government for services like PDS and drinking water, they do not depend so much on the state for road transport, health services and primary education. Drinking water and health services score better on reliability whereas PDS, primary schools and road transport are found wanting in this aspect. But it is on the overall satisfaction of the user, where the scores are the lowest. A significant proportion of users are only partially satisfied. An important point is that, aspects of services that required a high level of human interaction show lower levels of satisfaction.

If we look at each service separately, then the top five rankers in the case of drinking water are Tamil Nadu, Karnataka, Gujarat, Himachal Pradesh and Maharashtra. The weakest are Nagaland, Bihar, Assam, Tripura and Sikkim. Around 40 per cent of the respondents across the country were willing to pay for better drinking water facilities.

**Health:** In the case of health services, Sikkim, Gujarat, Maharashtra, Punjab and Tamil Nadu have done well. The states that performed poorly are Andhra Pradesh, Nagaland, Tripura, Arunachal Pradesh and Meghalaya. One of the difficulties that the government faces in health care, especially in states like Andhra Pradesh is a human resource problem. There are several posts just lying vacant, and not enough doctors willing to work in remote locations. In states like Nagaland, Punjab, Haryana and Kerala, private hospitals and doctors are preferred to government facilities, and usage of private sources reaches 50 per cent.

**Bus Transport:** Road transport facilities provided by governments are best in Gujarat, Tamil Nadu, Karnataka Andhra Pradesh and Mizoram. At the bottom of the list are Bihar, Orissa, Assam, Tripura and Meghalaya. In Bihar and Orissa, people had little access to government buses. Often vans and jeeps are used to fill the gaps in availability. In Kerala, in spite of government buses being available, people tend to use the private service.

**Public Distribution System:** Tamil Nadu, Sikkim, Andhra Pradesh, Karnataka and Maharashtra perform very well in relation to the public distribution system. Nagaland, Rajasthan, Arunachal Pradesh, West Bengal and Uttar Pradesh are the backbenchers. Though 81 per cent of people own ration cards only 8 per cent are fully satisfied with the service, indicating significant gaps in service delivery. An important reason can be traced to the fact that only one fourth of cardholders reported regular availability of food grains.

**Education:** On primary education, Tamil Nadu, Gujarat, Karnataka, Andhra Pradesh and Maharashtra that share the top honours. Arunachal Pradesh, Tripura, Meghalaya, Punjab, and Mizoram are the poor performers. In rural areas, across the country, three quarters of families with children in school going age reported easy access to schools and use of government schools. The mid-day meal scheme has had its impact with 68 per cent of the respondents being aware of it and 83 per cent of those aware benefiting from it.

**Weaker Sections:** More SC/ST households depend on public services compared to the other communities, even though the former have less ease of access to some of these services. Ease of access to health facilities, fair price shops and buses is lower for SC/ST households compared to other communities. This could be due to the typical rural settlement pattern where SC/ST households generally live together in a settlement (hamlet). The other communities often live in the main village where most public services are located.

**Small Villages:** Households in small villages face significant disadvantages too. Respondents from small (Class C villages with population less than 1000) had significantly lower ease of access to health centres, fair price shops and bus stops, compared to the bigger villages. It is evident that economies of scale and norms for locating facilities in places where they are likely to be used more intensively, explain this phenomenon to a large extent.

**Poor Households:** A significantly smaller proportion of very poor households have easy access to health care, public transport, and PDS compared to the rest of the households, but have more or less equal access to drinking water and primary schools. But a higher proportion of very poor households utilise all services except public transport. There are no significant differences between very poor and other households in terms of the reliability and full satisfaction with the services. One reason is that the poor and non-poor are using the same service facility once they have access to it (e.g., a government hospital).

**Satisfaction as a Robust Measure:** The study also offers important contributions to the body of knowledge on studying user feedback and reaffirms the validity of measures of satisfaction. While sceptics have doubted the validity of measures of something as 'subjective' as satisfaction with services, second order analysis has confirmed that aspects such as greater ease of access, greater reliability, etc. are closely related to satisfaction. This analysis was carried out in relation to drinking water, health care, education and public distribution system.

## Conclusions

This study on the State of India's Public Services is a unique survey with a distinct focus. It does not merely attempt to assess the reach of these services, but does an in-depth analysis of various aspects of these services from a user perspective and their impact on the people they intend to benefit. It is based on feedback from people who actually use these services and who interact with the service providers. Therefore, it is not just an opinion poll but is based on experiences and facts. While it cannot completely rule out bias, every effort has been made to minimise such tendencies through careful research design and field supervision.

This study is not meant to merely provide national estimates on public services. It hopes to motivate better levels of performance across governments by providing adequate information on states and enabling comparisons between them. It also tries to put into context the variations between states and between different regions within a state. These variations could exist because of differences in resources, in location, the history of local administrative and political systems, and the political leadership in that region. This should help both government and civil society to make an informed assessment of what the ground realities are and to start the process of looking for solutions and remedies through dialogue and discussion.

A summary of the findings of this study has already been published (EPW, February 2004). It has also been presented to both the central and state governments and different civil society institutions. Discussions that emerged have served to get stakeholders to take a closer look at gaps in services, and to stimulate them to improve service delivery. We believe that studies of this nature can provide a much needed corrective to the widely prevalent tendency of governments to focus only on public spending.

# 1

# Introduction

There is broad agreement among most development professionals that human development, through improved access to basic services, is indispensable for sustainable and sound economic growth. The human development approach argues that creation of social opportunities through expansion of education, health care services and social security, contributes directly to the expansion of human capabilities and improvement in the quality of life, and thereby further contributes to economic growth. The Millennium Development Goals[1] (UNDP, 2002) directly relate to providing universal primary education, reduced infant mortality and improved maternal health, all of which reinforce the strong conviction that governments across the world hold to improving related services. These services help address the other goals relating to elimination of hunger, gender equality and environmental sustainability. Indeed, the greatest challenge is in making services that contribute to better health and education (including water, sanitation, energy and transport) deliver what is required for poor people (World Bank, 2004).

## Role of the State in Service Delivery

The significance of these goals, as an agenda for action, is tied to the very direct role governments play in the lives of their citizens. Be it drinking water, bus transport or primary schools, Indians overwhelmingly depend on state and local governments for these services, although the extent of dependence may vary from location to location, depending on the policies of state governments. While some of these basic needs are met through self provisioning, as with private wells in rural areas, or private provisioning in the case of private schools and buses in urban areas, a large majority of households in India depend heavily on the government for most essential public services.

There are strong reasons why governments play such a major role in providing basic services. The infrastructure to offer standardised and cost

1. The Millennium Development Goals were set at the UN General Assembly in 2002 which comprise quantifiable, monitorable targets to be achieved by 2015.

efficient service is usually large and complex, and thus, prone to uncertainties that private producers would be unable to bear. On the other hand, many services such as law and order or preventive health are 'public goods,' from the benefits of which no one can be excluded. The argument for equity and social justice also weighs heavily on government policy. Given the commitment to serve the disadvantaged sections, it becomes incumbent on governments to create and maintain a service infrastructure capable of ensuring equitable and universal use.

The strategy for planned development that has guided governments in India has over the years, given importance to economic growth as well as public provision of basic services. In recent years, the Government of India (GoI) and state governments have invested an increasing share of their budgets to expand the reach of these services. The Economic Survey (2002-03) states that the expenditure on social services (combined centre and states) as a percentage of GDP or as a percentage of total expenditure has increased in recent years. The expenditure on social services, as a percentage of GDP, is about 6.5 per cent, and as a percentage of the total expenditure is about 22 per cent. These magnitudes reflect the importance given to the social services through the budgetary process of the state.

Recent years have witnessed a sharper focus in India's development strategy to address the basic issues of human development through programmatic interventions in education and health (Dev and Mooij, 2002; Shariff and Ghosh, 2002). While this shift has been taking place, there is also a widespread feeling that India's performance in the social sector is far from satisfactory (Dreaze and Sen, 1995), and that the new investments have neither resulted in a more efficient and equitable delivery of public services nor helped reduce inter-state disparities.

## Gaps in Service Delivery

Recent studies on public expenditure in the social sector suggest that mere provision of basic services will not automatically lead to human development outcomes. The Mid-Term Appraisal of the Ninth Plan points out that the benefits of government programmes have not percolated to the target group at the desired level, which is a poor reflection on the quality of governance of these schemes. Unless people have easy access, are able to use the services and these services are of adequate quality, the intent with which investment in these services are made, would not be realised. But comprehensive studies of public services are conspicuous by their absence (PROBE, 1999). The diversity of public services and difficulties in tracking their delivery are some of the reasons why the problems of public service access, productivity and quality have received only limited attention.

Purposive targeting of public expenditure and policy consistency with respect to services contribute in significant measure when it comes to making an impact. (Dreaze and Sen, 1989), while comparing human development across Kerala and Uttar Pradesh, highlight the role played by early political commitment in Kerala to basic universal services in schooling, health care, child immunisation, and public food distribution. A comparison of expenditure between these states highlight the massive expenditure on state administration in contrast to the investment in education and health in Uttar Pradesh. What happened in Kerala was exactly the opposite.

The absence or inadequacy of basic services is a major dimension of poverty experienced by poor people across the world. The brunt of deficiencies in service, leave "poor people vulnerable to rudeness, humiliation and inhuman treatment by both private and public agents of the state" (Narayan *et al.*, 1999: 26), even when they seek services they are entitled to under the law of the land. The difficulties in accessing services are aggravated by the physical and social environment that the poor live in. The World Development Report 2004 highlights limitations in the institutional environment that make services fail when the poor seek access to public services. They include:

a. only a small part of budget provisions for serving the poor are actually spent for the specified purpose,
b. money meant for serving the poor does not reach the front line service provider who is to deliver the service,
c. weak incentives and poor supervision of the machinery that has been set up to deliver services, and
d. weak demand for services, because of missing materials, absent workers, abusive treatment and the like.

Hence, lack of access and inability to pay are only two among the various factors why services fail to serve the poor.

The belief that the existence of democracy ensures the speedy redress of such problems is far from the truth. Despite the growth in decentralisation and strengthening of local governments, people do not automatically get responsive local governments or effective service agencies. "The ineffectiveness of political pressure through elected representatives is reflected in the striking cynicism of poor people in every continent. People especially disparage elected officials for turning their backs on campaign promises to deliver much needed services" (Narayan *et al.*, 2000: 205). These deficiencies are compounded by the helplessness among poor people about public institutions, which they see as not accountable or as responsive only to the powerful and rich segments of society. Reforms are seen as a process that has generated opportunities and mechanisms which empower better-off citizens over others, since they require legally literate ways that are beyond the poor (Goetz and Gaventa, 2001: 11).

## Institutional Factors Affecting Public Service Delivery

While the factors underlying poor service delivery are diverse, there is a strong perception that many public agencies in India are inefficiently managed. Most public service agencies in the developing world are state owned and managed, primarily because service provisioning is capital intensive. But the rapid growth of populations they serve has brought these monopolies under a tremendous overload of demand (Paul, 2000). On the other hand, these agencies work under severe resource constraints with large umbers of incompetent and unmotivated staff, and deal with poorly organised citizenry and weak civil society.

The monopolistic structure of service provider agencies is a major factor that explains this situation. Given the protection these agencies enjoy, expansion and increases in expenditure may occur without commensurate improvement in scale or quality of service. Antiquated systems and practices, which originated in colonial times, do not lend to professional work ethics in government, much less to service orientation. Many believe that inadequate reforms in the provider agencies and the limited 'exit' options available to the people who use the services, continue to make it difficult for the weaker sections of society to access these services.

The role of subsidies in service provision has also become a major issue. When basic services are highly subsidised, ostensibly for providing the poor with free services, hidden costs have emerged. The differential has provided room for widespread corruption, and an excuse for substandard service, particularly for the poor who are unable to afford private alternatives. Since these services are often provided under conditions of material scarcity and excess demand, service standards are neither specified by the provider nor sought by poor clients.

The close overlap between policymakers, who also supervise performance, and the agency that actually delivers service, further weakens the control system that is supposed to act as a watchdog on performance. The long route to accountability through political representation (World Bank, 2004) also fails under these circumstances, because the power wielded by elected representatives lends to abuse of power through patronage and corruption, which clients often fail to observe.

The scenario of systemic weakness described above suggests that mere shrinking of the role of the state through deregulation, liberalisation and privatisation is not necessarily the solution to address the problem of service delivery. Any improvement requires a review and change of prevalent institutional arrangements to make those vested with power accountable. Institutions which audit performance such as the Office of the Comptroller and Auditor General also seem to be unable to significantly impact on these problems. It is evident that new mechanisms would need to be fostered and an empowered citizenry brought in as a strong stakeholder.

The failure of oversight and supervision is another factor that play a key role. As mentioned earlier, public expenditure on basic services represents a significant allocation of the scarce resources of the nation. The outcomes and effectiveness of this expenditure, however, are not easy to observe and measure. Governments typically monitor the progress of expenditure on each and every service and scheme, and measure achievement in terms of the physical assets and benefits created as recorded by the officials involved. Other reports, including Human Development Reports, present a wide range of comparative information between the state and the rest of India. Most of the variables in these reports reflect long-term outcomes—they include literacy, availability of schools and hospitals, and extent of access to safe drinking water, to name a few.

Whether these services and assets are actually delivered efficiently and meet the real needs of the people cannot be determined by expenditure monitoring or head counts alone. Services may be delivered, but they may be of low quality or entail unwarranted delays or other costs for the people. Assets may be created, but yield low benefits because of the neglect of maintenance or lack of responsiveness on the part of public officials. Policy statements may declare certain services as freely available, yet in reality hidden costs such as bribes and delays may negate these benefits. Public expenditure's productivity and effectiveness can be greatly reduced by these shortcomings. Yet the latter are seldom monitored, let alone analysed and remedied.

On the other hand, experts have always evinced much interest in assessing long term outcomes of governmental performance. A common practice is to assess the performance of a government and its development strategy by tracking outcome measures such as poverty reduction, infant mortality, life expectancy and literacy levels. Comparing countries in terms of these measures enables the experts to pronounce a verdict on the efficacy of governments, efficiency of public expenditure and the like. While such an effort is a useful practice, it cannot shed much light on the issues of quality, effectiveness and productivity of services raised above. As an approach to judging the performance of governments as service providers, there are two problems here that deserve to be noted.

The first problem is that the outcome measures mentioned above are long term in nature and may be influenced by a multiplicity of factors. Poverty reduction may occur over time, but it does not necessarily mean that anti-poverty programmes have been efficiently managed and delivered. Health services will certainly have an impact on the levels of infant mortality and the average life span of the population. But the latter are also influenced by factors such as general economic conditions, increased public awareness, growing role of non-governmental initiatives and communications, etc. These are not all factors within the control of the health ministry or its service providers. Such long term trends in outcomes, while useful for tracking the progress of countries, are not sharp enough to shed light on the performance of government policies and service providers in the short term. If we desire to hold the government accountable for performance, we need to look for a different approach.

A second limitation of this approach is that the findings come too late to help the government make mid-course corrections to its strategy and to manage its operations more effectively in the short or medium term. Once a government adopts a development strategy and allocates resources in pursuit of its policies, programmes and services, it needs systematic feedback on how its plans are working on the ground. In the absence of such timely assessments, it will be difficult for the government and its service providers to remedy the problems in the field and improve productivity and performance.

Accountability implies taking responsibility for the tasks one has undertaken to do. These tasks include implementing current policies and deploying budgets and personnel to this end. These are the tasks that are within the control of the government and for which it should be held accountable. It is not of much use to the current policymakers if the assessment of their work shows 10 years later that it did not contribute to certain desired long term outcomes. If their services are not reaching the people or are being delivered inefficiently, they obviously could not have been contributing to the desired outcomes. It is best to get this feedback to them as early as possible, while their operations are still in progress. The approach should enable them to move closer to the optimal use of the funds and people entrusted to them. We need new benchmarks and comparisons across states and districts to stimulate and facilitate this process.

In theory, governments could easily fill this monitoring gap. Yet all evidence points to a poor track record on their part to monitor public service delivery and its effectiveness. Planning new projects and spending public funds are often higher priority for governments than monitoring performance and outcomes. There are several reasons behind this phenomenon. There are some services that are difficult to monitor. For example, how a doctor treats his/her patient is not easy for a superior authority to monitor. A more important problem is that the kind of systems and practices needed to perform the monitoring function are seldom put in place by governments. Even when systems are in place, collusion between service providers and their superiors (e.g., between bureaucrats and politicians) may make them toothless. One would have expected political leaders to highlight the issues pertaining to services at least at the time of elections. But such issues are seldom on the agenda in elections, perhaps because of ignorance of people and their inability to articulate their concerns. In the absence of external pressure by an informed public, it is unlikely that government's monitoring of services will improve (Paul, 2002).

## Concept and Approach to Involving Citizens in Monitoring Service Delivery

Like service providers, users of services also experience and observe how services are being delivered. Even when service providers and their field staff neglect their monitoring function, feedback from the people who use public services can be used to assess the state of service delivery and to identify important gaps in their quality and productivity. Because the average citizen is not an expert on the technology and delivery systems of these services, his/her experience is usually ignored. This is an important lacuna in conventional attempts at evaluation of public services. For example, citizens can verify whether in fact they are able to make use of a service according to the conditions promised by the provider. They can comment on aspects of quality and cost that the provider may not be able to, or want to monitor. Delays in services, repeated visits to the agencies to solve problems, the investments people make to compensate for the unreliability of services, and corruption in services entail costs to citizens that governments do not monitor. User's level of satisfaction with a service may well reflect the quality of responsiveness of the service provider in its interaction with the public.

Citizens' feedback on the services is also a more cost effective and systematic way of articulating the voice of the people. It is collective 'voice' that can exert pressure on governments to improve services when people have no exit option. If the feedback is positive, it speaks well for the government and its service providers. But if the feedback is negative in major aspects, then the chances are that scarce resources are being wasted or poorly utilised.

When user feedback is converted into voice backed by large numbers of people, it can stimulate governments to better utilise public funds, redesign services and rectify problems people face. It can also signal whether the long term outcomes expected from the services will be within reach. Long term service outcomes cannot be efficiently achieved when services are not being delivered properly in the short term.

User feedback as a basis for monitoring and assessing public services is a relatively new phenomenon. It has been in vogue in the business world for a much longer period than in the public sector. In the developed countries, there are some examples of governments seeking user feedback on their services and programmes (Samuels, 1998). In developing countries, however, there are hardly any examples of governments adopting this approach. The few initiatives in developing countries have come from civil society organisations such as the Public Affairs Centre (PAC) that pioneered the 'citizen report cards' on urban services (Goetz and Gaventa, 2001; Paul, 2002). PAC has used its report cards not only to create public awareness, but also to advocate policy and governance reforms. The feedback from the people who are at the receiving end of public services was observed to effectively fill the gaps in assessing the impact of public expenditure and holding providers accountable.

## Scope of the Citizen Feedback Survey on Public Services

Citizens who interact with service providers and receive their services are not experts on the technologies and delivery systems of the services. Nor can they produce overall assessments of the performance of the public agencies involved. These are some of the reasons why such feedback is neglected in conventional evaluation and monitoring exercises. Nevertheless, experience based user feedback can shed useful light on the efficiency and effectiveness of those who plan and deliver these services. For example, citizens can testify whether in fact they are able to avail of a service on the conditions specified by the provider. They can comment on aspects of quality and cost that the provider may not be able or motivated to monitor. Their degree of satisfaction with a service may also reflect the responsiveness of the service provider in its interactions with the public. This perspective on how services perform across the 'last mile' can only be reflected in user feedback collected in a purposive and systematic manner.

Citizen feedback on services is a cost effective way to articulate the 'voice' of the people. If the feedback is positive, there is a good chance that public expenditure is leading to desired outcomes and impact. If it is negative in important respects, the chances are that scarce resources may have been wasted. Citizen feedback can thus provide early warning signals that could be used by governments to redesign services and make mid-course corrections so as to improve the service outcomes. The variations in service standards across different regions and states also provide insights into factors and measures that have a bearing on quality of service that gets delivered. In the Indian context, this offers the additional advantage of inter-state comparisons based on citizen feedback, which may act as a catalyst to nudge the state governments to upgrade their quality of service provisioning and governance.

There is a need to assess the specific strengths and weaknesses of the service delivery system, by generating systematic and reliable information and benchmarking service standards. The success of citizen report cards at the city and sector level provided the foundation for a wider and nationwide assessment of key basic services in India. The underlying purpose of this study was to establish the significance of user feedback in managing service delivery, and help evolve a system or method by which the public service providers would receive and respond to feedback from users, on the performance and qualitative aspects of public services, to improve the delivery mechanism. Although, this initiative was conceived outside government, it was expected to motivate the state and its institutions to learn from the experience.

It is in this context that the Millennial Survey of basic services was taken up. The survey has concentrated on aspects of performance, from a user perspective (such as providing ease of access to facilities, the immediate benefit in terms of quality of service and qualitative assessment in terms of user satisfaction). These indicators on quality and satisfaction with services (e.g. frequency of breakdown of hand pumps, satisfaction with behaviour of doctors and display of prices at ration shops) are measures of current performance, and provide a basis for corrective action. It may be borne in mind that long term outcomes, like infant mortality, are influenced by many other factors, only some of which are within the control of the government. Needless to say, positive long term outcomes cannot occur without effective service provision by the state and its agencies.

Comparisons of services over time, using public feedback, are an efficient way to assess provider agencies and make them more accountable for their performance. The survey of public services reported below was completed in 2001. Repeated surveys at reasonable intervals of time (say three to five years) can be used to benchmark progress of the services over time. It is the kind of information that civil society institutions can use to demand improved performance and accountability from public service providers.

A service is completely effective only if the user is satisfied with it in all respects. This study, therefore, collected feedback from users on four key aspects of public service:

- Access—proximity of the users to the service provided,
- Usage—the extent to which the service is used,
- Reliability—how dependable or regular the service is, and
- Satisfaction—user's assessment of the overall effectiveness of the service.

Access refers to the proximity of the service facility to the household or the user of the service. Government norms for access often tend to be based on population criteria. For example, the location of primary health centres is based on population norms. But from a user perspective, it is the distance or nearness to the facility that matters most. The adoption of the latter approach in the present study will yield results that are different from the application of government norms. Sometimes, the service infrastructure may exist somewhere in the proximity of the user, but the service may not be available in a convenient manner, making access nominal. Therefore, from a user perspective, it is effective and easy access that matters.

Use of a service tells us whether a household actually utilises a public service. In a monopoly situation, access and use may be identical. But when other options are available, people may prefer to use facilities other than that provided by governments. The reasons for such choices could be many, but this study does not probe them in depth, since the focus was only to ascertain if people to use a public facility when accessible.

Quality/reliability is a more complex dimension of a service from the standpoint of measurement. It refers to the features of a service that are not self-evident from the physical good or infrastructure involved. Households may not be able to observe or assess all such features, especially the technical aspects of quality. But they can comment on other important aspects of quality. One such is the reliability of a service. The user of a service, for example, may find the processes and interactions with the service provider (predictability, responsiveness, corruption, etc.) unsatisfactory. He/she then may attribute low quality or reliability (an aspect of quality) to that service.

Satisfaction reflects the overall assessment of a service by the user, based on his/her experience. In this assessment, the person implicitly brings in his/her expectations or standards that in turn may also be influenced by the past experience of others in the community, one's educational level and awareness of the working of government. Given the low levels of education, income and mobility of many people in the Indian context, it is likely that their expectations from services are more modest in contrast to those of people in more developed countries. Irrespective of how a person arrives at his/her assessment of satisfaction, it is an internal assessment on which he/she may act. Admittedly, satisfaction reflects personal judgments of users and can be measured only through the information provided by them.

## User Satisfaction as a Core Indicator of Service Quality

The concept and determinants of satisfaction have attracted growing attention among economists and psychologists in recent times. Though there has been much scepticism among economists about the feasibility and value of measuring utility or happiness, there has been a recent shift from this view, largely influenced by the evidence from psychological research on the subject (Frank, 1997; Diener *et al.*, 1999). Some authors have identified expectations, comparisons with others, and 'baseline happiness' of individuals as the main factors that determine the state of self reported well being. Marketing research literature has also paid considerable attention to the measurement of satisfaction (Sasser *et al.*, 1978; Driver, 2002). Experts have developed different models that link performance and expectations. One model, for example, assumes that satisfaction measures the gap between performance and expectations. Another model assumes that customers continually adjust their expectations to their recent experience of specific services. As a result, performance and expectations will not vary a great deal and both may then be positively related to satisfaction levels. Expectations act as an anchor for the assessment of performance of a service provider (Deichmann and Lall, 2003).

In the survey reported here, explicit statements and questions were not raised about expectations. As will be clear from the sections below, it would have been difficult for us to probe expectations about multiple public services in a survey covering large populations with limited education. An alternative would have been to explain to the people the standards of service stipulated by the government and ask them to express their satisfaction in relation to them. But most government service providers have not announced such standards, thus ruling out this line of investigation. Responses to the survey questions, therefore, reflect the implicit expectations about services that people have. In reasonably homogeneous populations and socio-economic environments, expectations could be very similar. Expectations of a person can also change over time. It is a point to bear in mind while comparing satisfaction scores across very different states.

## Objectives of the Study

The study specifically aimed to:

- Provide an independent assessment of key public services, based on citizen's feedback, as well as independent observation of the facilities set up.
- Build an independent database and set benchmarks, to measure the progress of these services over time.
- Create public awareness and motivate people to act on the information that the report now provides.

This monograph reports on the first national initiative to generate user feedback on public services. The monograph presents a user perspective on five basic services provided by the government, namely, drinking water, healthcare, primary education and childcare, road transport, and public distribution system in India. It provides an assessment of the state of these services in the different states of India based on user feedback gathered through a stratified random sample survey of households. The information thus generated has been used to compare and rate the states in terms of their performance.

The concept, scope and approach of the survey are presented in Chapter 1 of the book. Chapter 2 reviews the existing literature on the services covered by the survey. Chapter 3 spells out the methodology of the survey and some of its limitations. The major findings of the study are discussed in Chapter 4. The Chapter 5 discusses the findings on how the poor and disadvantaged are being served. Chapter 6 explores the conceptual framework of user satisfaction as a key indicator in assessing public service delivery, and empirical findings from the study. The major conclusions and policy implications of the study are presented in Chapter 7.

## Limitations of the Study

The design of the study was prepared for an assessment across all states of India; hence some aspects on which data was collected turned out to be less relevant for a few states. For example, some states did not have bus transport service in the government sector, and therefore, no data on that service could be collected. Special characteristics of different states in terms of water availability and PDS policy were not addressed in the study.

Services can be assessed on a number of supply related dimensions, which have a bearing on the quality that users receive. But the study limited itself to collecting information reported by users rather than physical measurement at the point of delivery. The study did not collect data from service providers on different aspects of their work and outputs.

In response to some questions in the survey, especially those related to satisfaction, respondents are likely to have used their own expectations and judgement. Given the variations in local conditions, expectations would vary from one state or region to another for obvious reasons, and in turn have a bearing on the degree of satisfaction.

The sampling plan was designed to obtain reliable estimates at state level both for rural and urban areas. However, the size of the sample was not large enough to provide valid estimates when data was disaggregated within the states to the district or regional levels. The sampling plan for the survey was based on 1991 census; hence it did provided for separate estimates for newly formed states of Chhattisgarh, Jharkhand and Uttaranchal. This limitation was also felt while analysing results in states with newly formed districts.

Comparison of our findings with those of other studies and surveys conducted by government agencies could indicate wide variations in some cases for two reasons. First, measures of reliability and satisfaction do not find a place in most surveys/studies. Quality of services may have been assessed in a few micro level studies. But unless the measures used are identical, comparisons with the present findings will be well nigh impossible. Second, even when other surveys have measured access and use of services, the definitions and norms used seem to have been quite different. Governments typically use population norms to define access to a service. For example, a health sub-centre is designed to cater to a population of 5000. A PDS shop is meant to cover a population of 2000. A drinking water source is supposed to serve households within a distance of 1.6 kms. As against this, the norm used in this survey is a distance of 100 metres from a household. Our norm of 100 metres is clearly a more user-friendly measure of access. Similar problems exist in the definitions of the use of service. Comparisons between the findings of this study and of others will be rendered difficult by the use of these varying norms. The only exception is in primary education where the access norm used (one km. from the household) is the same as the Government's Education Survey.

Given these limitations, it would be appropriate to indicate that the study served to benchmark performance of services at the state level, and highlighted the problems being encountered. The estimates enable comparison across states on many key performance parameters. However, the study did not attempt state-wise analysis to derive policy options or remedies for issues, beyond general conclusions relevant across the country.

# 2

## Provision of Public Services in India: A Review

Given the long history and active involvement of the government in provision of public services, the pool of secondary data on this theme is both vast and diverse. Official records over the years and research on service delivery were reviewed, and an overview presented here. The review provides insights into the manner in which five public services *viz.*, drinking water, health facilities, road transport, public distribution system (fair price shops) and primary school education, are being provided to citizens across India. The chapter also provides an overview of the extent to which services are distributed, norms for provision and budget allocations, and quality of service, wherever available.

### Drinking Water

It was during the Fifth Five Year Plan that the Government of India incorporated provision of potable water to rural areas as part of the Minimum Needs Programme (MNP). The Seventh Five Year Plan envisaged providing safe drinking water to all sections of the population. It is in this context that the Government of India in 1986 launched the National Drinking Water Mission (NDWM), popularly known as the 'Technology Mission', to ensure that potable water for the rural population in a time bound manner; it was renamed Rajiv Gandhi Drinking Water Mission in 1991. The Tenth Five Year Plan (2002-07) reiterated the goal of providing potable drinking water to every settlement in the country on a sustainable basis. To achieve the goal the Department of Drinking Water Supply under Ministry of Rural Development has been mandated to provide safe drinking water to all rural habitations by April 2004.

The Central and State investments on drinking water and sanitation have increased from Rs.10306 million in Fifth Five Year Plan to Rs.395380 million in Ninth Five Year Plan (Table 2.1). The investment on the sector (drinking water and sanitation) as percentage of total plan outlay has increased from 2.6 per cent in Fifth Five Year Plan to 4.6 per cent in Ninth Five Year Plan.

## Table 2.1

*Plan Investments in Water Supply and Sanitation*

*(Rs. Million)*

| *Plan Period* | *Central and State Investments* |
|---|---|
| Fifth Plan (1974-79) | 10306 |
| Sixth Plan (1980-85) | 40470 |
| Seventh Plan (1985-90) | 65224 |
| Eighth Plan (1992-97) | 167110 |
| Ninth Plan (1997-2002) | 395380 |

*Source:* Planning Commission, Government of India, *India Assessment 2002, Water Supply & Sanitation.*

As on January 2003, 91 per cent of rural habitations have been fully covered and 7.9 per cent are partially covered with drinking water facility, with an investment of over Rs.340,000 million (MoF, 2003). On the urban water supply front, the Accelerated Urban Water Supply programme was launched in 1993-94 to provide water supply to 2151 towns having population less than 20,000. Provision of protected water supply is a component of the Integrated Development of Small and Medium Towns (IDSMT) programme launched in 1979-80 for development of urban infrastructure. Under the programme, 1310 small and medium towns have been assisted for development of infrastructure.

In terms of coverage of rural population, 95 per cent of the rural population had access to a safe source of water, but only 52 per cent were fully covered as per norms (40 lpcd or more) while 48 per cent were partially covered (between 10 and 40 lpcd) (World Bank, 1999). Another estimate by the IIPS (2000), indicated that 92.6 per cent of urban and 72.2 per cent of rural households have access to safe drinking water sources. Among the drinking water sources, 74.5 per cent of urban households are covered by piped water supply and 18.1 per cent by hand pump. In rural areas 25 per cent of households are covered by piped water supply and 47.2 per cent are covered by hand pump. (Table 2.2).

A household is considered as having access to safe drinking water if the drinking water source is a tap, hand-pump/tube well, within or outside the residential premises (as per the definition used by the Census of India). The Census of 1991 reported that 62 per cent of households in India have access to safe drinking water, with the spread being 81 per cent among urban and around 56 per cent among rural households. The 54th Round of National Sample Survey (NSSO, 1999) estimated that 50 per cent of rural households are served by tube well/hand pumps and 19 per cent by taps. The population

## Table 2.2

*Source of Drinking Water for Urban and Rural Households*

*(Per cent)*

| *Source of Drinking Water* | *Urban* | *Rural* | *Total* |
|---|---|---|---|
| Piped water supply | 74.5 | 25.0 | 38.7 |
| Hand pump | 18.1 | 47.2 | 39.2 |
| Well water | 6.0 | 23.5 | 18.7 |
| Surface water | 0.4 | 3.5 | 2.6 |
| Others | 1.0 | 0.7 | 0.8 |
| **Total Per cent** | 100.0 | 100.0 | 100.0 |

*Source: National Family Health Survey (NFHS-2),* 1998-99.

## Table 2.3

*Distribution of Household by Source of Drinking Water*

*(Per cent)*

| *Source of Drinking Water* | *1981* | | | *1991* | | | *1993* | | *1998* | |
|---|---|---|---|---|---|---|---|---|---|---|
| | *Total* | *Rural* | *Urban* | *Total* | *Rural* | *Urban* | *Rural* | *Urban* | *Rural* | *Urban* |
| Tap | 23.03 | 10.29 | 63.24 | 32.26 | 20.64 | 65.06 | 8.72 | 70.50 | 18.70 | 70.10 |
| Well | 51.71 | 61.63 | 20.40 | 32.23 | 38.01 | 15.91 | 52.28 | 12.78 | 25.80 | 6.70 |
| Tube well/Hand pump | 15.16 | 16.21 | 11.82 | 30.04 | 34.90 | 16.32 | 27.36 | 14.34 | 50.10 | 21.30 |
| Tank/Pond | 2.77 | 3.38 | 0.86 | 1.33 | 1.69 | 0.31 | 3.78 | 0.58 | 1.90 | 0.30 |
| River, Canal, Lake | 3.92 | 4.93 | 0.74 | 2.01 | 2.58 | 0.35 | 5.15 | 0.60 | 1.30 | 0.20 |
| Spring | - | - | - | - | - | - | - | - | 1.70 | 0.10 |
| Others | 3.41 | 3.56 | 2.94 | 2.13 | 2.17 | 2.04 | 2.71 | 1.20 | 0.40 | 1.10 |
| **Total** | 100.00 | 100.00 | 100.00 | 100.00 | 100.00 | 100.00 | 100.00 | 100.00 | 100.00 | 100.00 |

*Source:* Statistical Abstract of India, 1999.
NSS 50th Round July 1993—June 1994.
NSS 54th Round January—June 1998; NSS Reports No. 449.

*Note:* Data for the Census year 1981 and 1991 exclude Assam and Jammu & Kashmir respectively.

census and NSS data on drinking water status, for rural and urban households, at two points of time, are presented in Table 2.3. The table suggests that though higher percentage of urban households continue to have access to safe drinking water over time, the gap in the access to safe drinking water has come down between urban and rural households overtime.

The Government of India's norm, for classifying a habitation as one where safe drinking water is available, requires user households to have access to the source of water within 1.6 km. in plains and within 100 meters elevation in the hilly areas. Most states appear to have achieved this norm to a large extent in providing drinking water to the rural households (CSTE&M, 2001). Despite the progress achieved in the provision of water supply, the level of water-related sickness continues to be high, which is also a reflection on the poor quality of water. The poor quality of water was also highlighted in a recent evaluation carried out in 122 countries by United Nations (UNESCO, 2003). The study ranked India as third from the bottom in the quality of water (120th rank).

An area of concern in the drinking water sector is the unstable status of water availability. Habitations, which had hitherto been classified as adequately covered by safe drinking water, are sliding into the category of uncovered villages due to the depletion of ground water levels (MoF, 2003). To ensure sustainability of the water systems, and to tackle the problem of water quality, reforms have been introduced in 1999 so as to gradually replace the government oriented, centralised, and supply driven programmes by a people-oriented decentralised, demand driven and community based one.

## Health Care

Historically, the State has taken responsibility for health care in India, and made considerable progress during the last five decades. The crude birth rate per 1000 population, which was 40.8 in 1951, has declined to 25.8 by 2000. Similarly, the infant mortality rate (per 1000 live birth) was 68 in 2000 as compared to 146 in 1951. The key statistics presented in Table 2.4 highlight progress achieved after Independence.

The scale of growth in health infrastructure has been very impressive. The number of sub-centres, PHCs and CHCs increased from 725 in 1951 to 57,363

**Table 2.4**

*Trends in Vital Statistics*

| *Parameter* | *1951* | *1981* | *1991* | *2000* |
|---|---|---|---|---|
| Crude Birth Rate (per 1000 population) | 40.8 | 33.9 | 29.5 | 25.8 (2000) |
| Crude Death Rate | 25.1 | 12.5 | 9.8 | 8.5 (2000) |
| Total Fertility Rate | 6.0 | 4.5 | 3.6 | 3.2 (1999) |
| Infant Mortality Rate (per 1000 live birth) | 146 | 110 | 80 | 68 (2000) |
| Child Mortality Rate (0-4 yrs., per 1000 children) | 57.3 (1972) | 41.2 | 26.5 | 20.4 (1999) |
| Couple Protection Rate (per cent) | 10.4 (1971) | 22.8 | 44.1 | 48.2 (1998-99)* |
| Life Expectancy at Birth: Male | 37.2 | 54.1 | 59.7 (1991-95) | 62.3 (1996-01) |
| Life Expentancy at Birth: Female | 36.2 | 54.7 | 61.7 (1991-95) | 64.0 (1996-01) |

*Source:* GoI, *Economic Survey,* 2002-2003, **National Family Health Survey,* 1998-99.

in 1981, and further to 1,63,181 in 1999. The number of dispensaries and hospitals increased from 9209 in 1951 to 23,555 in 1981 and further to 43,322 in 1996. The distribution of sub-centres, PHCs and the population covered by the centres are presented in Table 2.5. The table shows that there are wide

**Table 2.5**

*Scale of Service of Sub-centres and PHCs across India (1995)*

| *Sl. No.* | *States and Union Territories* | *No. of Sub-centres* | *No. of PHCs* | *Avg. Rural Population per sub-centre* | *Avg. Rural Population per PHC* | *Population per bed* |
|---|---|---|---|---|---|---|
| 1. | Andhra Pradesh | 7894 | 1283 | 6159 | 37896 | 1526 |
| 2. | Arunachal Pradesh | 203 | 42 | 3714 | 17950 | 349 |
| 3. | Assam | 5280 | 619 | 3774 | 32191 | 1968 |
| 4. | Bihar | 14799 | 2209 | 5069 | 33962 | 2969 |
| 5. | Goa | 175 | 21 | 3943 | 32859 | 326 |
| 6. | Gujarat | 7284 | 956 | 3715 | 28309 | 706 |
| 7. | Haryana | 2299 | 397 | 5397 | 31256 | 2584 |
| 8. | Himachal Pradesh | 1906 | 240 | 2477 | 19673 | 1184 |
| 9. | Jammu & Kashmir | 1700 | 335 | 3458 | 17550 | 868 |
| 10. | Karnataka | 7793 | 1428 | 3986 | 21757 | 1283 |
| 11. | Kerala | 5094 | 929 | 4204 | 23055 | 391 |
| 12. | Madhya Pradesh | 11936 | 1376 | 4259 | 36949 | 3770 |
| 13. | Maharashtra | 9725 | 1695 | 4976 | 28551 | 1023 |
| 14. | Manipur | 420 | 72 | 3170 | 18493 | 1357 |
| 15. | Meghalaya | 333 | 88 | 4339 | 1641 | 978 |
| 16. | Mizoram | 244 | 43 | 1523 | 8846 | 633 |
| 17. | Nagaland | 244 | 33 | 4104 | 30343 | 1238 |
| 18. | Orissa | 5927 | 1055 | 4627 | 25995 | 2314 |
| 19. | Punjab | 2964 | 472 | 4820 | 30272 | 1509 |
| 20. | Rajasthan | 8000 | 1493 | 4242 | 22732 | 2347 |
| 21. | Sikkim | 142 | 23 | 2601 | 16063 | 843 |
| 22. | Tamil Nadu | 8681 | 1436 | 4236 | 25614 | 1120 |
| 23. | Tripura | 535 | 63 | 4365 | 37070 | 1817 |
| 24. | Uttar Pradesh | 20153 | 3761 | 5532 | 29648 | 2593 |
| 25. | West Bengal | 7873 | 1556 | 6271 | 31729 | 1351 |
| 26. | Andaman & Nicobar | 96 | 17 | 2142 | 12100 | 372 |
| 27. | Chandigarh | 12 | 0 | 5515 | - | 1540 |
| 28. | Dadra & Nagar Haveli | 34 | 6 | 3728 | 21125 | 1435 |
| 29. | Daman & Diu | 19 | 4 | 2844 | 13510 | 680 |
| 30. | Delhi | 42 | 8 | 22595 | 118627 | 585 |
| 31. | Lakshadweep | 14 | 7 | 1613 | 3227 | 886 |
| 32. | Pondicherry | 79 | 26 | 3681 | 11184 | 310 |
|  | **All India** | 131900 | 21693 | 4766 | 28981 | 1498 |

*Note:* Based upon the 1991 census population.

*Source: Bulletin of Rural Health Statistics in India,* June 1995.

variations across states in the coverage of health facilities to the population. Among the major states, Gujarat, Kerala, Karnataka and Tamil Nadu have relatively better coverage of health facilities. At an aggregate level, most of the states appear to have more or less fulfilled the stipulated norms on provision of health facilities (one sub-centre for every 5000 population in plain area and for 3000 in tribal and hilly areas; one PHC for population of 30,000 in plain areas and 20,000 in hilly and tribal areas).

The urban population has better access to government health services compared to rural population. Estimates by the CSO indicate that the availability of hospitals per lakh of urban population is 6.3 times more than that for rural population. Similarly the number of beds per lakh of urban population is 11.2 times more than the availability for rural population. Further, the extent of access to and utilisation of health care varied substantially between states, districts and different segments of society (MoF, 2003).

Though, the government has provided a large network of health institutions, the extent and frequency of utilisation of these facilities is considerably low. The variations in availability of services across urban and rural areas are very large (MoH&FA, 2002). Several factors have come in the way of utilisation of public health services, such as distance to the facility, shortage of health personnel and medicines, absence of doctors, poor quality of services, unhygienic atmosphere, non-responsive behaviour of health staff and corruption. The National Health Policy 2002 aims at to increase the utilisation of public health facilities from the current level of less than 20 per cent to over 75 per cent by 2010.

## Road Transport

A well-developed road network and transport system accelerates the pace of economic development. It helps in triggering trade, sustaining economic activities and creating employment opportunities. Between 1950 and 2000, length of roads in India grew at more than 4 per cent per annum. Today, India has more than 3 million kilometres of road network, perhaps making it one of the largest road networks in the world. However, almost half of the roads are un-surfaced. Long distance traffic is served by National Highways and State Highways and they account for about 8 per cent the total road length.

Only 37 per cent of villages are connected by *pucca* roads, and 64.5 per cent of villages have bus stop within a distance of two kilometres (Table 2.6). Among the states, Bihar, Orissa, West Bengal, Madhya Pradesh and Northeast region have large proportions of villages, which are not connected yet by *pucca* roads. A larger proportion of villages in southern states have a bus stop within a distance of two kilometres.

**Table 2.6**

*Villages Connected by Pucca Road and Bus Stop*

*(in per cent)*

| *States* | *Connected with Pucca Road* | *Bus Stop within Two Kms.* |
|---|---|---|
| Haryana | 61.1 | 76.7 |
| Himachal Pradesh | 23.8 | 61.9 |
| Punjab | 81.4 | 68.6 |
| Bihar | 19.0 | 42.2 |
| Uttar Pradesh | 34.3 | 44.4 |
| Madhya Pradesh | 21.2 | 40.1 |
| Orissa | 15.7 | 44.1 |
| Rajasthan | 40.6 | 53.8 |
| North-eastern Region | 21.2 | 21.2 |
| West Bengal | 14.1 | 14.1 |
| Gujarat | 54.6 | 85.2 |
| Maharashtra | 45.0 | 81.5 |
| Andhra Pradesh | 44.3 | 92.0 |
| Karnataka | 25.9 | 85.9 |
| Kerala | 85.3 | 94.7 |
| Tamil Nadu | 40.8 | 93.4 |
| **All India** | 36.8 | 64.5 |

*Source:* Abusaleh Shariff, (1999). *India Human Development Report,* National Council of Applied Economic Research, Oxford University Press, New Delhi.

State Highways, district and rural roads are being constructed and maintained by various agencies of the state governments. The scale of road construction has accelerated different poverty alleviation programme in rural areas. These programmes have taken up this activity as a means to provide employment. The roads are also being developed under minimum needs programme. The larger aim of the Government of India is to link all villages with population of 1,500 and more with all weather roads. A major programme, titled The Pradhan Mantri Gram Sadak Yojana (PMGSY), was launched in December 2000 to provide road connectivity to 1.6 lakh unconnected habitations (with population of 500 persons or more) by the end of the Tenth Plan Period (2007), at an estimated cost of Rs. 60,000 crore. The National Rural Roads Development Agency (NRRDA), a registered society, has been set up to provide operations and management support for the programme.

The Road Transport Corporation Act, 1950 strengthened public sector participation in passenger road transport services. At present, there are 71 State Transport Undertakings in the country (Sriraman S., 1998). There were around 1,11,200 buses in the public sector by 1995 with a total investment of over Rs. 6,000 crore and formed 27 per cent of the country's bus population. The number of breakdowns went down from 1.03 to 0.54 and the rate of accidents from 82 to 31 per 10,000 km. However, there are considerable variations in the performance of different State Transport Undertakings.

The emerging demand for road passenger traffic has called for significant expansion in capacity of bus transport. With the State Transport Undertakings facing an acute shortage of resources to keep their fleet intact, let alone provide for expansion, there is a strong view that the private sector should play a larger role especially in bus transport. The dependence on a state monopoly to provide this service serves to restrict user choice and often increases cost—which has possibly been the case in states, which opted for total nationalisation of the passenger road transport sector such as Maharashtra, Gujarat, etc. Studies on deregulation and privatisation of urban bus transit services in the countries have shown that most parties have gained from such policies (Gomez and Meyer, 1993).

## Public Distribution System

India has a large programme of food distribution through fair price shops, in order to ensure adequate availability of foodgrains and essential commodities across the country. This programme is operated jointly by the state governments and the Central Government. Through the Public Distribution System, governments ensure availability of essential commodities like rice, wheat, sugar, edible oils and kerosene to the consumers with a network of outlets called Fair Price Shops or Ration Shops. Hence, PDS involves two services *viz.*, procurement of foodgrains under minimum support prices and distribution of foodgrains through the network of Fair Price Shops in the country. The Central Government looks after procurement, storage and transport operations through Food Corporation of India whereas, the distribution aspect rest with the state governments.

The PDS, which was evolved in the wake of foodgrain shortages during the World Wars and the sixties (Radhakrishna *et al.*, 2002), is now the recipient of a major part of the government's subsidies, and operates as a producer price-support-cum-consumer subsidy programme. In the early years of planned development, the focus of PDS was price stability for consumers in urban and major food deficit areas. In the subsequent plan periods, some form of equitable distribution was also envisaged as the objective of PDS and thereby the coverage has been extended to rural areas since mid-80s (George, 1996). In the, nineties, PDS was perceived as the major safety net to protect the poor from short-run, price induced, adverse effects of economic reforms (Mooij, 1994). With this change in the focus of PDS, the number of fair price shops increased from 2.78 lakh in 1982 to 3.45 lakh in 1987 and further to 4.61 lakh in 2000.

The gap between the economic cost incurred by the FCI towards procurement, storage, distribution and wastage of foodgrains and average realisation through issue prices under PDS is the food subsidy borne by the Central Government. The subsidy on foodgrains incurred by the Central Government has increased over time. The food subsidy increased from Rs. 835 crore in 1983-84 to Rs. 2450 crore in 1990-91 and further to Rs. 17,612 crores in 2001-02. But the percentage of households using PDS is around 33 per cent (Table 2.7). The percentage of households using PDS is only around 5 per cent in the states of Punjab, Bihar, Uttar Pradesh and Orissa.

### Table 2.7

*Consumption of Foodgrains and Utilisation of the PDS in States*

| *States* | *Percentage of Households using PDS* | *Quantity of Cereals (kg) Bought from PDS (per hh/month)* | *Percentage of Requirement of Cereals met by PDS* |
|---|---|---|---|
| Haryana | 9.0 | 18.1 | 32.4 |
| Himachal Pradesh | 75.6 | 43.8 | 41.4 |
| Punjab | 5.6 | 23.4 | 5.5 |
| Bihar | 5.0 | 49.5 | 29.2 |
| Uttar Pradesh | 5.2 | 33.4 | 24.5 |
| Madhya Pradesh | 34.2 | 15.7 | 20.4 |
| Orissa | 5.2 | 18.6 | 16.7 |
| Rajasthan | 23.6 | 33.1 | 14.7 |
| North-eastern Region | 21.7 | 20.5 | 31.9 |
| West Bengal | 11.3 | 38.4 | 45.6 |
| Gujarat | 47.6 | 17.3 | 18.1 |
| Maharashtra | 50.7 | 13.8 | 13.2 |
| Andhra Pradesh | 66.4 | 18.6 | 30.6 |
| Karnataka | 70.1 | 15.0 | 22.8 |
| Kerala | 78.0 | 23.7 | 51.9 |
| Tamil Nadu | 82.4 | 12.0 | 21.6 |
| **All India** | 33.2 | 19.0 | 23.5 |

*Source:* Abusaleh Shariff, (1999). *India Human Development Report*, National Council of Applied Economic Research, Oxford University Press, New Delhi, 1999.

Several attempts have been made to modify the scope and coverage of PDS to better serve the poor. Studies have pointed out that the dependence on PDS by the non-poor is much higher than by the poor, and that of the moderately poor is higher than the very poor (Radhakrishna *et al.*, 1997). Many empirical studies have shown severe biases in the inter-regional distributions of the PDS supplies—states with the high incidence of poverty such as Bihar, Orissa and Madhya Pradesh received a lower share. Further, with few exceptions, the PDS remained an untargeted programme. The states of Andhra Pradesh, Assam, Gujarat, Jammu & Kashmir, Kerala, Rajasthan and Tamil Nadu have shown comparatively better performance in targeting the poor than the other states (Radhakrishna *et al.*, 1997).

Studies have also pointed out that the cost effectiveness of reaching the poorest 20 per cent of households through PDS cereals is small (Parikh, 1994). For every rupee spent, less than 22 paise reach the poor in most of the states (except in Goa, Daman and Diu where 28 paise reach the poor). Radhakrishna and others (1997) observed that Central Government spent Rs. 4.35 to transfer one rupee to the poor. In Andhra Pradesh, one rupee of income was transferred to the poor at a cost of Rs. 6.35 (the state also subsidises PDS). On the other hand, the impact of PDS on poverty and nutritional status has been negligible in most of the states except Kerala and Andhra Pradesh. They further observed that the country as a whole, there could be a decline of two percentage points in poverty ratio due to the combined effect (income gains) of food and non-food subsidies.

Comparisons of the PDS with other anti-poverty programmes, on cost efficiency in distributing food to the poor, indicate that PDS is perhaps the costliest (Radhakrishna *et al.*, 1997). PDS has been found to deliver 100 kcal of nutrients at three times the cost under the direct nutrition programmes like Integrated Child Development Scheme (ICDS). In terms of cost of per rupee income transferred, PDS has also been found to be inferior to employment programmes.

To make PDS more targeted and focussed towards the poor, the Government of India launched Antyodaya Anna Yojana in December 2000. The scheme envisages identification of 100 million poor families and providing 25 kg. of foodgrains per family per month at a low price of Rs. 2 per kg. of wheat and Rs. 3 per kg. of rice. The estimated annual allocation of foodgrains for *Antyodaya* families would be 30 lakh tonnes involving a subsidy of Rs. 2315 crore.

## Primary Education

Article 45 of the Directive Principles of the Constitution urges the State to provide free and compulsory education for all the children until they complete 14 years of age. In this direction the National Policy on Education, 1968 stressed the need for strenuous efforts for early fulfilment of the goal laid down in the Constitution. The Constitutional Amendment of 1976 included education in the concurrent list. The National Policy on Education, 1986 and the Programme of Action 1992 envisage free and compulsory education for all children up to the age of 14 years. The Programme of Action of the Central Government directs the state governments to have their own State Programme of Action for implementing the thrust areas of the national policy based on local conditions. The 93rd Constitutional Amendment declared free and compulsory elementary education as a fundamental right for all children in the age group of 6-14 years. To fulfil the Constitutional obligation, the Government of India launched Sarva Shiksha Abhiyan programme in partnership with the states. The programme aims to improve the performance of the school system and improve the quality of elementary education in a mission mode to all children in the age group of 6-14 years by 2010 through a community owned approach.

Literacy rates have shown substantial improvement over the decades. The total literacy rate, which was only 18.33 per cent in 1951, rose to 52.21 per cent in 1991 and further increased to 65.4 per cent in 2001. During the last decade, the female literacy rate has shown much higher growth and reduced the male-female differential in literacy rates from 24.84 in 1991 to 21.7 in 2001.

The total expenditure on education in India is currently 3.99 per cent of GDP (2001-02) against the goal of 6 per cent of GDP. The government increased the allocation for education in successive Five Year Plans. The plan outlay on education increased from Rs. 153 crore in the First Five Year Plan to Rs. 24,908 crore in the Ninth Five Year Plan and to Rs. 43,825 crore in the Tenth Plan. The allocation for elementary education in Tenth Plan is Rs. 28,750 crore, which accounts for 66 per cent of allocation for the education sector.

The number of primary and upper primary schools has gone up from 2.23 lakh in 1950-51 to 8.17 lakh in 1998-99. According to the Sixth All India Education Survey 1999, 83 per cent of the rural habitations and 94 per cent of the rural population have access to primary schools within a distance of one km., and 84 per cent of the rural population have access to upper primary schools within a distance of three kms.

The enrolment ratio of children in the age group of 6-11 years (Primary Schools) has increased from 43.1 per cent in 1950-51 to 90 per cent in the early 1980s, and further to a little over 95 per cent in the year 2000-2001. Similarly, about 13 per cent of the total children in the age group of 11-14 years were enrolled in the schools during 1950-51 and their proportion has gone up to over 58 per cent in 2000-01. However, the proportion of female children enrolled in the schools (both 6-11 and 11-14 age groups) was lower when compared with male children.

The dropout rate for children in primary classes decreased from 53.5 per cent in 1981-82 to 39.58 in 1998-99 (GoI, 2002). The difference between dropout rates between boys and girls has come down from 6 percentage points in 1981-82 to 3 percentage points in 1998-99. The dropout rate for children (1998-99) is 50 per cent and more in the states of Bihar, Manipur, Meghalaya, Mizoram, Orissa, Uttar Pradesh and West Bengal.

In 1950-51, the pupil-teacher ratio for primary schools was 24 and it increased to 38 during 1980-81 and more than 40 in the 1990s. The student-teacher ratio for middle school has gone up from 20 to more than 35 between 1950-51 and 1990. To improve the quality of education in the schools, Operation Blackboard was launched in 1987-88 with the objective to provide essential facilities (two teachers and teaching/learning material) in all primary schools in the country. The scheme was expanded during 1993-94 and provided a third teacher to primary schools having enrolment of more than 100. The scheme also covered upper primary schools and provided additional teacher and teaching aids. As many as 5,22,902 primary schools and 1,27,257 upper primary schools received teaching learning equipment under the scheme during 1987-88 to 1999-2000.

## Assessment of the Service Delivery System

Major surveys by the Government of India *viz.*, Population Census, National Sample surveys, NCERT surveys, National Family Health surveys, ICMR surveys as well as periodical surveys by state governments and private organisations like NCAER provide information on scale and operations of public services. Evaluation studies on public services provide insights into delays and cost escalations in execution of works, in addition to the general assessment of targets and achievements. Information generated by these surveys enables government agencies to account for expenditure on public services.

The aggregate data on access to services, in terms of distance, are available for drinking water, schools and bus stops in different surveys. Access to health facility for each village is available in the population census. But the qualitative aspects of delivery of public services from the users' perspective, apart from access, are usually not addressed in these studies. The major exception is the recent survey sponsored by UNICEF on rural water supply (National Survey of Rural Community Water Supplies), which covered, in addition to the conventional aspects of sectoral surveys, the users' attitudes, perceptions and levels of satisfaction with the water supply schemes at community level. The study also looked into water quality, by testing water samples both at source and household points. This was an important improvement in the scope of sectoral studies, since it started assessing services from the users' perspective, even though this sample survey only covered the households mainly depending on hand pumps as the major source of water. Studies of this nature for other public services are not available at the state level. There are however, a few village surveys portraying socio-economic aspects of the villages, which include assessments of the public services. These studies are location specific and do not provide an assessment of delivery systems of public services at the aggregate level.

# 3

# Approach and Methodology

The gap in empirical data on the delivery of public services, described in the concluding part of Chapter 2, provided the impetus for this study. Hence, this study was taken up to focus on aspects of performance of public services, from a user perspective (such as ease of access to facilities, the immediate benefit in terms of quality of service and qualitative assessment in terms of user satisfaction). Indicators on quality and satisfaction with services (e.g. frequency of breakdown of hand pumps, satisfaction with behaviour of doctors and display of prices at ration shops) are measures of current performance, and provide a basis for corrective action.

## Approach

As was evident from the review of available research on public services reported in the earlier chapter, data on performance of public services is not collected by the service providers or researchers, in any significant scale. Hence, the study had to establish a comprehensive pool of primary data that could be analysed to assess service delivery. Primary data for the study was collected using household surveys, independent observation of selected public facilities, village profiles for the selected villages, and case studies. The design and methodology of the study were jointly designed by PAC and AC Nielsen-ORGMARG, and the field work was executed by AC Nielsen-ORGMARG.

The study made use of three complementary tools:

- sample household survey,
- key informant interviews or village profile sheets, and
- case studies.

The core of the study was the sample survey of households. However, the information common to all households in a sample village, such as availability of health care, road transport, fair price shop and primary school, were not collected from households. Instead, this information on availability and accessibility to services was collected through discussions with key informants in the sample villages, as a part of the profile of the villages. A limited number of case studies were taken up to illustrate the details on which data was collected and the issues reported by rural respondents and communities in accessing and using public services.

An important priority for the study was to collect data in a manner that captured the actual experiences of users of services. Hence, data was collected only from households which had first hand and recent experience in using the particular service. Hence, primary data was entirely based on user feedback collected through the structured interviews by trained investigators using an elaborate questionnaire.

The design of the study was tested out with a pilot survey in Karnataka, and the revised survey instruments field tested in four states (Gujarat, Karnataka, Uttar Pradesh, and West Bengal), prior to commencing the fieldwork for the study. A panel of highly experienced researchers reviewed the research design and analysis at each stage of the study.

## Sampling and Reliability of Estimates

### *Sampling*

The household survey covered 36,542 households selected from rural and urban areas of 24 states. The rural component of the sample consisted of 26,797 households selected from 2502 villages spread over 148 districts of the 22 states.[2] The urban component of the sample consisted of 9745 households selected from 107 towns spread over 24 states.

A multistage stratified random sampling procedure was adopted to select rural and urban households. While selecting the sample villages in each state, representation was given to all its socio-cultural regions, within which representation was ensured both to better and lesser-developed districts, and also to villages of different sizes.[3] At the regional level, districts were listed in order of their development index and one district each from below and above the median value of the development index were selected using random numbers. From each selected district, the villages were listed according to their population, classified by village class into A B and C class, and number allocated to each category chosen using Probability Proportionate to Size[4] (refer Table 3.2 for details).

2. The states of Jammu & Kashmir and Manipur were not included for reasons of security. Goa and Delhi were covered but are not part of this analysis.

3. The census definition of Village classes A, B and C was used. A: population > 5,000, B: population 1,000-5,000, C: population < 1,000

4. For each selected district, four: A class villages, six: B class villages and eight: C class villages were selected. From each selected A class village 15 to 20 households were selected based on the village population. Similarly, 10 households were selected from B class villages and 8 households from C class villages.

At the village level, a social map of the village was drawn showing the geographic layout of the village as well as the concentration of habitation by community/class/category. The proportions of the population by each category were determined, and the required number of households from that village was distributed across the categories of communities in proportion. Respondent households were selected in each pocket using systematic sampling with a random start following the right hand rule. For information on availability of and access to services, key informants such as the *sarpanch* (if he lived in the village), *panchayat* member (if there was one for the village) and the school teacher, were used to fill in the village profile sheet for each village. In select villages, observers carried out observations on the status and functioning of some of the facilities such as public taps, hand pumps, health centres, schools, ration shops and public transport. This information is however, not used in this report.

Similarly in the selection of urban households, representation was given for all the size groups of towns, (metro cities were excluded). Within the selected town, representation was given to all geographical zones.[5] In each geographical zone one to four wards were selected using systematic sampling. In the selected ward 10 households were selected using systematic sampling combined with the right hand rule with a random start.

At each household, the main respondent gave answers to the general questions and then for each of the service sections, the household member who was the most frequent user of the service was asked to respond to questions related to that service. Every Household that was selected had not necessarily used all the five services.

## Reliability of Estimates

The sample size in each state for rural and urban areas was determined with a view to keeping the error margin of the estimates within 5 per cent and at 95 per cent confidence level. The sample size for rural and urban areas in a state is adequate to make reliable estimates of the different dimensions of the five services. The lowest level at which the analysis was carried out for the state reports, was at the district level. At that level, however, the reliability was at 90 per cent confidence level. The sample is self-weighted to obtain estimates for each state. The state-wise distribution of the sample and the number of

---

5. The towns in each state were classified in to four size classes based on population *viz.*, class I (population 10,00,000 – 100,00,000), class II (population 50,000 – 10,00,000), class III (population 20000—50000) and class IV (population < 20,000). From each size class one to two towns were selected randomly. Each selected town was divided into four geographical zones. A sample size ranging from 50 to 150 households was allotted to the town based on its population. The allotted sample was proportionately distributed to the four geographical zones based on population.

villages/towns from which the sample was drawn are presented in the following tables.

### Table 3.1

*Distribution of Sample Household by Rural & Urban and by States*

| Sl. No. | State | Rural | Village Class | | | Urban | Total |
|---|---|---|---|---|---|---|---|
| | | | A | B | C | | |
| 1 | Andhra Pradesh | 1346 | 417 | 548 | 381 | 508 | 1854 |
| 2 | Arunachal Pradesh | 500 | 50 | 222 | 228 | 200 | 700 |
| 3 | Assam | 1229 | 408 | 422 | 399 | 510 | 1739 |
| 4 | Bihar | 1372 | 475 | 503 | 394 | 460 | 1832 |
| 5 | Delhi | 0 | 0 | 0 | 0 | 203 | 203 |
| 6 | Goa | 0 | 0 | 0 | 0 | 200 | 200 |
| 7 | Gujarat | 1356 | 480 | 525 | 351 | 510 | 1866 |
| 8 | Haryana | 957 | 347 | 364 | 246 | 510 | 1467 |
| 9 | Himachal Pradesh | 611 | 0 | 339 | 272 | 200 | 811 |
| 10 | Jharkhand | 690 | 152 | 313 | 225 | 65 | 755 |
| 11 | Karnataka | 1408 | 500 | 374 | 534 | 511 | 1919 |
| 12 | Kerala | 797 | 480 | 287 | 30 | 509 | 1306 |
| 13 | Madhya Pradesh | 2203 | 697 | 784 | 722 | 512 | 2715 |
| 14 | Maharashtra | 3091 | 1373 | 1233 | 485 | 600 | 3691 |
| 15 | Meghalaya | 758 | - | 400 | 358 | 600 | 1358 |
| 16 | Mizoram | 405 | 25 | 240 | 140 | 200 | 605 |
| 17 | Nagaland | 408 | - | 242 | 166 | 200 | 608 |
| 18 | Orissa | 835 | 223 | 360 | 252 | 404 | 1239 |
| 19 | Punjab | 971 | 364 | 377 | 230 | 401 | 1372 |
| 20 | Rajasthan | 1414 | 493 | 539 | 382 | 510 | 1924 |
| 21 | Sikkim | 393 | 75 | 177 | 141 | 200 | 593 |
| 22 | Tamil Nadu | 1345 | 390 | 517 | 438 | 511 | 1856 |
| 23 | Tripura | 453 | 160 | 179 | 114 | 200 | 653 |
| 24 | Uttaranchal | 441 | 67 | 199 | 175 | 0 | 441 |
| 25 | Uttar Pradesh | 2842 | 937 | 1029 | 876 | 511 | 3353 |
| 26 | West Bengal | 972 | 342 | 376 | 254 | 510 | 1482 |
| | **Total** | 26797 | 8455 | 10549 | 7793 | 9745 | 36542 |

## Table 3.2

*Number of Sample Villages and Towns by States*

| *Sl. No.* | *State* | *Districts* | *Village Class* | | | *Total Villages* | *Towns* |
|---|---|---|---|---|---|---|---|
| | | | *A* | *B* | *C* | | |
| 1 | Andhra Pradesh | 6 | 24 | 43 | 44 | 111 | 6 |
| 2 | Arunachal Pradesh | 3 | 2 | 13 | 22 | 37 | 1 |
| 3 | Assam | 7 | 25 | 47 | 49 | 121 | 6 |
| 4 | Bihar | 7 | 28 | 48 | 55 | 131 | 5 |
| 5 | Gujarat | 6 | 26 | 36 | 46 | 108 | 6 |
| 6 | Haryana | 6 | 24 | 41 | 40 | 105 | 6 |
| 7 | Himachal Pradesh | 4 | 0 | 28 | 33 | 61 | 3 |
| 8 | Jharkhand | 4 | 10 | 32 | 28 | 70 | 1 |
| 9 | Karnataka | 8 | 32 | 37 | 64 | 133 | 6 |
| 10 | Kerala | 6 | 24 | 20 | 3 | 47 | 6 |
| 11 | Madhya Pradesh | 13 | 42 | 84 | 93 | 219 | 6 |
| 12 | Maharashtra | 10 | 80 | 126 | 63 | 269 | 6 |
| 13 | Meghalaya | 4 | 0 | 10 | 17 | 27 | 3 |
| 14 | Mizoram | 2 | 1 | 14 | 14 | 29 | 3 |
| 15 | Nagaland | 2 | 0 | 15 | 14 | 29 | 3 |
| 16 | Orissa | 10 | 16 | 40 | 49 | 105 | 6 |
| 17 | Punjab | 6 | 25 | 40 | 40 | 105 | 6 |
| 18 | Rajasthan | 9 | 33 | 57 | 65 | 155 | 6 |
| 19 | Sikkim | 2 | 3 | 12 | 17 | 32 | 2 |
| 20 | Tamil Nadu | 8 | 28 | 52 | 54 | 134 | 6 |
| 27 | Tripura | 2 | 8 | 15 | 19 | 42 | 2 |
| 22 | Uttaranchal | 3 | 5 | 20 | 22 | 47 | 0 |
| 23 | Uttar Pradesh | 14 | 72 | 101 | 105 | 278 | 6 |
| 24 | West Bengal | 6 | 25 | 39 | 43 | 107 | 6 |
| | **Total** | 148 | 533 | 970 | 999 | 2502 | 107 |

*Services Covered*

The study covered the following five basic public services, provided mainly by the government; they are:

- drinking water,
- health care,
- road transport,
- public distribution system, and
- primary education and child care.

## Design of the Questionnaire

The questionnaire was designed in such a way that it covered important aspects but did not become too long for a household respond to with ease. The structure of the questionnaire consisted of an introductory part on demographic details of the household, separate sections on each of the five services, some questions on experiences with judicial and police services and a section on rights and entitlements.

The section for each service was designed taking into consideration the manner in which it was provided, the aspects of quality and reliability that users could provide valid feedback on and key dimensions of the service on which users could indicate the extent of satisfaction. Care was taken to avoid questions on aspects on which respondents would not be able to give valid assessments, such as quality of medicines or efficiency of doctors—instead, queries were limited to aspects such as regular availability of medicines, and availability of doctor when treatment was sought.

The elaborate preparations and pilot surveys helped to convert a major part of the questionnaire into closed ended queries, with response options pre-coded. This approach was also applied for measuring numerical responses such as distance and time taken. A small set of open-ended questions was retained in the questionnaire, particularly in relation to elaboration of problems encountered.

Questions to assess the degree of satisfaction with services used a two-step approach. The respondent was first asked whether the household was satisfied or dissatisfied with the quality of the service or did not know or could not say whether they were satisfied or dissatisfied. In the next step they were asked to specify the level of their satisfaction/dissatisfaction (choosing between two options). This therefore resulted in a five-point scale being used but in two steps. The five points were: very/fully satisfied, satisfied, don't know/can't say, dissatisfied and very/fully dissatisfied.

Conducting interviews in local language was seen as critical to ensuring valid responses; hence the questionnaires needed to be translated for the investigators to conduct the interview with ease and reliability. The basic questionnaire was first prepared in English, and vetted by the panel of experts. After the pilot survey, the questionnaire was revised. Thereafter, the questionnaire was translated into several languages. The translated versions were independently assessed by another individual who was well versed in the local language as well as in English to ensure that the translation truly reflected the content of the original questionnaire.

## Fieldwork/Data Collection Modalities

The fieldwork was carried out in 2001. AC 7Neilsen ORG-MARG carried out the data collection on behalf of Public Affairs Centre. There was a team of around 30 investigators in each state, who were divided into smaller teams of five with one senior (more experienced) investigator supervising each team. The supervisor would not conduct any interviews but would allocate households according to the sampling plan and also monitor the interviews conducted by each member of his team. In addition it was also the supervisor's responsibility to collect information for the village profile from key informants in each village. A separate team of investigators was delegated the task of observation of facilities.

All investigators were drawn from a panel of field resource persons who had previously worked with ORG-MARG on other surveys. Selected investigators were provided with systematic briefing on the survey, content of the questionnaire, and opportunity for mock interviews, in order to ensure adequate preparation for fieldwork. Briefing notes and scrutiny manuals were prepared and given to the team to assure uniformity of data collection at All-India level.

## Quality Assurance

AC Nielsen ORG-MARG as well as Public Affairs Centre put in place a monitoring mechanism to assure the quality of the data collected. Field supervisors accompanied investigators to the field and spot checked a reasonable proportion of interviews. They also back checked 30 per cent of the interviews. This was further reinforced by random checks by senior executives. Field supervisors also scrutinised the schedules/questionnaires for errors (missed entries, wrong entries or filling in of questions that were to be skipped) on the field as well as before data was entered. Research officers from

Public Affairs Centre visited the field in several states and monitored the work of the investigators.

## Framework of Analysis

The data collected from the three methods—village profiles, household survey and case studies—were analysed separately and the findings triangulated for arriving at conclusions and preparing the report.

The analysis was carried out at several levels. While the principal objective was to make estimates at the state level, in order to make comparisons across states, analysis was also carried out at the level of socio-cultural region and districts, depending on sample size for the particular variable being analysed. Other significant frames of analysis were across rural and urban areas, by economic status (to be defined later), across important caste categories and by different size of villages—these were carried out for the country as a whole, and for each state.

The analysis focused on four sets of indicators: ease of access, extent of use, quality and reliability, and satisfaction with services. Proximity of the users to the service provided was the measure of access, extent to which the respondents used the service was considered usage, and the dependability of the service measured its reliability. The user's rating of the overall effectiveness of the service was measured in terms of overall satisfaction with the service.

Specifically, 'access' was defined as follows for each service:

- *Drinking Water*: access to drinking water from a protected water source within 100 metres of the residence.
- *Public Transport*: access to public buses within one kilometre of the village, and access to a pucca road.
- *Primary Education*: presence of a primary school within one kilometre of the village.
- *Primary Health Care*: presence of a primary health care centre within one kilometre of the village.
- *Public Distribution System*: presence of a ration shop within one kilometre of the village.

While data from the village profiles was used for estimating rural access to four services *viz.*, health care, road transport, public distribution system and primary education and childcare, for drinking water the household survey findings were used to measure access. In the case of the urban data, the household data was used to measure access for all services.

Since estimation of patterns and standards were central to the study, the analytical tools applied widely were estimation of proportions and means. This made possible extensive use of two way cross tabulations to draw insights into significant variations across demographic groups. Second order analysis was carried out using regression analysis to assess the influence of several factors (individually and collectively) on the level of satisfaction with services.

'Usage' was measured as follows:

- *Drinking Water*: usage of public sources of drinking water.
- *Public Transport*: usage of Government/private buses.
- *Primary Education*: percentage of households with primary school-going age children sending their children to primary school.
- *Primary Health Care*: usage of government health facility for major ailment or minor ailment.
- *Public Distribution System*: usage of the ration card at least once in two months.

'Reliability' was measured differently for each service that was covered:

- *Drinking Water*: frequency of breakdown–percentage of households reporting breakdown in source once in three months.
- *Public Transport*: satisfaction with punctuality of buses.
- *Primary Education*: satisfaction with behaviour of teacher.
- *Primary Health Care*: presence of doctors and paramedics.
- *Public Distribution System*: regular availability of commodities.

'Satisfaction' was measured for more than one aspect of quality of service for each service. The measures used were as given below:

- *Drinking Water*: satisfaction with quality and quantity (adequacy) of water.
- *Public Transport*: satisfaction with frequency of service and behaviour of conductor.
- *Primary Education*: satisfaction with building and toilets.
- *Primary Health Care*: satisfaction with behaviour of doctors and paramedics.
- *Public Distribution System*: satisfaction with quality and quantity of commodities and with the fairness of the shopkeeper.

# 4

## State of Public Services in India

The analysis presented in this chapter is based on the data collected through the survey covering 36,542 households spread over 24 states used in tandem with the village profile data. Response related to particular services was collected only when the household had made use of the service recently.

The demographic characteristics of the sample households show that about 64 per cent of respondents are above 36 years of age and 73 per cent of respondents are literate (Annexure 1). The economic status of the respondent households, using type of housing as a proxy for economic status, indicated that 34.2 per cent dwell in *kutcha* houses, 38.1 per cent in semi-*pucca* houses and the remaining 27.7 per cent in *pucca* houses. If the sample was analysed by self-reported income, using the Planning Commission criteria for poverty (Rs.20,000 per annum per household), about one third of responding households were below the poverty line. The proportion of the poor in the sample, therefore, is close to the Planning Commission estimate of 26.1 per cent of households below poverty line for the year 1999-00 (MoF, 2003).

### Drinking Water

Safe drinking water is a basic requirement for all households. The main sources of protected water supply for the households in the country are:

1. Domestic piped supply by local/state government.
2. Public taps provided by local/state government.
3. Hand pumps—private or provided by local/state government.
4. Bore wells—private or provided by local/state government

Other non-protected public sources, used by some sections of the population are common/village wells, tanks, streams, etc.

*Availability and Use*

Protected sources (government and private) serve 80 per cent of households in the country. Around two-thirds of the households (62 per cent) use protected water supply from government sources, while 18 per cent use private protected sources. High levels of use of public water supply takes place in the states of Sikkim (90 per cent), Tamil Nadu (90 per cent) and Arunachal Pradesh (87 per cent); low level of use is in Assam (10 per cent), Bihar (18 per cent) and Nagaland (20 per cent).

> **Box 4.1**
>
> ***Kuliana*** village located in the Bada Sahi Block of the Mayurbhanj district of Orissa faced with inadequate supply of water through government sources. A group of villagers approached NABARD who helped construct an overhead tank and an elaborate network of pipelines to provide drinking water to every household. Villagers manage the system, and dependence on Village Common Well and Handpumps has reduced considerably. This has induced a sense of hygiene among the villagers. Although, the village still lacks a proper drainage system, villagers keep surroundings clean—a small yet significant step towards a better tomorrow.

About 55 per cent of households in the country enjoy ease of access (within 100 meters) to public water supply. Ease of access to the households is more in the states of Sikkim (90 per cent), Tamil Nadu (83 per cent) and Arunachal Pradesh (81 per cent) and less in the states of Assam (9 per cent), Nagaland (19 per cent), and Bihar (16 per cent).

The lower dependency of rural households on public water sources in the state of Punjab and parts of Uttar Pradesh could be due to the high prevalence of irrigation pump sets. Rural households in these areas use the same irrigation source for domestic and drinking water purposes and hence, may not be feeling the necessity for a separate public source.

Public protected water is used more in urban areas (72 per cent) than in rural areas (58 per cent). Similarly, the ease of access to the households is more in urban areas (68 per cent) than in rural areas (50 per cent).

*Reliability of Service*

The 'use' of a given source of drinking water by a household does not say anything about the regularity of supply. If the supply is irregular or infrequent, it implies a more limited use of the water supply source in contrast to a case where water supply is available throughout the day. Table 4.2 below reports on this aspect of water supply from public tap and piped water supply for the states where these are important sources.

A positive feature is that the vast majority of households using public water supply sources report water availability on a daily basis though the duration of supply might vary. But it also shows that daily availability is high in terms of coverage (over 90 per cent) only in four states with respect to public taps and in six states with respect to piped water supply. Nearly 20-30 per cent of the households do not enjoy this facility in the remaining states.

### Table 4.1

*Public Drinking Water Facilities: Access, Use, Reliability and Full Satisfaction*

*(per cent households–rural and urban combined)*

| Sl.No. | States | Access | Use[1] | Reliability (breakdown) | | Full Satisfaction (piped supply) | |
|---|---|---|---|---|---|---|---|
| | | | | Taps | Hand pumps | Adequacy | Quality |
| 1 | Andhra Pradesh | 69 | 82 | 24 | 27 | 25 | 27 |
| 2 | Arunachal Pradesh | 81 | 87 | 17 | Ns | 3 | 4 |
| 3 | Assam | 9 | 10 | 30 | Ns | 25 | 33 |
| 4 | Bihar | 16 | 18 | 33 | 34 | 17 | 18 |
| 5 | Gujarat | 70 | 75 | 27 | 21 | 46 | 61 |
| 6 | Haryana | 42 | 50 | 23 | 33 | 27 | 39 |
| 7 | Himachal Pradesh | 80 | 84 | 20 | Ns | 12 | 18 |
| 8 | Karnataka | 71 | 79 | 19 | 22 | 35 | 45 |
| 9 | Kerala | 28 | 30 | 17 | Ns | 16 | 22 |
| 10 | Madhya Pradesh | 61 | 75 | 12 | 20 | 30 | 47 |
| 11 | Maharashtra | 77 | 79 | 11 | 11 | 11 | 13 |
| 12 | Meghalaya | 69 | 77 | 22 | 0 | 14 | 9 |
| 13 | Mizoram | 68 | 72 | 33 | 7 | 1 | 9 |
| 14 | Nagaland | 19 | 20 | 29 | Ns | 0 | 0 |
| 15 | Orissa | 56 | 80 | 12 | 16 | 11 | 18 |
| 16 | Punjab | 30 | 31 | 21 | Ns | 2 | 3 |
| 17 | Rajasthan | 56 | 75 | 45 | 60 | 9 | 23 |
| 18 | Sikkim | 90 | 90 | Ns | Ns | 17 | 25 |
| 19 | Tamil Nadu | 83 | 90 | 40 | 68 | 52 | 60 |
| 20 | Tripura | 49 | 63 | 46 | 37 | 7 | 8 |
| 21 | Uttar Pradesh | 36 | 39 | 52 | 16 | 50 | 46 |
| 22 | West Bengal | 61 | 81 | 8 | 20 | 14 | 15 |
| | **National average** | 55 | 62 | 25 | 24 | 20 | 27 |

*Notes:* Ns: Percentage is not computed when the number of sample users is less than 30.

[1] Use exceeds access in some cases as respondents are getting water from sources beyond 100 meters (the norm for access in the study).

## Table 4.2

*Frequency of Water Supply by Source*[6]

*(per cent of households)*

| Sl.No. | States | Public Tap | | | Piped Water Supply | | |
|---|---|---|---|---|---|---|---|
| | | Daily | Alternate Day | Once in 3 to 7 days | Daily | Alternate day | Once in 3 to 7 days |
| 1 | Andhra Pradesh | 84.8 | 14.0 | 1.1 | 78.7 | 16.0 | 5.3 |
| 2 | Assam | 77.0 | 22.3 | 0.7 | 92.0 | 5.3 | 2.7 |
| 3 | Bihar | 75.0 | 20.8 | 4.2 | 95.7 | 2.1 | 2.1 |
| 4 | Gujarat | 89.4 | 8.2 | 2.3 | 86.7 | 11.3 | 2.0 |
| 5 | Haryana | 95.5 | 2.6 | 1.8 | 84.6 | 8.8 | 6.6 |
| 6 | Himachal Pradesh | 91.9 | 6.3 | 1.8 | 90.1 | 5.7 | 4.2 |
| 7 | Karnataka | 78.3 | 16.2 | 5.5 | 76.7 | 11.7 | 11.7 |
| 8 | Kerala | 78.3 | 10.6 | 11.1 | 69.9 | 27.2 | 2.9 |
| 9 | Madhya Pradesh | 69.5 | 25.2 | 5.3 | 79.2 | 13.6 | 7.2 |
| 10 | Maharashtra | 82.5 | 14.1 | 3.4 | 89.0 | 7.5 | 3.5 |
| 11 | Orissa | 95.8 | 3.0 | 1.2 | 98.6 | 1.4 | 0 |
| 12 | Punjab | 89.8 | 6.8 | 3.4 | 90.6 | 3.7 | 5.7 |
| 13 | Rajasthan | 75.4 | 11.4 | 13.2 | 54.0 | 30.9 | 15.1 |
| 14 | Tamil Nadu | 80.6 | 11.1 | 8.3 | 43.3 | 17.6 | 39.1 |
| 15 | Uttar Pradesh | 73.2 | 18.6 | 8.2 | 92.9 | 4.9 | 2.2 |
| 16 | West Bengal | 99.7 | 0.3 | 0.0 | 100.0 | 0.0 | 0.0 |

> **Box 4.2**
>
> Having access to protected sources of drinking water is clearly not a solution, as evidence from the field revealed. When the hand pump breaks down or runs dry most of the summer, villagers in Jhagaria, Madhya Pradesh, have to depend on unprotected open wells. In Jalalpur, Gujarat, women trudged 3 kms to access water from an Ashram, just because the installed borewell handpump in the village broke down years back.

The reliability of protected water supply is adversely affected by breakdown in the supply or source. One fourth of the households in the country reported that water supply through public taps breaks down at least once in three months (Table 4.1). Similarly, about one-fourth (24 per cent) of households using public hand pumps also reported breaks down of hand pumps at least once in three

6. Analysis of the main 16 states.

months. Breakdowns of public taps are reported more by users in rural areas (27 per cent) as compared to urban users (18 per cent). On the other hand, breakdowns of public hand pumps reported more by users in urban areas (31 per cent) as compared to rural users (24 per cent).

Breakdowns in supply of public taps are reported by a large number of households in Uttar Pradesh (52 per cent), Tripura (46 per cent), Rajasthan (45 per cent) and Tamil Nadu (40 per cent). In contrast, a small number of households reported lower incidence of breakdowns in West Bengal (8 per cent), Maharashtra (11 per cent), Orissa (12 per cent), and Madhya Pradesh (12 per cent). In the case of public hand pumps, breakdowns are reported by larger number of households in Tamil Nadu (68 per cent) and Rajasthan (60 per cent) and lower incidence of breakdowns are reported in Mizoram (7 per cent), Maharashtra (11 per cent), Orissa (16 per cent) and Uttar Pradesh (16 per cent).

The proportion of households involved in maintenance of public sources is relatively high in Kerala (65 per cent), Rajasthan (51 per cent), Bihar (46 per cent) and Uttar Pradesh (40 per cent). A lower involvement in maintenance is reported in West Bengal (4 per cent), Orissa (7 per cent) and Himachal Pradesh (9 per cent). Schemes emphasising community management have been implemented in recent years in Kerala, Maharashtra, Karnataka, Rajasthan and Gujarat. These initiatives appear to be yielding results in the states of Kerala and Rajasthan.

*Willingness to Pay for Better Service*

There seems to be widespread consensus on a willingness to pay more for better water supply services—40 per cent of households in the country reported willingness to pay more. The extent of willingness to pay more for better water supply services varied across states. Large numbers of users in Rajasthan (75 per cent), Uttar Pradesh (63 per cent), Karnataka (57 per cent), Andhra Pradesh (50 per cent) and Bihar (50 per cent) indicated willingness to pay more. Lower levels of willingness to pay more are reported in Kerala (17 per cent), Tamil Nadu (18 per cent) and West Bengal (21 per cent).

Participation in maintenance of the public sources seems to have a bearing on willingness to pay more for better services (correlation coefficient 0.46). It is stands to reason to expect

> **Box 4.3**
>
> Bhadgaon village *panchayat*, Maharashtra provides piped water supply to 1885 households. There are also 85 public handpumps at various locations. The *Panchayat* collects a monthly tariff of Rs. 30 and the rate of recovery is reported to be very good.

## Table 4.3

*Maintenance and Willingness to Pay for Drinking Water*

*(per cent of households)*

| *Sl. No.* | *States* | *Households Involved in Maintenance* | *Willingness to Pay More* |
|---|---|---|---|
| 1 | Andhra Pradesh | 18 | 50 |
| 2 | Arunachal Pradesh | 29 | 29 |
| 3 | Assam | 11 | 30 |
| 4 | Bihar | 46 | 50 |
| 5 | Gujarat | 26 | 31 |
| 6 | Haryana | 30 | 44 |
| 7 | Himachal Pradesh | 9 | 44 |
| 8 | Karnataka | 23 | 57 |
| 9 | Kerala | 65 | 17 |
| 10 | Madhya Pradesh | 14 | 38 |
| 11 | Maharashtra | 29 | 43 |
| 12 | Meghalaya | 10 | 22 |
| 13 | Mizoram | 24 | 39 |
| 14 | Nagaland | 22 | 30 |
| 15 | Orissa | 7 | 35 |
| 16 | Punjab | 11 | 30 |
| 17 | Rajasthan | 51 | 75 |
| 18 | Sikkim | - | - |
| 19 | Tamil Nadu | 17 | 18 |
| 20 | Tripura | 16 | 36 |
| 21 | Uttar Pradesh | 40 | 63 |
| 22 | West Bengal | 4 | 21 |
| | **National Average** | 23 | 40 |

persons involved in maintaining public sources to be aware of costs of reliable services, leading to willingness to pay enough to ensure operation and maintenance. Hence, higher percentage of households involved in maintenance might be more willing to pay more for better services compared to others.

Willingness to pay also needs to be examined in the context of unofficial payments that users make. Among the households using public water sources, about 11 per cent reported to have paid bribes for getting the sources repaired when there was breakdown. Among the households using public water sources, about 5 per cent of them have paid the amount voluntarily and the remaining 6 per cent paid on demand by the maintenance staff. The practice of unofficial payments for maintenance of public water sources are relatively more in the states of Bihar, Uttar Pradesh, Rajasthan, Punjab and Haryana.

*Satisfaction with Service*

Adequacy and quality of water is a major concern in many parts of India. One-fifth of households using public piped supply are fully satisfied with the adequacy of water. The percentage of households fully satisfied with the adequacy of water from other protected sources is about 24 per cent. About one-fourth (27 per cent) of households using public piped supply are fully satisfied with the quality of water. The percentage of households fully satisfied with the quality of water from other protected sources is about 32 per cent. Full satisfaction with quantity is more widespread among users of piped water supply in Tamil Nadu (52 per cent), Uttar Pradesh (50 per cent), and Gujarat (46 per cent) while, users in Nagaland (0 per cent), Mizoram (1 per cent) and Punjab (2 per cent) reported low full satisfaction.

In the case of other protected sources, full satisfaction with quantity is reported more in the states of Uttar Pradesh (49 per cent), and Tamil Nadu (41 per cent), and less in the states of Tripura (1 per cent), Nagaland (3 per cent), Punjab (3 per cent), Mizoram (5 per cent) and Orissa (5 per cent). In the quality of piped water supply, Gujarat (61 per cent) and Tamil Nadu (60 per cent) reported higher full satisfaction while Nagaland (0 per cent), Punjab (3 per cent), and Arunachal Pradesh (4 per cent) reported lower full satisfaction. Full satisfaction with quality of water from other public sources is high in Uttar Pradesh (54 per cent) and Tamil Nadu (53 per cent), and low in Nagaland (0 per cent) and Tripura (3 per cent).

*Summary on Drinking Water*

The picture suggests that easy access to a public protected drinking water source is available to just above half of the population. One out of every five citizen still depends on unprotected sources for the vital daily requirement. It appears the programmes of Government of India to provide potable water to rural habitations have narrowed rural and urban disparities in the access and use of drinking water from public protected sources. Frequent breakdown in the supply from public sources are affecting one-fourths of users. There seems to be widespread recognition and willingness to pay more for better water supply services. There is a need to encourage public participation in the maintenance of public sources of water supply. In drinking water, private provision is not a substitute for public provision. The low levels of full satisfaction are indicative of the need for service providers to closely examine the range of local issues that are affecting service delivery.

## Health Care

State governments have attached a significant priority to provide minimum health facilities to the population. A variety of health facilities have been set up in a hierarchical way at different levels ranging from village level to state level. The private sector also plays an important role in providing health care, which includes private hospitals and medical practitioners, as well as practitioners of local medical traditions. Proximity of health care facility is critical to ensuring timely and convenient treatment.

### *Access*

The location and density of health care facilities by the government are governed by population norms, and distance from habitations is not a criterion for extending health care facilities. As there is no existing norm to provide health care facility based on distance, and that ease of access has to be measured in terms of distance, one kilometre distance either from a village or from an urban household is considered an appropriate criterion for ease of access to health care for the present analysis. This criterion may seem rigorous, but it serves the purpose of bringing out the relative performance of the states in provision of access to health care facilities to the people. Further, the present status of access serves as a benchmark for future comparisons in the provision of services.

**Box 4.4**

Having easy access to a health care facility is of vital importance to those needing immediate treatment. The trauma citizens face is highlighted by the experience of pregnant women living in Sankal, located in the hill tract of Vadodara, Gujarat, who have to travel 13 kms to the nearest health facility. This is the reality that many others, across the country experience, in accessing health care.

About 40 per cent of sample villages and 41 per cent of urban households reported ease of access to government health care facilities (Table 4.4). Ease of access to government health care facilities for rural area is high in Sikkim (97 per cent), Mizoram (82 per cent) and Punjab (62 per cent), and relatively low in Nagaland (12 per cent), and Bihar (21 per cent). Similarly, the ease of access is more for urban households in Orissa (73 per cent) and Arunachal Pradesh (72 per cent) and low in Meghalaya (15 per cent) and Bihar (17 per cent).

### *Usage of Government Health Care Facilities*

The medical facilities are used for treatment of minor[7] and major[8] ailments. For treatment of minor ailments, 45 per cent of households in the country use

---

7. Cough, cold, fever, wounds, loose motions, etc.

8. Surgery, fractures, complicated deliveries, heart attacks, etc.

## Table 4.4

*Access and Usage of Health Care Facilities*

*(per cent of households)*

| Sl. No. | States | Government Health Facility within 1 km. | | Usage: Minor Ailments | | Usage: Major Ailments | |
|---|---|---|---|---|---|---|---|
| | | Rural* | Urban | Govt. | Private | Govt. | Private |
| 1 | Andhra Pradesh | 36 | 55 | 55 | 22 | 48 | 33 |
| 2 | Arunachal Pradesh | 36 | 72 | 95 | 2 | 76 | 8 |
| 3 | Assam | 38 | 49 | 68 | 14 | 68 | 26 |
| 4 | Bihar | 21 | 17 | 7 | 14 | 13 | 49 |
| 5 | Gujarat | 36 | 43 | 43 | 13 | 58 | 40 |
| 6 | Haryana | 35 | 21 | 23 | 5 | 28 | 53 |
| 7 | Himachal Pradesh | 53 | 59 | 51 | 4 | 58 | 36 |
| 8 | Karnataka | 26 | 46 | 48 | 14 | 49 | 46 |
| 9 | Kerala | 57 | 59 | 60 | 37 | 46 | 52 |
| 10 | Madhya Pradesh | 44 | 53 | 49 | 16 | 65 | 23 |
| 11 | Maharashtra | 51 | 38 | 50 | 9 | 69 | 23 |
| 12 | Meghalaya | 23 | 15 | 38 | 22 | 38 | 47 |
| 13 | Mizoram | 82 | 64 | 84 | 5 | 94 | 4 |
| 14 | Nagaland | 12 | 23 | 44 | 30 | 24 | 68 |
| 15 | Orissa | 28 | 73 | 83 | 4 | 92 | 6 |
| 16 | Punjab | 62 | 24 | 24 | 12 | 42 | 52 |
| 17 | Rajasthan | 52 | 65 | 74 | 5 | 87 | 8 |
| 18 | Sikkim | 97 | 45 | 92 | 2 | 97 | 1 |
| 19 | Tamil Nadu | 44 | 42 | 53 | 24 | 60 | 33 |
| 20 | Tripura | 53 | 34 | 59 | 6 | 72 | 13 |
| 21 | Uttar Pradesh | 34 | 23 | 19 | 4 | 41 | 37 |
| 22 | West Bengal | 33 | 57 | 47 | 3 | 88 | 6 |
| | **National Average** | 40 | 41 | 45 | 12 | 55 | 33 |

*Note:* * percentage of villages

government health facilities and 12 per cent use private hospitals. For treatment of major ailments 55 per cent of households use government health facilities and 33 per cent use private hospitals. Though, the dependency on government health facilities is high among rural and urban households, it is relatively higher for rural households. On the other side, the dependency on private hospitals is relatively more for urban households. It is interesting to note that private hospitals are more used by households for major ailments than minor ailments. It was also observed that households tend to use private hospitals more for major ailments rather than for treatment for minor ailments.

Households in Arunachal Pradesh (95 per cent), Sikkim (92 per cent), Mizoram (84 per cent) and Orissa (83 per cent) reported higher dependence on government health facilities for minor ailments while the households in Bihar (7 per cent) reported lower dependence. Both rural and urban households in Bihar reported more dependence on private hospitals than government health facilities for minor ailments. In contrast, the dependence on private hospitals for minor ailments is more in the states of Kerala (37 per cent), Nagaland (30 per cent), Tamil Nadu (24 per cent), Meghalaya (22 per cent) and Andhra Pradesh (22 per cent).

For major ailments, the households in Sikkim (97 per cent), Mizoram (94 per cent) and Orissa (92 per cent) reported higher dependence on government health facilities, and the households in Bihar (13 per cent), and Nagaland (24 per cent) reported lower dependence. Households in Bihar, Haryana, Kerala, Meghalaya, Nagaland and Punjab reported greater dependence on private hospitals than government health facilities, for major ailments. This pattern continues when it comes to major ailments even among rural households in Bihar, Himachal Pradesh and Kerala where a higher percentage of depend upon private hospitals compared to their urban counterparts.

The intensity of use of healthcare facilities depends heavily on ease of access. Data from the survey across the states on ease of access to government health facilities for rural areas and use of government health facilities for minor and major ailments by rural households highlight this association, through correlations of 0.47 in case of minor ailments and 0.55 in case of major ailments. This association indicates that proximity of health care facilities is an important factor that influences use of government health facilities.

*Reliability of Health Care*

Services cannot be provided at healthcare facilities, without the presence of trained personnel. 83 per cent of users of government health facilities found

## Table 4.5

*Government Health Care: Reliability and Full Satisfaction*

*(per cent households–rural and urban combined)*

| Sl. No. | States | Reliability (Presence) | | Full Satisfaction (Behaviour) | |
|---|---|---|---|---|---|
| | | Doctors | Paramedics | Doctors | Paramedics |
| 1 | Andhra Pradesh | 28 | 59 | 6 | 7 |
| 2 | Arunachal Pradesh | 64 | 65 | 1 | 0 |
| 3 | Assam | 72 | 84 | 5 | 5 |
| 4 | Bihar | 79 | 89 | 8 | 5 |
| 5 | Gujarat | 95 | 96 | 30 | 27 |
| 6 | Haryana | 75 | 83 | 14 | 12 |
| 7 | Himachal Pradesh | 80 | 95 | 10 | 8 |
| 8 | Karnataka | 74 | 93 | 31 | 27 |
| 9 | Kerala | 58 | 89 | 9 | 8 |
| 10 | Madhya Pradesh | 63 | 78 | 8 | 8 |
| 11 | Maharashtra | 88 | 93 | 22 | 21 |
| 12 | Meghalaya | 64 | 63 | 15 | 15 |
| 13 | Mizoram | 54 | 75 | 2 | 1 |
| 14 | Nagaland | 68 | 78 | 1 | 1 |
| 15 | Orissa | 79 | 89 | 3 | 2 |
| 16 | Punjab | 85 | 85 | 2 | 3 |
| 17 | Rajasthan | 59 | 73 | 5 | 5 |
| 18 | Sikkim | 77 | 94 | 20 | 16 |
| 19 | Tamil Nadu | 71 | 90 | 29 | 29 |
| 20 | Tripura | 39 | 47 | 1 | 1 |
| 21 | Uttar Pradesh | 72 | 76 | 18 | 18 |
| 22 | West Bengal | 63 | 77 | 11 | 3 |
| | **National Average** | 70 | 83 | 14 | 12 |

paramedical personnel at the time of their visit, while 70 per cent reported the presence of doctor. Higher proportion of urban users reported availability of doctors and paramedical staff at the time of their visit compared to rural users. A high proportion of users in Gujarat (95 per cent), Maharashtra (88 per cent) and Punjab (85 per cent) reported availability of doctors at the time of their visit to government health facilities. While low proportion of users in Andhra Pradesh (28 per cent) and Tripura (39 per cent) reported availability of doctors.

*Satisfaction with Health Care*

Although, about 55 per cent of the households in the country make use of government health facilities, few among them are fully satisfied with the service they get. The extent of full satisfaction with the behaviour of doctors and paramedical staff (out-patients) is 14 per cent and 12 per cent respectively. Full satisfaction with behaviour of doctors (out-patients) seems to be high in Karnataka (31 per cent), Gujarat (30 per cent) and Tamil Nadu (29 per cent), and as low as one per cent in Arunachal Pradesh, Nagaland and Tripura. Full satisfaction with behaviour paramedical staff is also high in Tamil Nadu (29 per cent), Gujarat (27 per cent) and Karnataka (27 per cent) and low in Arunachal Pradesh, Mizoram, Nagaland and Tripura (about 1 per cent). The full satisfaction with the behaviour of doctors and paramedical staff is relatively more in urban areas compared to rural areas.

**Box 4.5**

Edira village is situated at a distance of 7 kms. from Mahabubnagar town. Edira village has a newly built PHC with all medical facilities. A lady doctor visits the PHC only twice a week and hardly attends to the patients. The villagers reported that, she refrains from even touching the patients at the time of examination. The villagers are reluctant to visit the PHC due to her behaviour. The villagers have made written complaints against the doctor. A *morcha* had been led by the village SHG members shouting slogans against the doctor "maaku mandulu voddu, doctoroo voddu" (we do not want medicines and doctor). This news had appeared in a few local papers.

For rural households, there appears to be an association between the presence of doctors at the health facilities and full satisfaction with the behaviour of doctors, as well as presence of paramedical staff at the health facilities and full satisfaction with the behaviour of paramedical staff. The correlation coefficients for these variables are 0.57, 0.47 respectively. The associations suggest that

**Box 4.6**

Villagers in Chahipeda, Madhya Pradesh are quite satisfied with their PHC because doctors and paramedical staff are present throughout the day. Inhabitants of Fardapur, Aurangdabad, Maharashtra located close to the famous Ajanta Caves too were satisfied, as the ANM lives in the village itself and visits houses regularly.

satisfaction of rural users of health facilities tends to be higher when the doctors and paramedical staff are more present regularly, and that full satisfaction with the government health service appears to significantly depend on the reliability of the services. In contrast, there was no significant relationship in data from urban areas; this is probably because urban households have greater choice in health service provision, and would move to another provider (even private) should there be an urgent need.

Further, there is significant correlation between the presence of doctors and the behaviour of paramedical staff (0.53). The presence of doctors at the health facilities appear to make the paramedical staff more responsive towards the patients. This could be due to the responsibility discharged by doctors in administering public health care facilities, whereby the regular presence of administrative head on the work spot makes a substantial difference in the behaviour of subordinate staff and makes them more responsive.

### *Cost of Health Care*

Health care facilities provided by the government are expected to cater to the needs of the poor and underprivileged through free or subsidised health care. Around 40 per cent of in-patients and 16 per cent of out-patients paid fee for the health care service. About 16 per cent of in-patients have reported payment of bribes.

**Box 4.7**

Cheap treatment is a major incentive for villagers to use the services of the PHCs. However, for the residents of Kodakkambur village in Kerala, located in the Western Ghats, the nearest PHC normally has no staff in attendance and the villagers are forced to seek the services of private clinics, for which they have to pay a great deal more.

### *Summary on Health Care Services*

Less than half of the population in rural as well as urban areas have easy access to government healthcare facilities. Both, rural and urban households, use government health facilities more than the private hospitals. The treatment in government health facilities is not completely free. Around 40 per cent of in-patients and 16 per cent of out-patients paid fee for the health care service. But full satisfaction with respect to government health services is very low. Regular presence of doctors is the primary requisite to treat the patients, and users' satisfaction may primarily depend on the outcome of the treatment. For rural households, the presence of doctors at the government health facilities appears to be a major factor for full satisfaction with the facility. There, however, seems to be no significant association between the presence of doctors and full satisfaction with government health facilities, among urban households.

## Road Transport

Road transport is an important infrastructure for social and economic development of developing countries. The government of India and the state governments have given importance for strengthening the road transport infrastructure. The resources invested on the sector have increased considerably over the years. Road transport includes roads, bridges and government and private owned and operated transport services. Private sector has come to play an important role in road transport sector in some of the states. Unlike some other basic services, there is no free entry for private players in passenger transport sector. The state governments control the operation of the private sector in passenger transport through licensing policy. In Andhra Pradesh, public transport is state monopoly. Most of the states allocate certain routes to private players and in some states both government and private buses operate on the same routes.

### *Access to Roads and Bus Transport*

Cemented/tarred roads seek to ensure that villages are accessible in all kinds of weather. Tarred roads are available in 39 per cent of the villages in the country. There are variations across the states in the access to tarred roads.

A higher percentage of villages in Kerala (86 per cent), Haryana (82 per cent) and Gujarat (66 per cent) have access to cemented/tarred roads and lower access to *pucca* roads is observed in the rural areas of Nagaland (0 per cent), Tripura (3 per cent), Arunachal Pradesh (8 per cent) and Andhra Pradesh (8 per cent). Bus stops are available within 1 km. in 44 per cent of villages. A higher percentage of villages in the states of Kerala (86 per cent), Tamil Nadu (74 per cent), and Gujarat (73 per cent), and have bus stops within 1 km.

> **Box 4.8**
>
> Residents of Jamalpur kala village, near Hardwar, Uttar Pradesh saw easy access to public transport as a means to secure livelihood opportunities, in and around Hardwar. When no government buses are available, as is the case for residents of Jhagaria village in Mandsour, Madhya Pradesh, they have no choice but to await private buses that follow no fixed schedule, and pay a price which they feel is very high.

### *Use of Government Bus Transport*

The state governments have a wide network of buses plying within and outside the states including the routes (particularly in rural areas) that may

**Table 4.6**

*Percentage of Villages having Access to Tarred Road and Bus Stops*

| *Sl. No.* | *States* | *Availability of Bus Stops within 1 Km.* | *Access to Tarred Road* |
|---|---|---|---|
| 1 | Andhra Pradesh | 57 | 8 |
| 2 | Arunachal Pradesh | 24 | 8 |
| 3 | Assam | 32 | 23 |
| 4 | Bihar | 17 | 23 |
| 5 | Gujarat | 73 | 66 |
| 6 | Haryana | 39 | 82 |
| 7 | Himachal Pradesh | 45 | 47 |
| 8 | Karnataka | 65 | 47 |
| 9 | Kerala | 86 | 86 |
| 10 | Madhya Pradesh | 32 | 25 |
| 11 | Maharashtra | 67 | 47 |
| 12 | Meghalaya | 35 | 42 |
| 13 | Mizoram | 67 | 22 |
| 14 | Nagaland | 8 | 0 |
| 15 | Orissa | 27 | 22 |
| 16 | Punjab | 54 | 50 |
| 17 | Rajasthan | 38 | 42 |
| 18 | Sikkim | 35 | 28 |
| 19 | Tamil Nadu | 74 | 58 |
| 20 | Tripura | 32 | 3 |
| 21 | Uttar Pradesh | 20 | 44 |
| 22 | West Bengal | 27 | 15 |
| | **National Average** | 44 | 39 |

not be profitable for private operators. Private buses operate mainly in shorter routes connecting villages to small towns.

Government buses are available within 1 km. for 50 per cent of villages and for 60 per cent of urban households in the country (Table 4.7). The availability of government buses is higher for the villages in the states of Andhra Pradesh

(96 per cent), Gujarat (93 per cent), and Karnataka (91 per cent). Further, the availability of government buses is higher for urban households in the states of Karnataka (100 per cent), Tamil Nadu (98 per cent) and Andhra Pradesh (96 per cent).

Private buses are available within 1 km. for 63 per cent of villages and for 64 per cent of urban households in the country. The availability of private buses is high for the villages in the states of Kerala (100 per cent), Mizoram (90 per cent), Punjab (86 per cent), and Tamil Nadu (84 per cent). The availability of private buses is also high for urban households in the states of Kerala (99 per cent), Tamil Nadu (95 per cent) and Himachal Pradesh (88 per cent).

Though, the access to private buses compared to government buses is high for rural areas, the usage of private and government buses by rural households is almost at the same level (36 per cent and 34 per cent respectively for private and government buses). The use of buses operated either by government or private is low in Tripura.

The use of government buses is high in the states of Andhra Pradesh (95 per cent), Maharashtra (89 per cent). On the other hand, the use of private buses is much higher in the states of Assam (89 per cent), Kerala (79 per cent) and Madhya Pradesh (76 per cent).

> **Box 4.9**
>
> **Jhagaria** village is located at a distance of 19 kms. from block HQ, Sitamau in Mandsour district of Madhya Pradesh. No proper **transport facility** is available to reach block HQ. A private bus makes two trips, one in the morning and another in the evening. The private bus has no fixed time schedule. During the daytime, the villagers have to travel about 7 kms. on foot to catch a govt. bus. As there is no alternative mode of transport, the villagers are forced to avail the private bus service, though, the fare is expensive and the bus is overloaded beyond the capacity by 35 to 40 passengers.

The use of government and private buses is at the same level when aggregated at the national level, and there is negative association between the use of government and private buses across the states. In many states there is either domination of public buses or private buses. This could be attributed to the state government policies in transport sector. Some states have nationalised bus services and left little room for private operators, whereas some other states left most of the bus routes to private operators (Annexure AII.7).

*Quality and Reliability of Service*

The effective use of transport facilities depends on punctuality in running the buses. Extent of full satisfaction with punctuality of buses is used as a measure of reliability.

The reliability of public bus services at aggregate level for the nation is 18 per cent for rural households and 25 per cent for urban households. The reliability of public buses is highest in Gujarat (43 per cent) followed by Tamil Nadu (34 per cent). The low reliability is observed in Arunachal Pradesh (2 per cent), Meghalaya (3 per cent), Nagaland (4 per cent), and Punjab (5 per cent).

The reliability of public buses is positively correlated with access to *pucca* roads (0.60 in rural and 0.62 in urban areas). These indicators suggest that better access (tarred roads) appears to facilitate the punctuality of buses. In other words, better road infrastructure seems to bring in greater reliability of government buses.

### *Satisfaction with Service*

The full satisfaction of users with respect to services of public buses is captured in terms of full satisfaction with the frequency of bus services and also with the behaviour of bus conductors. About 21 per cent of public bus users expressed full satisfaction with the frequency of bus services as well as with the behaviour of conductors. Full satisfaction is higher among urban households compared to rural households, both with the frequency of public bus services as well as with the behaviour of conductors.

Full satisfaction with respect to frequency of public buses is more in the states of Gujarat (40 per cent), Tamil Nadu (34 per cent) and Uttar Pradesh (29 per cent). Full satisfaction with respect to the behaviour of bus conductors is relatively higher in the states of Gujarat (38 per cent), Tamil Nadu (37 per cent) and West Bengal (27 per cent).

User satisfaction seems to be significantly related to reliability of service. There is high association between the reliability and full satisfaction with government bus services. The correlation coefficient between punctuality and frequency of public buses is 0.96, punctuality and behaviour of bus conductors is also 0.96.

Availability of tarred roads also has a positive influence on quality of bus services that rural and urban households receive. Access to tarred roads has a correlation of 0.49 with frequency of buses in rural areas and 0.59 with the satisfaction with behaviour of conductors. Similarly urban access to tarred roads has a correlation of 0.59 with the frequency of buses and 0.60 with the behaviour of conductors.

### *Summary on Road Transport*

The extent of availability of government bus transport depends largely on state government policy. Reliability of service and satisfaction with the public

## Table 4.7

*Government Buses: Access, Use, Reliability and Full Satisfaction*

*(per cent households—rural and urban combined)*

| Sl. No. | States | Access | | Use | Reliability (Punctuality) | Full Satisfaction | |
|---|---|---|---|---|---|---|---|
| | | Rural* | Urban | | | Frequency of Service | Behaviour of Conductor |
| 1 | Andhra Pradesh | 96 | 96 | 95 | 13 | 20 | 21 |
| 2 | Arunachal Pradesh | 23 | 12 | 39 | 2 | 3 | 1 |
| 3 | Assam | 22 | 34 | 2 | 13 | 20 | 21 |
| 4 | Bihar | 2 | 7 | Neg | Ns | Ns | Ns |
| 5 | Gujarat | 93 | 88 | 67 | 43 | 40 | 38 |
| 6 | Haryana | 58 | 59 | 35 | 21 | 20 | 22 |
| 7 | Himachal Pradesh | 76 | 86 | 48 | 15 | 12 | 14 |
| 8 | Karnataka | 91 | 100 | 65 | 22 | 21 | 23 |
| 9 | Kerala | 76 | 84 | 13 | 13 | 14 | 13 |
| 10 | Madhya Pradesh | 19 | 32 | 8 | 17 | 21 | 15 |
| 11 | Maharashtra | 88 | 86 | 89 | 15 | 15 | 16 |
| 12 | Meghalaya | 15 | 10 | 4 | 3 | 3 | 3 |
| 13 | Mizoram | 83 | 80 | 46 | 14 | 18 | 18 |
| 14 | Nagaland | 48 | 78 | 32 | 4 | 4 | 5 |
| 15 | Orissa | 10 | 38 | 1 | Ns | Ns | Ns |
| 16 | Punjab | 71 | 72 | 20 | 5 | 4 | 4 |
| 17 | Rajasthan | 46 | 66 | 26 | 9 | 10 | 10 |
| 18 | Sikkim | 69 | 51 | 40 | 13 | 13 | 12 |
| 19 | Tamil Nadu | 88 | 98 | 73 | 34 | 34 | 37 |
| 20 | Tripura | 15 | 39 | 5 | Ns | 6 | 0 |
| 21 | Uttar Pradesh | 25 | 62 | 8 | 28 | 29 | 26 |
| 22 | West Bengal | 15 | 45 | 7 | 25 | 28 | 27 |
| | **National Average** | 50 | 60 | 35 | 20 | 21 | 21 |

*Note:* * percentage of villages

Ns: Percentage is not computed when the number of sample users is less than 30.

transport is better for urban households compared to rural households. Lack of cemented/tarred roads and poor availability of public buses are affecting more than half of the population, particularly the rural population. Punctuality of public buses appears to depend on the tarred roads; hence provision of tarred approach roads to rural areas could significantly improve the quality of public bus services.

## Public Distribution System

The Public Distribution System (PDS) is a network through which food grains, sugar and kerosene are provided at subsidised rates to the ration cardholders. PDS outlets are called fair price shops (popularly known as ration shops) through which these supplies are made available. The PDS was serving all sections of the community for many decades, but recent efforts point towards eliminating the higher income groups from the scope of the PDS with a view to better target this subsidised service and make it a safety net for the vulnerable sections of the community.

### *Access and Usage*

The state governments have expanded the number of fair price shops to cover the rural and urban population. For the present analysis, availability of PDS outlets within one kilometre from the sample villages and from urban sample households is considered as easy access.

About 60 per cent of villages in the country have easy access to PDS outlets. About 85 per cent of urban households have easy access to PDS outlets. Among the states, rural Nagaland is poorly served (12 per cent) in terms of easy access to PDS outlets, while those in Maharashtra, Mizoram, Sikkim and Tamil Nadu, both rural and urban areas are better served (above 80 per cent).

Households need to possess ration cards in order to get supplies from the PDS outlets. About 82 per cent of rural and 76 per cent of urban households possess ration cards. Card ownership is particularly high (above 90 per cent) among rural households in the states of Gujarat, Haryana, Himachal Pradesh, Kerala, Mizoram, Orissa, Tamil Nadu, West Bengal and Rajasthan.

The benefit of access and the possession of ration cards are realised only through the regular use in drawing ration from the PDS outlets. About 75 per cent of rural and 62 per cent of urban households possessing ration cards use PDS at least once in two months. More than 90 per cent of rural households in the states of Assam, Karnataka, Orissa, and West Bengal use PDS at least once in two months. Similar high usage by urban households is observed only in the states of Orissa and Tamil Nadu. The usage of PDS is significantly lower in Nagaland (8 per cent) and Meghalaya (10 per cent).

> **Box 4.10**
>
> Villagers use the PDS for buying different items supplied by the outlets, of which foodgrains are the most important. Usage is high even in states where foodgrain off-take is low, because villagers use the PDS outlet to procure subsidised kerosene and sugar. This is the case in many parts of the Punjab.

*Quality of Service*

The main benefit PDS provides is the supply of staple foodgrains at subsidised prices. The regular availability is defined in the study as the availability of staple foodgrains from PDS outlets at least once in two months to the households. In spite of a large proportion of households using ration cards, only one fourth (24 per cent) of rural and one fifth (20 per cent) of urban households report regular availability of staple foodgrains.

Regular availability is reported by more than half of rural households in the four southern states *viz.*, Andhra Pradesh, Karnataka, Kerala, and Tamil Nadu. In other states, the regular availability for rural households is less than 50 per cent. The regular availability is as low as 2 per cent or less in the states of Bihar, Haryana, Punjab, and Uttar Pradesh.

The regular availability of staple foodgrains for rural areas appears to be associated with the ease of access to PDS outlets (correlation coefficient is 0.72). Given that PDS outlets receive stocks for distribution at varying intervals, ease of access to outlets probably enables households to be in frequent touch with outlets, and draw supplies as soon as stocks are received.

> **Box 4.11**
>
> Most inhabitants of Ludkibeda, Balangir, Orissa are seasonal workers. There has been numerous skirmishes between the villagers and the PDS shopkeeper over erratic supply of foodgrains and anomalies in the distribution of foodgrains.

In addition to the provision of subsidised items, the PDS outlets are also required to display the prices of the supplies. About 47 per cent of users in the country reported display of prices by PDS outlets. Display of prices by PDS outlets appears to be more in urban areas than in rural areas. 45 per cent of rural and 56 per cent of urban households reported display of prices.

Display of prices is reported by higher percentage of households in the states of Kerala (81 per cent), Gujarat (79 per cent), Sikkim (75 per cent), and Tamil Nadu (71 per cent) and lower percentage of households in Nagaland (2

## Table 4.8

*PDS: Access, Use, Reliability and Full Satisfaction*

*(per cent of households–rural and urban combined)*

| Sl. No. | States | Access | | Use | Reliability (Regular Availability) | Full Satisfaction | | |
|---|---|---|---|---|---|---|---|---|
| | | Rural* | Urban | | | Quantity | Quality | Fairness |
| 1 | Andhra Pradesh | 64 | 85 | 68 | 51 | 13 | 18 | 18 |
| 2 | Arunachal Pradesh | 40 | 97 | 40 | 12 | 0 | 0 | 0 |
| 3 | Assam | 72 | 89 | 99 | 10 | 2 | 6 | 7 |
| 4 | Bihar | 53 | 87 | 75 | 1 | 6 | 15 | 10 |
| 5 | Gujarat | 57 | 89 | 86 | 41 | 12 | 12 | 14 |
| 6 | Haryana | 53 | 92 | 85 | 2 | 9 | 9 | 9 |
| 7 | Himachal Pradesh | 47 | 83 | 82 | 11 | 6 | 6 | 6 |
| 8 | Karnataka | 67 | 81 | 93 | 47 | 7 | 14 | 20 |
| 9 | Kerala | 69 | 92 | 86 | 45 | 4 | 3 | 3 |
| 10 | Madhya Pradesh | 73 | 82 | 76 | 23 | 6 | 9 | 8 |
| 11 | Maharashtra | 84 | 96 | 56 | 38 | 2 | 4 | 4 |
| 12 | Meghalaya | 54 | 57 | 10 | 14 | 5 | 5 | 5 |
| 13 | Mizoram | 89 | 98 | 89 | 27 | 10 | 1 | 1 |
| 14 | Nagaland | 12 | 68 | 8 | 6 | 4 | 4 | 4 |
| 15 | Orissa | 58 | 94 | 99 | 10 | 0 | 1 | 2 |
| 16 | Punjab | 64 | 96 | 79 | 0 | 2 | 4 | 3 |
| 17 | Rajasthan | 46 | 90 | 83 | 6 | 7 | 6 | 5 |
| 18 | Sikkim | 93 | 98 | 82 | 34 | 15 | 14 | 14 |
| 19 | Tamil Nadu | 88 | 88 | 89 | 73 | 22 | 19 | 24 |
| 20 | Tripura | 47 | 97 | 50 | 10 | 16 | 16 | 1 |
| 21 | Uttar Pradesh | 43 | 78 | 78 | 1 | 13 | 15 | 14 |
| 22 | West Bengal | 44 | 96 | 85 | 9 | 2 | 1 | 2 |
| | **National average** | 60 | 85 | 72 | 23 | 8 | 9 | 10 |

*Note:* * percentage of villages

per cent), Meghalaya (15 per cent), Haryana (21 per cent), and Uttar Pradesh (21 per cent).

Heavily used PDS outlets, which are located close to users, seem to be doing well not only on regularity of supply but also on displaying price information. The display of prices by PDS appears to be associated with the ease of access in rural and urban areas (0.53 and 0.50), regular usage of PDS (0.52 and 0.60) and regular availability (0.58 and 0.51).

### *Satisfaction with Service*

Notwithstanding the major achievements in extending the reach of the PDS, satisfaction with service is low. The three aspects of service considered for assessing full satisfaction with PDS are quantity and quality of supplies and the fairness of the shopkeepers. Only a small section of users across the country (less than 10 per cent) are fully satisfied with the three aspects of the PDS, while 30 per cent reported dissatisfaction. Only 8 per cent of the households in the country are fully satisfied with quantity of supplies, 9 per cent with quality of supplies and 10 per cent with the fairness of shopkeepers.

The percentage of households reported full satisfaction was highest, in relative terms, in Tamil Nadu (22 per cent with respect to quantity, 19 per cent with quality, and 24 per cent with fairness of shopkeepers). Sikkim and Andhra Pradesh were the two other states that did relatively better, than the rest where users have given very poor ratings.

### *Summary on PDS*

PDS has achieved wide coverage in the country with 81 per cent of households owning ration cards and 72 per cent of card holders use PDS at least once in two months. But there is no regularity in the supply of foodgrains to the cardholders. Only one fourth of cardholders reported regular availability of foodgrains. Further, few households reported full satisfaction with the quality of services. The performance of PDS in relatively poor states where it is really required does not rise to the level where we can say that it has adequately addressed its primary goal of serving the poor.

## Primary Schools

Education is viewed as a major long-term investment to bring about sustainable improvements in large sections of the country's population. There is a large network of government-supported schools in all the states of which primary schools form a major part. In addition, there are also a good number of primary schools run by private institutions providing primary education.

## Table 4.9

*Government/Aided Primary Schools: Access, Use, Reliability and Full Satisfaction*

*(per cent households–rural and urban combined)*

| Sl. No. | States | Access | | Use | Reliability (Behaviour of Teacher) | Full Satisfaction | |
|---|---|---|---|---|---|---|---|
| | | Rural* | Urban | | | Quality of Building | Quality of Toilet |
| 1 | Andhra Pradesh | 92 | 54 | 82 | 16 | 18 | 4 |
| 2 | Arunachal Pradesh | 23 | 37 | 93 | 1 | 0 | 0 |
| 3 | Assam | 74 | 38 | 82 | 14 | 6 | 2 |
| 4 | Bihar | 80 | 44 | 70 | 9 | 4 | 1 |
| 5 | Gujarat | 93 | 56 | 86 | 23 | 22 | 9 |
| 6 | Haryana | 81 | 32 | 56 | 5 | 5 | 3 |
| 7 | Himachal Pradesh | 75 | 38 | 83 | 6 | 4 | 3 |
| 8 | Karnataka | 82 | 53 | 80 | 26 | 23 | 7 |
| 9 | Kerala | 75 | 22 | 74 | 17 | 16 | 10 |
| 10 | Madhya Pradesh | 87 | 29 | 86 | 20 | 13 | 3 |
| 11 | Maharashtra | 83 | 53 | 93 | 21 | 17 | 13 |
| 12 | Meghalaya | 73 | 13 | 20 | 0 | 0 | 0 |
| 13 | Mizoram | 62 | 39 | 84 | 2 | 16 | 5 |
| 14 | Nagaland | 82 | 9 | 31 | 0 | 0 | 0 |
| 15 | Orissa | 89 | 54 | 93 | 3 | 3 | 1 |
| 16 | Punjab | 74 | 33 | 57 | 1 | 1 | 1 |
| 17 | Rajasthan | 85 | 51 | 75 | 6 | 6 | 2 |
| 18 | Sikkim | 52 | 17 | 63 | 16 | 17 | 12 |
| 19 | Tamil Nadu | 71 | 67 | 86 | 38 | 30 | 18 |
| 20 | Tripura | 41 | 24 | 91 | 1 | 1 | 0 |
| 21 | Uttar Pradesh | 82 | 40 | 71 | 15 | 18 | 8 |
| 22 | West Bengal | 60 | 41 | 94 | 21 | 14 | 4 |
| | **National Average** | 76 | 42 | 78 | 16 | 14 | 6 |

*Note:* *percentage of village

### *Access and Use of Government Schools*

The main users of primary education are young children, for whom travelling long distances on a daily basis is a difficult and expensive proposition. Hence, provision of primary schools within walking distance to the young children is a primary requisite in achieving the objective of universal literacy. Government/aided primary schools are accessible within one kilometre for 76 per cent of the villages and for 42 per cent of urban households in the country. Private primary schools are accessible within one kilometre for 25 per cent of the villages and also for 25 per cent of urban households.

In both rural and urban areas, ease of access (within one kilometre) is greater among users of government/aided primary schools. The ease of access (within one kilometre) to government and aided schools is high in rural areas of Gujarat (93 per cent) and Andhra Pradesh (92 per cent), Orissa (89 per cent), Madhya Pradesh (87 per cent), and Rajasthan (85 per cent). Easy rural access to primary schools is lower in the states of Arunachal Pradesh (23 per cent) and Tripura (41 per cent).

> **Box 4.12**
>
> Notwithstanding the wide network of private schools in Kerala, a large number of villagers make use of the government schools (primary, middle and high) in Kalliyoor near Trivandrum.

In spite of the growing spread of private schools, 83 per cent of rural and 61 per cent of urban households with children of school going age, depend on government run schools for primary education. The dependence on government/aided schools is more than 90 per cent in the rural areas of Arunachal Pradesh, Gujarat, Madhya Pradesh, Maharashtra, Orissa, Tripura and West Bengal. The dependence on government/aided schools is more than 80 per cent in the urban areas of Arunachal Pradesh, Orissa, Tamil Nadu and West Bengal. In rural areas there is predominant use of government/aided schools in all the states except in the states of Meghalaya and Nagaland. The dependence of urban households on private schools is more than that on government schools in the states of Haryana, Nagaland and Uttar Pradesh.

### *Quality of Schools*

The indicator considered to measure the quality of primary education in government/aided schools is the full satisfaction with the behaviour of teachers. Among households who are sending their children to government run and aided primary schools, only 16 per cent reported full satisfaction. Relatively higher percentage of households in the states of Tamil Nadu (38 per cent), Karnataka (26 per cent) and Gujarat (23 per cent) reported full satisfaction with the behaviour of teachers. Less than two per cent of households reported full satisfaction with the behaviour of teachers in the states of Arunachal Pradesh, Meghalaya, Nagaland, Punjab and Tripura. The mid-day meal scheme is an important initiative promoted by governments to improve the health of children as well as school attendance. About 68 per cent of households in the country reported awareness of the scheme. Awareness of the households about mid-day meals scheme is low in the states of Meghalaya, Tripura, and Nagaland.

### *Satisfaction with Schools*

Parents of school going children may have better awareness of the physical infrastructure of the schools compared to other aspects of education that take place within classrooms. Toilet facilities are an important part of the infrastructure of the school, particularly for girl children. Hence, satisfaction of households with respect to primary schools is assessed in relation to quality of facilities such as school buildings and toilets.

Around 14 per cent of households using government run and aided primary schools reported full satisfaction with quality of the school buildings. Higher proportions reported full satisfaction in Tamil Nadu (30 per cent), Karnataka (23 per cent) and Gujarat (22 per cent). Only six per cent of households using government primary schools reported full satisfaction with the quality of the toilets; Tamil Nadu faired relatively better (18 per cent) followed by Maharashtra (13 per cent), and Sikkim (12 per cent).

> **Box 4.13**
>
> Mudhol in Karnataka has one primary school with three classrooms. But the contractor has locked up two rooms for which his payments have not been made. All children from classes 1 to 4 sit in the same room or in the narrow corridor outside. Inhabitants of remote villages find that their schools have an inadequate number of teachers to handle the classes, as in Sankal in Vadodara, Gujarat or very irregular teachers as in Elumyuo, Nagaland.

There is a strong association among the variables *viz.*, full satisfaction with the behaviour of teachers, quality of school buildings and quality of toilets. The correlation coefficient between full satisfaction with the behaviour of teachers and quality of school buildings is 0.87, behaviour of teachers and quality of toilets is 0.80 and quality of buildings and toilets is 0.87. These correlations suggest that schools with good teachers, tend to be ones with good infrastructure too.

### *Summary on Schools*

Government-supported primary schools are available within one kilometre to more than three-fourth of villages in the country. Dependence of households

## Table 4.10

*Access, Use, Reliability and Full Satisfaction with Child Care System*

*(per cent rural households)*

| Sl. No. | States | Access* | Usage | Reliability (Regular Opening) | Full Satisfaction (Staff Behaviour) |
|---|---|---|---|---|---|
| 1 | Andhra Pradesh | 49 | 31 | Ns | Ns |
| 2 | Arunachal Pradesh | 52 | Ns | Ns | Ns |
| 3 | Assam | 43 | 30 | 87 | 91 |
| 4 | Bihar | 32 | 8 | Ns | Ns |
| 5 | Gujarat | 85 | 40 | 95 | 94 |
| 6 | Haryana | 84 | 29 | 91 | 88 |
| 7 | Himachal Pradesh | 71 | 32 | Ns | Ns |
| 8 | Karnataka | 92 | 40 | 99 | 74 |
| 9 | Kerala | 71 | 29 | 96 | Ns |
| 10 | Madhya Pradesh | 87 | 26 | 83 | 68 |
| 11 | Maharashtra | 96 | 40 | 99 | 86 |
| 12 | Meghalaya | 58 | Ns | Ns | Ns |
| 13 | Mizoram | 85 | 49 | 89 | 75 |
| 14 | Nagaland | 96 | 35 | 12 | 62 |
| 15 | Orissa | 87 | 50 | 92 | 76 |
| 16 | Punjab | 70 | 15 | Ns | Ns |
| 17 | Rajasthan | 76 | 26 | 80 | 64 |
| 18 | Sikkim | 66 | Ns | Ns | Ns |
| 19 | Tamil Nadu | 82 | 33 | 99 | 75 |
| 20 | Tripura | 79 | 9 | Ns | Ns |
| 21 | Uttar Pradesh | 42 | 19 | 64 | 64 |
| 22 | West Bengal | 72 | 15 | Ns | Ns |
| | **National Average** | 71 | 30 | 87 | 78 |

*Note:* * Percentage of villages

Ns: Percentage is not computed when the number of sample users is less than 30.

on government schools is very high in most of the states. The dependence is greater among rural households compared to urban households. Among the households using government run and aided primary schools, only about one-sixth of them reported full satisfaction with the behaviour of teachers. There is good awareness among the households about the mid-day meal scheme and most of the households are the beneficiaries of the scheme. Many rural households who are sending their children to government schools continue to send their children to government schools irrespective of the quality of schools due to lack of better choice. The low access to private schools, the inability of households to afford private schools, and the incentive of mid-day meal programme in government schools could be the reason for the high dependency of rural households on government schools.

## Child Care System

The state government provides childcare facilities through *anganwadis*. One kilometre distance to *anganwadi* from the rural habitations is used as criterion

**Table 4.11**

*Relative Performance of Public Services by States*

| Sl. No. | States | DW | Health | Transport | PDS | Education | Overall Rank |
|---|---|---|---|---|---|---|---|
| | | | | *First Level* | | | |
| 1 | Andhra Pradesh | 7 | 16 | 4 | 2 | 4 | 5 |
| 2 | Karnataka | 2 | 6 | 3 | 3 | 3 | 3 |
| 3 | Kerala | 13 | 7 | 7 | 5 | 8 | 6 |
| 4 | Tamil Nadu | 1 | 4 | 2 | 1 | 1 | 1 |
| 5 | Gujarat | 3 | 1 | 1 | 6 | 2 | 2 |
| 6 | Maharashtra | 5 | 2 | 5 | 4 | 4 | 4 |
| | | | | *Second Level* | | | |
| 7 | Haryana | 11 | 9 | 8 | 11 | 13 | 10 |
| 8 | Himachal Pradesh | 4 | 5 | 6 | 13 | 15 | 7 |
| 9 | Punjab | 14 | 3 | 10 | 10 | 16 | 11 |
| 10 | Madhya Pradesh | 6 | 10 | 13 | 8 | 6 | 8 |
| 11 | Uttar Pradesh | 9 | 7 | 9 | 14 | 7 | 9 |
| | | | | *Third level* | | | |
| 12 | Assam | 15 | 10 | 14 | 7 | 11 | 14 |
| 13 | West Bengal | 7 | 15 | 11 | 15 | 13 | 13 |
| 14 | Orissa | 10 | 13 | 15 | 9 | 10 | 12 |
| 15 | Rajasthan | 12 | 12 | 12 | 16 | 9 | 15 |
| 16 | Bihar | 16 | 14 | 16 | 12 | 12 | 16 |

for ease of access here. Over two-thirds of villages (71 per cent) in the country have ease of access to *anganwadis* and about one-third of the rural households (having children in the age group of 1 to 6 years) are using the facility. More than 90 per cent of villages in Karnataka, Maharashtra and Nagaland offer easy access to *anganwadis* and only less than one-third of villages (32 per cent) in Bihar have ease of access to *anganwadis*. Yet, *anganwadis* are covering only 30 per cent of the target households. The reasons given by the households for not sending their children to the *anganwadis* include inadequate time to take the children to *anganwadis* and that *anganwadis* are not located in the neighbourhood. Those using this service gave reasons as immunisation (79 per cent), pre-school facility (76 per cent) and supplementary diet (40 per cent).

On the whole, the satisfaction of the households with the services of *anganwadis* appears to be better compared to the other public services. Most of the households (87 per cent) using *anganwadis* reported that these institutions are working regularly. Many users (78 per cent) rated the behaviour of *anganwadi* workers as good.

*Relative Performance of States in Public Services*

The major states (16 states) have been ranked on the basis of the overall performance of each service. The indicators that are considered for the overall performance of a service are access, reliability and satisfaction with the service. 'Use' has been left out of this analysis as it can be overly influenced by the lack of private options. For each indicator of a service, average scores were computed and these average scores aggregated across all the indicators to obtain the overall score for a service. The overall scores for a service across states were used for ranking and obtaining the relative performance of states for each service. The ranks of the states for the five services are aggregated to obtain relative ranks for the states in the overall performance across the five public services.

The relative performance of public services for the major states show that except for health care in Andhra Pradesh, and drinking water in Kerala, the four southern states (Andhra Pradesh, Karnataka, Kerala and Tamil Nadu) and two western states *viz.*, Maharashtra and Gujarat have performed consistently well in all the five public services. In the overall performance of public services, Tamil Nadu comes first followed by Gujarat, Karnataka, Maharashtra, Andhra Pradesh and Kerala. The six states are contiguous. The other contiguous states, which form the second level in the overall performance of public services, are Haryana, Himachal Pradesh and Punjab from the North and Madhya Pradesh and Uttar Pradesh from the North-Central part of the country. For these states the overall performance ranks ranged from 7 to 11. The states that figured in the third level in the overall performance of public services are

Assam, West Bengal, Bihar and Orissa from the East and Rajasthan in the North West.

The bottom five states are way below the top states with respect to access in drinking water, health care and transport. The gap is smaller in primary schools and PDS. The use patterns between the two sets of states are more similar, except in public transport. In terms of reliability, the gap is indeed wide except in drinking water and health care. In the matter of full satisfaction, the bottom states are significantly below the top states.

It is significant that the ranking of the states given above does not follow the widely used ranking of the states by per capita income or other conventional measures of development. Of the six states in the top category, three are somewhere in the middle when ranked by per capita income. Some of the states with the highest per capita income are found in our middle category. It is only in our bottom category that we see a convergence of low per capita income and poor public services. A plausible hypothesis is that factors other than per capita income also influence the efficacy and quality of public services. Some observers have noted that the quality of governance is distinctly better in the higher ranked public service performers than in the rest of the states. But quantifying measures of governance is by no means easy.

*Variations in Ease of Access*

This analysis highlights the issues, which were central to the study. Even though, all states have lofty goals on service provision, and make huge

**Figure 4.1**

*Access to Public Services*

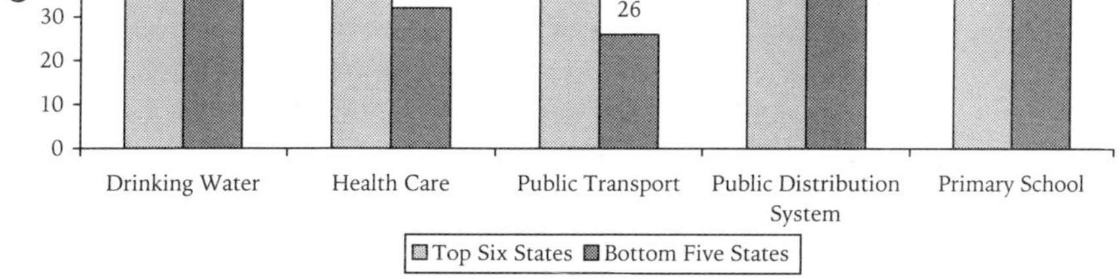

investments for the same, there are wide differences between the better performing states and the under performing ones, on providing access to these services. Ease of access is significantly higher for drinking water, health care and bus transport. In the case of PDS and primary schools, where achievements have also been good, and the gap is small. But the gap is largest in relation to government bus transport, which probably receives a low priority in poorer states, given the other developmental priorities.

*Variations in Use of Services*

In striking contrast to this picture of variations in access, we have a scenario of very small difference in extent of use of services, except in the case of government bus transport, which is not available in most parts of the poorer states. In other words, the inadequacy or difficulty to access services is compensated by extra effort and cost by residents of poorer states to use these services, particularly in health care, PDS and schools, and to a lesser extent in water.

**Figure 4.2**

*Use of Public Services*

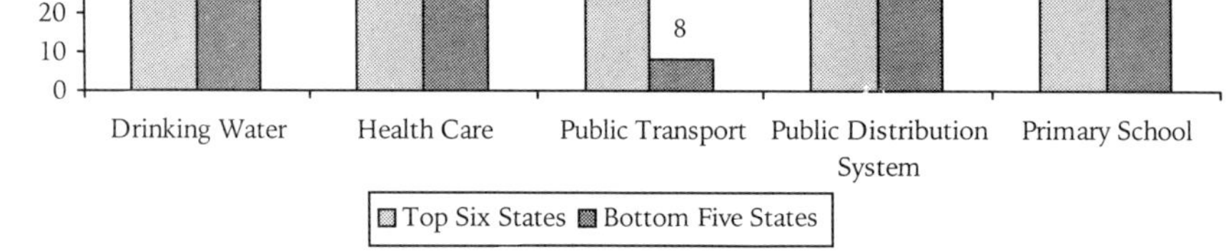


*Variations in Reliability of Services*

The impressive picture about ease of access to services, in the case of PDS and schools, falters when it comes to reliability and quality. The reliability of drinking water supply and health care seem to be more reliable (for those who are able to access them) at similar levels across the better and worse-off states, while those where we have observed greater equity in access, namely schools and PDS seem to fall, and the extent of fall is sharper in the poorer states. Clearly, easy access on a large scale has provided reliable service.

**Figure 4.3**

*Reliability of Public Services*

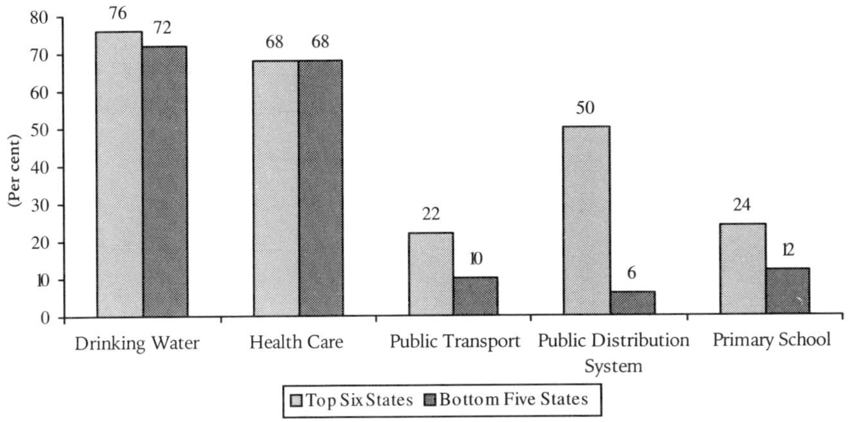


### *Variations in Satisfaction with Services*

The big variations are starker when it comes to satisfaction with services. While overall levels are low, even in the better performing states, the extremely low levels of satisfaction in the worse-off states are of major concern. Given that usage is of high order, it is a message of deep dependence and deprivation under which these services are being used by a large majority of citizens.

**Figure 4.4**

*Full Satisfaction with Public Services*

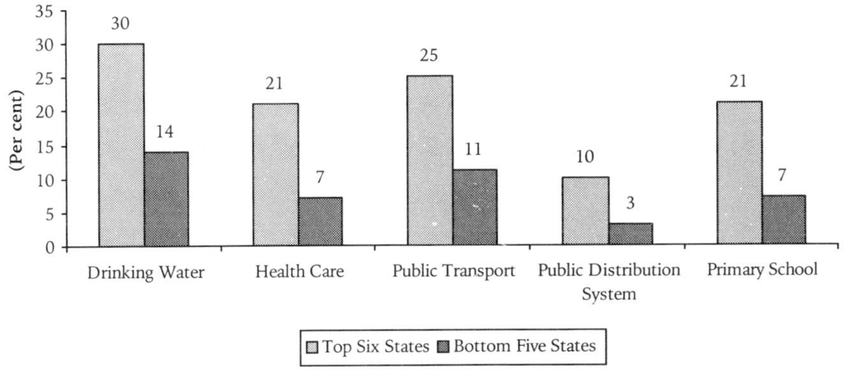

# 5

## Public Services and the Disadvantaged Sections

Planned development in India has improved incomes of rural and urban people. This is also reflected in the reduction of poverty levels in the country. The poverty ratio has decreased from 54.9 per cent in 1973-74 to 36 per cent in 1993-94 and further declined to 26.1 per cent in the year 1999-2000 (MoF, 2003). The achievements in income generation and reduction in poverty are accompanied by improvements in other indicators such as life expectancy, infant mortality and severe child under-nourishment. It is the distribution of income and public services across different sections and different regions is of paramount importance in the development process. This section examines the access, use and quality of services experienced by the disadvantaged sections in the country.

Given the limitations in reliability of self-reported income as the basis for identifying the very poor, this analysis used a combination of three criteria to define poor households in terms of both income and other handicaps. A household is considered to have a significant Income Capability Disadvantage (ICD), when:

- Living in a *kutcha* house (hut).
- The head of the household is illiterate or has not received formal schooling.
- The head of the household is a daily wage earner (e.g. farm worker).

Disadvantages arise not only from low income or illiteracy, but also from other factors such as caste or isolated locations of the households. A detailed analysis was done on households classified as weaker sections in the following manner:

- Scheduled Caste and Scheduled Tribe households (41 per cent of the total sample).
- Households from small villages—'C' villages with population less than 1000 persons (29 per cent of the rural sample).
- Very poor households with income capability disadvantage (30 per cent of the total sample).

Continuing from the previous section, the major 16 states are classified into top 6, middle 5 and bottom 5 states based on the overall performance of the five public services. It is interesting to observe that middle 5 states have higher proportion of SC/ST and ICD sample households compared top 6 states (Table 5.1). This trend is further accentuated when we observe the bottom 5 states, which have higher proportion of SC/ST and ICD households compared to the top 6 and middle 5 states. But the extent of variation is more in the case of ICD households (24.4 per cent to 42 per cent) than the SC/ST households (32 per cent to 36.5 per cent) across the three groups of states. Among the SC/ST households, 37.6 per cent households belong to ICD in the top 6 states. The proportion increased to 46.8 per cent in middle 6 states and to 54.5 per cent in the bottom 5 states. The bottom 5 states, thus, reflect higher proportion of ICD households both in SC/ST and general households, along with relatively lower performance of public services.

**Table 5.1**

*Distribution of Sample Households by Weaker Section Categories*

| *Group of States* | *% of SC/ST* | *% of ICD* | *% ICD among SC/ST* |
|---|---|---|---|
| Top 6 States | 32.0 | 24.4 | 37.6 |
| Middle 5 States | 35.2 | 33.1 | 46.8 |
| Bottom 5 States | 36.5 | 42.0 | 54.5 |
| Total (Major 16 States) | 34.2 | 31.9 | 45.5 |

## Variations in Service Quality Experienced by SC/ST Communities

The variations in service quality experienced by SC/ST and other communities, small villages and large villages and poor and other households are presented in Table 5.2.

*Drinking Water*

A larger segment (67 per cent) of SC/ST households use public protected drinking water, when compared to other communities (59 per cent). But ease of access to public protected drinking water (within 100 metres) is also high among SC/ST households (58 per cent) compared to other communities (53 per cent). This is probably explained by norms applied in setting up drinking water supply schemes, with special consideration for weaker sections. However, the full satisfaction with respect to adequacy and quality of supply of protected public sources is on the lower side for SC/ST households when compared to other communities.

## Table 5.2.1

*Performance of Drinking Water Supply: SC/ST vis-á-vis Other Communities*

*(per cent of households)*

| *Indicators* | *Community Groups* | | |
|---|---|---|---|
| | *SC/ST* | *O* | *T* |
| Access to public protected source 100 mts | 58 | 53 | 55 |
| Usage of public protected water | 67 | 59 | 62 |
| Breakdown within 3 months—protected public tap | 23 | 26 | 25 |
| Breakdown within 3 months—public hand pumps | 25 | 23 | 24 |
| Involvement of community in maintenance | 22 | 24 | 23 |
| Bribes paid for repair of protected public water sources | 11 | 10 | 11 |
| Willingness to pay for better service | 37 | 43 | 40 |
| Full satisfaction with adequacy of supply in protected piped water | 17 | 22 | 20 |
| Full satisfaction with quality of supply in protected piped water | 21 | 31 | 27 |
| Full satisfaction with adequacy of supply in protected public source | 22 | 26 | 24 |
| Full satisfaction with quality of supply in protected public source | 31 | 33 | 32 |

*Note:* O-Others, T-Total.

### *Health Care*

Households from SC/ST communities enjoy slightly lower ease of access to health centre facilities (37 per cent) compared to other communities (43 per cent). Higher proportion of SC/ST households depends on government facilities for treating major as well as minor ailments (61 per cent and 51 per cent respectively), compared to households of other communities (52 per cent and 42 per cent respectively). There is little variation in full satisfaction across households of SC/ST and other communities with respect to behaviour of doctors and paramedical staff.

## Table 5.2.2

*Performance of Public Services: SC/ST vis-á-vis Other Communities*

| *Indicators* | *Community Groups* | | |
|---|---|---|---|
| | *SC/ST* | *O* | *T* |
| Access to health care within one km. | 37 | 43 | 40 |
| Dependence on govt. facility for minor ailments | 51 | 42 | 45 |
| Dependence on govt. facility for major ailments | 61 | 52 | 55 |
| Presence of doctors at time of visit | 69 | 70 | 70 |
| Presence of paramedical staff at time of visit | 82 | 83 | 83 |
| Fee paid for service by out-patients | 16 | 16 | 16 |
| Bribe paid for service | 14 | 18 | 16 |
| Full satisfaction with behaviour of doctors-out-patient | 13 | 14 | 14 |
| Full satisfaction with behaviour of paramedics-out-patient | 11 | 13 | 12 |

*Bus Transport*

Ease of access to government and private buses is lower for SC/ST households (43 per cent and 49 per cent respectively) compared to other communities (52 per cent and 58 per cent respectively). However, there is little variation between SC/ST households and other segments of the population in the extent of use and full satisfaction with the public buses. This may more a function of remoteness of houses of SC/ST households from roads, rather than a problem of bus services.

**Table 5.2.3**

*Performance of Bus Transport: SC/ST vis-á-vis Other Communities*

*(per cent of households)*

| *Indicators* | *Community Groups* | | |
|---|---|---|---|
| | *SC/ST* | *O* | *T* |
| Public bus available within one km. | 43 | 52 | 48 |
| Private bus available within one km. | 49 | 58 | 55 |
| Public buses used | 33 | 36 | 35 |
| Private buses used | 34 | 34 | 34 |
| Full satisfaction with punctuality of public buses | 18 | 21 | 20 |
| Full satisfaction with frequency of public buses | 19 | 22 | 21 |
| Full satisfaction with behaviour of conductors | 20 | 22 | 21 |

*Public Distribution System*

The proportion of SC/ST households owning ration cards is lower than that of other communities (75 per cent and 85 per cent respectively). The ease of

**Table 5.2.4**

*Performance of PDS: SC/ST vis-á-vis Other Communities*

*(per cent of households)*

| *Indicators* | *Community Groups* | | |
|---|---|---|---|
| | *SC/ST* | *O* | *T* |
| Availability of ration shop within one km. | 73 | 79 | 77 |
| Households possessing own ration cards | 75 | 85 | 81 |
| Use of PDS by card owners at least once in two months | 68 | 74 | 72 |
| Regular availability of staple foodgrains | 25 | 21 | 23 |
| Display of prices always | 46 | 48 | 47 |
| Full satisfaction with quantity of supply | 7 | 8 | 8 |
| Full satisfaction with quality of supply | 9 | 10 | 9 |
| Satisfaction with fairness of shopkeeper | 9 | 10 | 10 |

access and use of PDS is also slightly lower for SC/ST households compared to other communities (73 per cent and 79 per cent for access and 68 per cent and 74 per cent for usage). No major differences are observed in relation to reliability and quality of services across the social groups.

*Primary School*

There is only marginal difference between the households of SC/ST and other communities, in relation to ease of access to government primary schools. The dependence on government run and aided primary schools for SC/ST households (82 per cent) is higher than the other communities (75 per cent). The extent of full satisfaction with the behaviour of teachers is slightly lower for SC/ST households compared to households of other communities. There is no major difference in full satisfaction with respect to other quality variables of the schools between SC/ST and other communities.

**Table 5.2.5**

*Performance of Government Schools: SC/ST vis-á-vis Other Communities*

*(per cent of households)*

| *Indicators* | *Community Groups* | | |
|---|---|---|---|
| | *SC/ST* | *O* | *T* |
| Availability of school within one km. | 76 | 77 | 76 |
| Dependence for education facility—Public | 82 | 75 | 78 |
| Dependence for education facility—Private | 18 | 25 | 22 |
| Full satisfaction with behaviour of teachers | 14 | 17 | 16 |
| Awareness of mid-day meal scheme | 68 | 69 | 68 |
| Use of mid-day meal | 83 | 82 | 83 |
| Satisfaction with school building | 13 | 14 | 14 |
| Satisfaction with toilet | 5 | 7 | 6 |

*Child Care*

*Anganwadis* are used more by SC/ST community (32 per cent) than the other communities (27 per cent). Availability of supplementary diet appears to be a motivating factor for SC/ST households to send their children to *anganwadis*. There is not much of difference in other variables pertaining to childcare between SC/ST and other communities.

**Summary:** The ease of access to public services, with the exception of drinking water and primary schools, is lower for SC/ST households compared to other communities. This could be due to the typical rural settlement pattern where SC/ST households generally live together in a settiement (hamlet) of a revenue village. The other communities often live in the main village where

### Table 5.2.6

*Performance of Public Services: SC/ST vis-á-vis Other Communities*

*( per cent of households)*

| *Indicators* | *Community Groups* | | |
|---|---|---|---|
| | *SC/ST* | *O* | *T* |
| Usage of *Anganwadi* | 32 | 27 | 29 |
| Regular opening of *Anganwadi* | 85 | 91 | 88 |
| Reasons—pre-school facility | 74 | 76 | 75 |
| Reasons—supplementary diet | 42 | 35 | 39 |
| Having Immunisation/medical check-up | 77 | 82 | 80 |
| Good behaviour of *Anganwadi* worker | 76 | 79 | 78 |

most public services are located. Hence, the access to the public services is more to the other communities than the SC/ST community. However, the dependence on public services is more for SC/ST households compared to the other communities, even though they have less ease of access. Many state governments are committed to provide drinking water to all the settlements and primary education to all the children in the schooling age. Since these services are being extended to all, even to hamlets, it facilitates ease of access to all sections of the communities. This probably explains the lack of difference in ease of access to these two services for SC/ST households.

## Variations in Service Quality Experienced in Small Villages

Population is the main criterion for the government when it comes to selecting a location for service provision. Hence, bigger villages are at a significant advantage compared to smaller ones, whereby ease of access to services becomes a bigger issue for inhabitants of small villages. Hence, the analysis examined the imbalances in service delivery experienced by households in small villages.

> **Box 5.1**
>
> **Somaliya** village is in Jaislmer district of Rajasthan, 35 kms. from the Jaislmer *taluka*. An irrigation tank provides drinking water for the village. But there is acute shortage of water in the tank for most of the year. The government. supplies drinking water by truck. The nearest market is at a distance of 35 kms. The only mode of transport is government bus which makes one trip to the village per day. There is no PHC/Sub-Centre or private doctor within the village. For any minor or major ailment they travel a distance of 35 kms. to reach the nearest health facility. There is no *Anganwadi* centre or FPS in the village. The FPS is located at a distance of two kms. The FPS is not opened regularly and the supply of wheat and sugar is also not regular. The only bright aspect of the village is the availability of primary school within the village.

Villages with population less than 1000 (Class C) have been termed small villages for this analysis. The quality of public services in small villages is compared with the quality of services in the big (rest of) villages, and based on feedback of rural households. Variations in service experienced by inhabitants of small villages *vis-á-vis* larger villages is presented in tables below.

### *Drinking Water*

Provision of drinking water to all settlements is a primary responsibility of the state governments. There are no major variations in ease of access, extent of usage and level of satisfaction in the delivery of service between small and big villages. However, satisfaction with piped water supply is a little better among households in the bigger villages (30 per cent) when compared to those who live in the smaller villages (24 per cent).

**Table 5.2.7**

*Performance of Drinking Water Supply: Small vis-á-vis Bigger Villages*

*(per cent of rural households)*

| *Indicators* | *Village Size* | | |
|---|---|---|---|
| | *A&B* | *C* | *T* |
| Access to public protected source 100 mts. | 51 | 48 | 50 |
| Usage of public protected water | 59 | 57 | 58 |
| Breakdown within three months—protected public tap | 27 | 28 | 27 |
| Breakdown within three months—public hand pumps | 23 | 24 | 24 |
| Involvement of community in maintenance | 24 | 22 | 23 |
| Bribes paid for repair of protected public water sources | 5 | 5 | 5 |
| Willingness to pay for better service | 41 | 40 | 40 |
| Full satisfaction with adequacy of supply in protected piped water | 22 | 20 | 21 |
| Full satisfaction with quality of supply in protected piped water | 30 | 24 | 29 |
| Full satisfaction with adequacy of supply in protected public source | 23 | 24 | 24 |
| Full satisfaction with quality of supply in protected public source | 31 | 34 | 32 |

*Note:* A&B—Big villages (Villages with more than 1000 population).
C—Small villages (villages with 1000 and less population).
T—Total.

### *Health Care*

Government healthcare facilities are more easily available (within one km.) for bigger villages (46 per cent) than for smaller villages (17 per cent). The population norms for setting up healthcare facilities favour bigger villages. There are no significant variations in use and satisfaction of services between big and small villages.

## Table 5.2.8

*Performance of Health Services: Small vis-á-vis Bigger Villages*

*(per cent of rural households)*

| *Indicators* | *Village Size* | | |
|---|---|---|---|
| | *A&B* | *C* | *T* |
| Access to health care within one km. | 46 | 17 | 40 |
| Dependence on government facility for minor ailments | 48 | 48 | 48 |
| Dependence on government facility for major ailments | 57 | 57 | 57 |
| Presence of doctors at time of visit | 67 | 66 | 67 |
| Presence of paramedical staff at time of visit | 82 | 80 | 82 |
| Fee paid for service by outpatients | 15 | 19 | 16 |
| Bribe paid for service | 17 | 16 | 17 |
| Full satisfaction with behaviour of doctors out-patient | 13 | 13 | 13 |
| Full satisfaction with behaviour of paramedical staff out-patient | 12 | 12 | 12 |

### *Bus Transport*

Small villages are in a relatively disadvantaged position with respect to bus transport compared to big villages. The ease of access to both public and private buses is less for small villages compared to big villages. Households in small villages use government buses to a lesser extent (30 per cent) compared to households in big villages (36 per cent); but there is not much of difference in use of private buses. The reliability and satisfaction of government buses in small villages is lower than that in bigger villages.

## Table 5.2.9

*Performance of Bus Transport: Small vis-á-vis Bigger Villages*

*(per cent of rural households)*

| *Indicators* | *Village Size* | | |
|---|---|---|---|
| | *A&B* | *C* | *T* |
| Public bus available within one km. | 55 | 42 | 50 |
| Private bus available within one km. | 69 | 52 | 63 |
| Public buses used | 36 | 30 | 34 |
| Private buses used | 35 | 37 | 36 |
| Full satisfaction with punctuality of public buses | 19 | 14 | 18 |
| Full satisfaction with frequency of public buses | 19 | 13 | 18 |
| Full satisfaction with behaviour of conductors | 20 | 18 | 20 |

### *Public Distribution System*

Households in small villages also face difficulties in using the services of PDS. The ease of access to PDS is less for small villages (41 per cent) compared to big villages (73 per cent). Lower proportion of households in small villages reported possessing ration cards. The use of ration cards is also less in small villages. But when it comes to satisfaction with respect to PDS, which is overall very low, there isn't much of difference between small and big villages.

**Table 5.2.10**

*Performance of PDS: Small vis-á-vis Bigger Villages*

*(per cent of rural households)*

| *Indicators* | *Village Size* | | |
|---|---|---|---|
| | *A&B* | *C* | *T* |
| Availability of ration shop within one km. | 73 | 41 | 60 |
| Households possessing own ration cards | 84 | 79 | 82 |
| Use of PDS by card owners at least once in two months | 76 | 73 | 75 |
| Regular availability of staple foodgrains | 24 | 22 | 24 |
| Display of prices always | 46 | 40 | 45 |
| Full satisfaction with quantity of supply | 7 | 8 | 8 |
| Full satisfaction with quality of supply | 9 | 10 | 9 |
| Satisfaction with fairness of shopkeeper | 9 | 11 | 10 |

*Primary School*

There is difference in ease of access to government run & aided primary schools between big villages (81 per cent) and small villages (67 per cent). There are other major variations in relation to primary education between big and small villages.

**Table 5.2.11**

*Performance of Government Primary Schools: Small vis-á-vis Bigger Villages*

*(per cent of rural households)*

| *Indicators* | *Village Size* | | |
|---|---|---|---|
| | *A&B* | *C* | *T* |
| Availability of school within one km. | 81 | 67 | 76 |
| Dependence for education facility—Public | 82 | 84 | 83 |
| Dependence for education facility—Private | 18 | 16 | 17 |
| Full satisfaction with behaviour of teachers | 15 | 16 | 16 |
| Awareness of mid-day meal scheme | 68 | 70 | 69 |
| Use of mid-day meal | 83 | 83 | 83 |
| Satisfaction with school building | 13 | 14 | 13 |
| Satisfaction with toilet | 5 | 4 | 5 |

### *Child Care*

Use of *anganwadis* by households is slightly more in small villages (34 per cent) compared to big villages (28 per cent). Using the facility for supplementary diet is also more in small villages (45 per cent) than in big villages (38 per cent). In the aspects of reliability and satisfaction there is not much of difference between small and big villages. The rural households, irrespective of the size of village, reported higher reliability and satisfaction with respect to the services of *anganwadis*.

**Table 5.2.12**

*Performance of Child Care Services: Small vis-á-vis Bigger Villages*

*(per cent of rural households)*

| *Indicators* | *Village Size* | | |
|---|---|---|---|
| | *A&B* | *C* | *T* |
| Usage of *Anganwadi* | 28 | 34 | 30 |
| Regular opening of *Anganwadi* | 89 | 84 | 87 |
| Reasons—pre-school facility | 77 | 74 | 76 |
| Reasons—supplementary diet | 38 | 45 | 40 |
| Having immunisation/medical check-up | 81 | 76 | 79 |
| Good behaviour of *Anganwadi* worker | 80 | 72 | 78 |

## Variations in Service Quality Experienced by Very Poor Households

About 30 per cent of households were found to be in the category earlier defined as ICD. The comparative assessment of services experienced by households with ICD against the rest of the households indicates the discrimination in public services if any against the very poor. Comparisons reported in this section are based on combined feedback of rural and urban households.

### *Drinking Water*

Ease of access to drinking water is slightly lower for ICD households (51 per cent) compared to other households. In use and satisfaction with respect to drinking water services there appears to be no significant difference across the poor and non-poor households. The willingness to pay for better services is lower in the case of poor households, but full satisfaction with quality of protected piped water supply is high. It is worth noting that the poor households reported higher full satisfaction with quality of supply of protected piped water compared to better-off households. The impact of poverty is also reflected in the slightly lower scale of willingness to pay more among the ICD households, as compared to the rest of the population.

## Table 5.2.13

*Performance of Drinking Water Supply: Very Poor vis-á-vis Rest*

*(per cent of rural households)*

| *Indicators* | *Economic Group* | | |
|---|---|---|---|
| | *ICD* | *O* | *T* |
| Access to public protected source 100 mts. | 51 | 56 | 55 |
| Usage of public protected water | 62 | 62 | 62 |
| Breakdown within three months—protected public tap | 23 | 25 | 25 |
| Breakdown within three months—public hand pumps | 24 | 25 | 24 |
| Involvement of community in maintenance | 23 | 23 | 23 |
| Bribes paid for repair of protected public water sources | 12 | 10 | 11 |
| Willingness to pay for better service | 36 | 42 | 40 |
| Full satisfaction with adequacy of supply in protected piped water | 22 | 20 | 20 |
| Full satisfaction with quality of supply in protected piped water | 29 | 21 | 27 |
| Full satisfaction with adequacy of supply in protected public source | 21 | 23 | 24 |
| Full satisfaction with quality of supply in protected public source | 30 | 31 | 32 |

*Note:* ICD—Income capability disadvantage.
O—Others.
T—Total.

### *Health Care*

The poor households depend on government health care facilities to a larger extent both for minor and major ailments compared to other households though their access to health care is less (34 per cent) than other households (43 per cent). The reliability experienced by poor households is lower than that by other households, which is also reflected in corresponding satisfaction ratings.

## Table 5.2.14

*Performance of Health Care Services: Very Poor vis-á-vis Rest*

*(per cent of rural households)*

| *Indicators* | *Economic Group* | | |
|---|---|---|---|
| | *ICD* | *O* | *T* |
| Access to health care within one kilometre | 34 | 43 | 40 |
| Dependence on government facility for minor ailments | 53 | 43 | 45 |
| Dependence on government facility for major ailments | 65 | 51 | 55 |
| Presence of doctors at time of visit | 67 | 72 | 70 |
| Presence of paramedical staff at time of visit | 81 | 83 | 83 |
| Fee paid for service by out-patients | 17 | 15 | 16 |
| Bribe paid for service | 18 | 16 | 16 |
| Full satisfaction with behaviour of doctors out-patient | 11 | 15 | 14 |
| Full satisfaction with behaviour of paramedical staff out-patient | 10 | 14 | 12 |

*Bus Transport*

Ease of access to public as well as private buses is lower for poor households. The poor households use less government buses and more private buses. The reliability and full satisfaction with the government buses is also low for poor households compared to other households.

**Table 5.2.15**

*Performance of Bus Transport Services: Very Poor vis-á-vis Rest*

*(per cent of rural households)*

| *Indicators* | *Economic Group* | | |
|---|---|---|---|
| | *ICD* | *O* | *T* |
| Public bus available within one km. | 36 | 53 | 48 |
| Private bus available within one km. | 47 | 58 | 55 |
| Public buses used | 29 | 37 | 35 |
| Private buses used | 39 | 31 | 34 |
| Full satisfaction with punctuality of public buses | 16 | 21 | 20 |
| Full satisfaction with frequency of public buses | 17 | 22 | 21 |
| Full satisfaction with behaviour of conductors | 18 | 22 | 21 |

*Public Distribution System*

There are no differences between poor and other households in owing ration cards (81 per cent) and regular availability of staple foodgrains (23 per cent). However, the usage of PDS is more with poor households (75 per cent). But the access and full satisfaction with respect to PDS is relatively low for poor households compared to other households.

**Table 5.2.16**

*Performance of PDS: Very Poor vis-á-vis Rest*

*(per cent of rural households)*

| *Indicators* | *Economic Group* | | |
|---|---|---|---|
| | *ICD* | *O* | *T* |
| Availability of ration shop within one km. | 70 | 80 | 77 |
| Households possessing own ration cards | 81 | 80 | 81 |
| Use of PDS by card owners at least once in two months | 75 | 70 | 72 |
| Regular availability of staple foodgrains | 23 | 23 | 23 |
| Display of prices always | 45 | 48 | 47 |
| Full satisfaction with quantity of supply | 6 | 9 | 8 |
| Full satisfaction with quality of supply | 8 | 10 | 9 |
| Satisfaction with fairness of shopkeeper | 7 | 11 | 10 |

### School Education

The poor households have better access to primary schools (78 per cent) compared to other households (75 per cent). The dependence on government primary schools is also high for poor households (89 per cent) than the other households (72 per cent). The dependence on private schools is very low for poor household (11 per cent) compared to other households (28 per cent). There is not much difference between poor and other households in the awareness of mid-day meals scheme and its use. But the full satisfaction with respect to behaviour of teachers, school buildings and toilets is low for poor households compared to other households.

**Table 5.2.17**

*Performance of Government Primary Schools: Very Poor vis-á-vis Rest*

*(per cent of rural households)*

| *Indicators* | *Economic Group* | | |
|---|---|---|---|
| | *ICD* | *O* | *T* |
| Availability of school within one km. | 78 | 75 | 76 |
| Dependence for education facility—public | 89 | 72 | 78 |
| Dependence for education facility—private | 11 | 28 | 22 |
| Full satisfaction with behaviour of teachers | 14 | 17 | 16 |
| Awareness of mid-day meal scheme | 69 | 68 | 68 |
| Use of mid-day meal | 82 | 83 | 83 |
| Satisfaction with school building | 11 | 15 | 14 |
| Satisfaction with toilet | 4 | 7 | 6 |

### Child Care

*Anganwadi* appears to be the only service where there are no significant differences between poor and other households in usage, reliability and full satisfaction with the service. Supplementary diet appears to be an incentive for poor households to send their children to *anganwadi*.

**Table 5.2.18**

*Performance of Child Care Services: Very Poor vis-á-vis Rest*

*(per cent of rural households)*

| *Indicators* | *Economic Group* | | |
|---|---|---|---|
| | *ICD* | *O* | *T* |
| Usage of *Anganwadi* | 30 | 29 | 29 |
| Regular opening of *Anganwadi* | 86 | 89 | 88 |
| Reasons—pre-school facility | 75 | 75 | 75 |
| Reasons—supplementary diet | 42 | 37 | 39 |
| Having immunisation/medical check-up | 80 | 80 | 80 |
| Good behaviour of *Anganwadi* worker | 77 | 79 | 78 |

The poor households are in a disadvantage situation with respect to many public services in the access, use, reliability and full satisfaction with respect to services. Though, the access and use of primary schools is better, the full satisfaction with the quality of services is low. *Anganwadi* appears to be a service, which does not discriminate against the poor.

## Summary of Findings on Services for Disadvantaged Sections

SC/ST households have more or less similar ease of access to public services as the rest of the population. They also report a higher dependence on public services except in transport compared to the rest. Small villages (class C) have lower access to all public services compared to the larger villages (A & B classes) except in drinking water. Despite lower access, smaller villages are on par with larger villages in the use of public services. A clear implication is that people in the small villages travel longer distances to avail of essential public services and in the process incur higher costs including lost wages.

The poor households are in a disadvantaged position to the access and use of most of the public services. In full satisfaction with respect to the services, there appears to be no significant difference between the disadvantaged sections and rest of the society.

The main finding from the 16 major states of India also show that a significantly smaller proportion of ICD households have ease of access to health care, public transport, and PDS compared to the rest of the households, but have more or less equal access to drinking water and primary schools. On the usage side, a higher percentage of ICD households utilise all services except public transport. There are no significant differences between ICD and other households in terms of the reliability and full satisfaction with the services. One reason is that the poor and non-poor are using the same service facility once they have access to it (e.g., a government hospital). In brief, the ICD households depend more on public services than the non-poor though, they are disadvantaged with respect to ease of access.

This aggregate picture, however, hides a very disturbing picture. A comparison of ease of access to public services for the poor and non-poor, in the top 6 and bottom 5 states indicates major disparities across states, in comparison with disparities between the poor and the rest within the states.

There are no significant differences in ease of access to most of the public services between ICD and other households in the top 6 states. Healthcare and PDS are two services where ICD households seem to have somewhat lower access.

### Table 5.3.1

*Access and Usage of Public Services by the Poor and the Rest*

(per cent)

| Public Services | Ease of Access | | Usage | |
|---|---|---|---|---|
| | ICD | Others | ICD | Others |
| Drinking water | 53 | 56 | 65 | 62 |
| Health care | 34 | 44 | 50 | 41 |
| Public transport | 46 | 59 | 28 | 42 |
| Public distribution | 70 | 81 | 79 | 75 |
| Primary school | 70 | 68 | 91 | 76 |

In the bottom 5 states, on the other hand, ICD households report lower ease of access to all services (compared to other households) except drinking water. Primary schools and drinking water are two services that seem to have better reached out to the poor.

### Table 5.3.2

*Access to Public Services by Economic Categories and Category of States*

(per cent)

| Public Services | Top 6 States | | Middle 5 States | | Bottom 5 States | |
|---|---|---|---|---|---|---|
| | ICD | Others | ICD | Others | ICD | Others |
| Drinking water | 69 | 71 | 48 | 42 | 47 | 45 |
| Health care | 43 | 49 | 38 | 43 | 25 | 37 |
| Public transport | 88 | 83 | 38 | 46 | 22 | 29 |
| Public distribution | 82 | 85 | 68 | 74 | 64 | 79 |
| Primary school | 77 | 71 | 75 | 66 | 59 | 64 |

Another disturbing finding is that the poor (ICD) households in the top 6 states have much higher access to all the five services than even the non-poor households in the bottom 5 states. This is true to a smaller extent of the middle states also, for four out of the five services. This is truly a sad reflection on the pathetic state of public services in several of India's major states. The bottom 5 states are also worse-off in terms of reliability and full satisfaction. It signifies the extreme disparities between our states in respect of the adequacy and quality of public services. In contrast, disparities between the poor and the non-poor within the states seem much less significant in comparison. This is not to say that the latter does not deserve careful attention. But the big challenge facing the country is how to bridge this wide gap between the states.

It is already observed that small villages (Class C) have lower access to all public services compared to the larger villages. A comparison of ease of access to public services for the villages across top 6, middle 5 and bottom 5 states indicates that villages in top 6 states have better ease of access to most of the public services compared to villages in middle 5 and bottom 5 states. Villages in middle 5 states have relatively better ease of access compared to the villages in bottom 5 states in drinking water, health care and public transport.

**Table 5.3.4**

*Access to Public Services by Village Size and Category of States*

*(per cent)*

| *Public Services* | *Top 6 States* | | *Middle 5 States* | | *Bottom 5 States* | |
|---|---|---|---|---|---|---|
| | *A&B* | *C* | *A&B* | *C* | *A&B* | *C* |
| Drinking water | 69 | 63 | 39 | 45 | 34 | 31 |
| Health care | 55 | 17 | 50 | 21 | 35 | 12 |
| Public transport | 94 | 86 | 41 | 29 | 27 | 18 |
| Public distribution | 85 | 55 | 66 | 32 | 65 | 38 |
| Primary school | 86 | 75 | 84 | 71 | 84 | 69 |

A&B—Big villages (Villages with more than 1000 population).
C—Small villages (villages with 1000 and less population).

Small villages in top 6 states have better access to most of the public services compared to villages in middle 5 and bottom 5 states. Similarly, small villages in middle 5 states have relatively better access compared to the villages in bottom 5 states in drinking water, health care and public transport. There is very little disparity in access to the villages of the same size across the group of states for primary school. The big challenge facing the bottom 5 states is to provide ease of access to the other four services.

# 6

# Satisfaction and Quality of Services: Validating the Linkage

The satisfaction ratings derived from our survey of households are based on the self-assessment of the utility of the selected services by their users. Not surprisingly, most technical experts tend to regard the measures of satisfaction expressed by respondents as rather subjective. It is evident that the reported level of satisfaction with a public service could be influenced by several factors such as the characteristics of the service (e.g., ease of access, reliability, cost and quality), the profile of households (e.g., income, social status, and education), as well as awareness of how the service provider functions. Whether an ordinary person can take all the relevant factors into account rigorously is the question that experts are likely to raise. Since the feedback on user satisfaction is an important component of the assessment of public services carried out in this study, a specific effort has been made to explore the significance of the relationship between satisfaction levels and the characteristics and quality of the service. If there are significant relationships, a case can be made for taking the satisfaction variable seriously. If the findings are negative, on the other hand, it would be difficult to reject the hypothesis that satisfaction measures are arbitrary and subjective.

## Approach to Analysis

As is evident from the earlier chapters, there are wide variations in the satisfaction levels associated with the different services covered by our survey. There is variability in the satisfaction levels of services between the states too. The hypothesis being tested in this chapter is that the measures of quality, quantity and other aspects of the provision of public services have a positive and significant relationship to the satisfaction ratings given by households. We do not have full information on all the variables relevant to the exercise. The survey, for example, has collected data on the levels of satisfaction of households for basic services using a four-point scale *viz.*, strongly dissatisfied,

dissatisfied, satisfied and strongly satisfied[9]. The four-point scale provided discrete choices of the households in rating public services. The evidence on the quality and quantity aspects of the services is limited to what the users were able to provide. Objective measures of quality and quantity certified by independent experts would have been more appropriate. Such data does not exist and is seldom collected even by governments. But this is not a serious lacuna as our objective here is confined to a test of the consistency between users' satisfaction ratings and their own assessments of quality, quantity and other features of service delivery based on their direct experience.

The users' ratings are qualitative, which are discrete choices. Discrete choice variables are classified into ordered and unordered variables. The level of satisfaction of the users is a discrete rated variable in four categories with ordinal numbers 1, 2, 3, and 4. The satisfaction rating associated with 4 (strongly satisfied) is better than 3 (satisfied). The rating associated with 3 is better than 2 and this in turn is better than 1. There is an order in the rating of satisfaction of the respondents for a particular attribute or service. The present analysis attempts to track the service characteristics of public services that have a bearing on the satisfaction ratings of households through an econometric model. This type of model is known as a qualitative choice model which is in contrast to a continuous dependent variable in a classical regression model. In a qualitative choice model the dependent variable is discrete, ordinal and having more than two outcomes and the appropriate methods followed for estimating the model are ordered logit and ordered probit (Greene, 2000 and Maddala, 1983). Between the two estimating methods (models) *viz.*, ordered logit and ordered probit, the ordered probit is most commonly used to explain the ordered discrete choices. Following the convention, in the present analysis, the ordered probit model was employed to track service characteristics that have a bearing on the satisfaction level of households with public services.

The analysis presented here covers three out of the five services *viz.*, drinking water, health care, and the public distribution system. The analysis excludes road transport, as government buses are not the predominant carriers of passengers in many states. Primary education has a smaller sample compared to other services and hence, has been left out. It may also be noted that the analysis is limited to data from rural users, in the interest of data homogeneity. The urban sample is excluded from the present analysis as the

---

9. Though the fifth point—don't know/can't say—was included, since there was negligible response on it, only four-points on the scale were used for this analysis.

provision of services significantly differs between rural and urban areas and they require separate analysis.

This analysis focuses on aggregate data for the 16 major states, and again separately for five major states to bring out the contrasts among the states. The five major states are chosen so as to give adequate spatial representation to all parts of India. The states chosen are Assam, Bihar, Gujarat, Madhya Pradesh and Karnataka. The purpose of choosing the states is to highlight the contrasts among the states and not to present regional comparisons. The total rural sample in the millennial survey for the major 16 states is 22749 households. All the sample households are not users of the four services and, therefore, the sample size varies from one service to another.

## The Analytical Model

First order outputs generated on SPSS were used in the ordered probit model to assess the statistical significance of the model, coefficients for the explanatory variables, threshold parameters and their statistical significance. The test of significance was performed using Wald $\chi^2$ statistic. The number of threshold parameters was one less than the number of response categories. For the four category responses in the model, the output contained three threshold parameters. The statistical significance and positive sign of the threshold parameters $\mu_{0,}$ $\mu_{1,}$ and $\mu_2$ and their ascending order $(0 < \mu_0 < \mu_1 < \mu_2)$ indicated that the categories of the responses were ordered. In other words, statistically significant positive and ordinal $\mu$ estimates served to indicate that the responses are ordered in the categories and also validate the use of ordered probit model for estimating the coefficients of the independent variables in explaining satisfaction (Liao, 1994). The present analysis is restricted only to the estimation of the coefficients of the independent variable in explaining satisfaction. Therefore, no further analysis is made to estimate the marginal effects of the independent variables.

In the ordered probit model, the independent or explanatory variables should be either continuous variables or dummy variables with binary choices. Therefore, some of the categorical variables with more than two outcomes were converted into dummy variables. The conversion of categorical variables with more than two outcomes into dummy variables was warranted as no meaningful interpretation can be given to the estimated coefficients of these variables. The description of the dependent and independent variables for each service is presented in the following paragraphs along with the empirical results.

The ordered probit model did not yield significant and appropriate threshold parameters for most of the regressions, particularly for the lower threshold, indicating the lack of ordering in the rating of dissatisfaction *viz.*, strong dissatisfaction and dissatisfaction. Hence, the study estimated coefficients of the variables in an iterative way by reducing the number of categories for the satisfaction rating. In the first run, we used four categories for the dependent variable and obtained the estimates, tests of significance of the model and threshold parameters. When the model was significant (model is significant in most of the regressions) and threshold parameters were either not significant or with a negative sign, we used three categories for the dependent variable *viz.*, dissatisfaction (clubbing strong dissatisfaction with partial dissatisfaction), satisfaction and strong satisfaction, and estimated the coefficients of the variables and their statistical significance. In the event the threshold parameters were not significant or had a negative sign, the categories for the dependent variable was further reduced to two, *viz.*, strong satisfaction and the rest of the satisfaction levels[10], and coefficients estimated for the model. In the special case where categories are reduced to two, the ordered probit model turns out to be the conventional binary probit model. The parameters of the ordered probit models[11] were estimated using SPSS package.

## Empirical Results

**Drinking Water:** Drinking water from public sources is mainly supplied through pipe connections to the houses, public taps and hand pumps. The problems associated with each of these modes of provision differ substantially. Water supply through pipe connections and public taps were assessed on frequency of supply (number of times per week) and duration of supply on the day of supply. These measures are not relevant to the provision of water through hand pumps. Similarly, there are common problems associated with public taps and hand pumps such as break down and downtime. Hence, the present analysis considered the three sources of drinking water supply as three different services.

The analysis attempted to explain the satisfaction of the households with the quantity of water supply through the following eight explanatory variables.

10. Two categories *viz.*, strong satisfaction and rest of the categories is considered instead of satisfaction and dissatisfaction as the data on rating of satisfaction for most of the services is in satisfaction category and relatively few rating are reported for strong dissatisfaction and dissatisfaction.

11. The specification of the model is same as the model presented by Tim Futing Liao in Interpreting Probability models—Logit, Probit, and Other Generalised Liner Models, pp.37-39.

Out of the eight explanatory variables—distance, frequency of water supply, duration of water supply, quality of water, break down and down time directly relate to the service provision. The other two variables *viz.*, village class and caste, served to capture any special impact these factors had on the manner in which agencies targeted these services. The explanatory variables and their specifications are given below in Table 6.1.

**Table 6.1**

*Specification of Variables for Drinking Water*

| *Explanatory Variables* | *Type of Variables* | *Specification of Variables* |
|---|---|---|
| Village class | Dummy | 0–Small village (less than 500 population)<br>1–Other villages |
| Caste | Dummy | 0–SC/ST community<br>1–Other communities |
| Distance to water source | Continuous | Number of meters |
| Frequency of water supply | Continuous | Number of days in a week |
| Duration of water supply | Continuous | Number of hours on the day of supply |
| Quality of water | Dummy | 0–Dissatisfied<br>1–Satisfied |
| Break down | Continuous | Number of times in a year |
| Down time | Continuous | Number of days |

### *Piped Water Supply*

The satisfaction rating of the user rural households on piped water supply is presented in Table 6.2 for the five states and all India. The table shows that the percentage of households strongly satisfied with piped water supply is highest in Gujarat (48.6 per cent) followed by Karnataka (41.4 per cent). The number of households reporting piped water supply is few in Assam and negligible in Bihar. Hence, the analysis for piped water supply was carried out for the states of Gujarat, Karnataka, Madhya Pradesh and all India.

The service quality variables that are relevant for the piped connection are frequency, duration and quality of water. Table 6.3 presents the results of ordered probit estimates for Gujarat, Karnataka, Madhya Pradesh and all India. The model is significant for the three states and all India. The threshold parameters are significant, positive and ordered for three categories for satisfaction (dissatisfied, satisfied and strongly satisfied) for Karnataka, Madhya Pradesh and all India and two categories (strongly satisfied and other satisfaction ratings) for Gujarat.

## Table 6.2

*Satisfaction with the Quantity of Water: Piped Water*

| *States* | *Strongly Dissatisfied* | *Dissatisfied* | *Satisfied* | *Strongly Satisfied* | *Total* |
|---|---|---|---|---|---|
| Assam | 1 (3.1) | 1 (3.1) | 19 (59.4) | 11 (34.4) | 32 (100.0) |
| Bihar | 0 (0.0) | 0 (0.0) | 1 (100.0) | 0 (0.0) | 1 (100.0) |
| Gujarat | 31 (5.3) | 38 (6.5) | 230 (39.5) | 283 (48.6) | 582 (100.0) |
| Karnataka | 9 (3.9) | 24 (10.3) | 103 (44.4) | 96 (41.4) | 232 (100.0) |
| Madhya Pradesh | 12 (5.2) | 23 (9.9) | 142 (61.2) | 55 (23.7) | 232 (100.0) |
| **All India** | 141 (4.4) | 337 (10.6) | 1948 (61.3) | 754 (23.7) | 3180 (100.0) |

*Note:* Figures in the parentheses are the percentages.

All the three service quality variables *viz.*, frequency, duration and the quality of water supply are significant at 1 per cent level in all the three states and all India (except frequency of water supply in Gujarat) indicating that the satisfaction with the piped water supply depends on the quality of service provision. In Gujarat, size of villages (small villages) and caste (SC/ST community) have a bearing on the satisfaction level. Deliberate policy measures might have been initiated to provide piped water supply to the small villages and to the SC/ST community in Gujarat. It is also interesting to observe such a relationship between SC/ST and satisfaction level at all India level.

## Table 6.3

*Satisfaction Estimates for the Quantity of Water: Piped Water*

| *Variables* | *Gujarat* | | *Karnataka* | | *Madhya Pradesh* | | *All India* | |
|---|---|---|---|---|---|---|---|---|
| | $\beta$ | *Sig.* | $\beta$ | *Sig.* | $\beta$ | *Sig.* | $\beta$ | *Sig.* |
| Village class | -0.368 | 0.070 | 0.234 | 0.278 | 0.033 | 0.904 | -0.036 | 0.558 |
| Caste | -0.335 | 0.015 | -0.182 | 0.340 | -0.098 | 0.633 | -0.084 | 0.075 |
| Frequency | 0.031 | 0.599 | 0.254 | 0.000 | 0.153 | 0.001 | 0.191 | 0.000 |
| Duration | 0.150 | 0.006 | 0.253 | 0.003 | 0.169 | 0.037 | 0.029 | 0.000 |
| Quality | 2.216 | 0.000 | 0.968 | 0.000 | 1.329 | 0.002 | 1.146 | 0.000 |
| $\mu_0$ | 1.477 | 0.001 | 1.651 | 0.001 | 1.223 | 0.032 | 1.144 | 0.000 |
| $\mu_1$ | - | - | 3.229 | 0.000 | 3.111 | 0.000 | 3.043 | 0.000 |
| Sample | 582 | | 232 | | 232 | | 3180 | |
| Model Chi-square (5df) | 313.45 | | 66.47 | | 30.52 | | 402.40 | |

*Public Tap*

The satisfaction ratings of rural user households, for public tap water supply, are presented in Table 6.4 for the five states and all India. The table shows that the percentage of households strongly satisfied with piped water supply is highest in Karnataka (42.7 per cent) followed by Gujarat (27.1 per cent). The proportion of households reporting supply of water from public tap is negligible in Bihar. Out of the 66 households reported to be using of public tap in Madhya Pradesh, only four households reported strong satisfaction and one household reported satisfaction. When the distribution is highly skewed towards dissatisfaction with a few observations on satisfaction, the model and the estimated coefficients will not be significant. Hence, Madhya Pradesh is omitted from the analysis for water supply from public taps and the analysis is carried out for the states of Assam, Gujarat, Karnataka and all India.

The service quality variables that are relevant for public tap are distance, frequency, duration, breakdown, downtime and quality of water. Table 6.5 presents the results of ordered probit estimates for Assam, Gujarat, Karnataka and all India. The model is significant for the three states and all India. The threshold parameters are significant, positive and ordered for three categories for satisfaction for Assam, Gujarat and all India and for two categories (strongly satisfied and other satisfaction ratings) for Karnataka.

**Table 6.4**

*Satisfaction Levels on the Quantity of Water: Public Tap*

| *States* | *Strongly Dissatisfied* | *Dissatisfied* | *Satisfied* | *Strongly Satisfied* | *Total* |
|---|---|---|---|---|---|
| Assam | 4 (4.8) | 14 (16.7) | 49 (58.3) | 17 (20.2) | 84 (100.0) |
| Bihar | 0 (0.0) | 0 (0.0) | 2 (100.0) | 0 (0.0) | 2 (100.0) |
| Gujarat | 10 (7.5) | 18 (13.5) | 69 (51.9) | 36 (27.1) | 133 (100.0) |
| Karnataka | 53 (9.5) | 37 (6.6) | 229 (41.1) | 238 (42.7) | 557 (100.0) |
| Madhya Pradesh | 16 (24.2) | 45 (68.2) | 1 (1.5) | 4 (6.1) | 66 (100.0) |
| **All India** | 245 (6.2) | 486 (12.4) | 2142 (54.5) | 1056 (26.9) | 3929 (100.0) |

*Note:* Figures in the parentheses are the percentages.

The coefficient for the distance variable is significant with a negative sign, for all India, while it is not significant in the three states. This implies that shorter the distance to water source, higher is the level of satisfaction. It suggests that ease of access is a major factor in determining satisfaction with public taps in rural India. But such a pattern has not emerged in the states of Assam, Gujarat and Karnataka. This could be because a large proportion of the households in Gujarat and Karnataka enjoy easy access to public taps, which leaves very few user households living at a great distance from public taps (Paul, *et al.*, 2004). In Assam, other water sources are the predominant water sources, and only about 7 per cent of sample households reported use of public tap. The absence of significant variations in level of satisfaction with increase in distance to the public tap could be explained by this small proportion of households in Assam, which rendered distance non-relevant for this analysis.

Aspects of service quality variables that are statistically significant in the all India analysis for supply through public tap are frequency of water supply, duration and quality of water. Quality of water is also separately significant in the three states. Frequency of water supply is significant in Assam and Gujarat, while duration of water supply is significant in Gujarat and Karnataka. Notwithstanding these state level variations, it can be concluded that the satisfaction with the quantity of water supply through public tap is explained by the quality of service variables.

Though, size of village does not show a significant relationship with level of satisfaction at all India level, it is significant when separately assessed for three states. The coefficient is positive in Assam and Gujarat and negative in Karnataka, signifying that higher satisfaction ratings are associated with bigger villages in Assam and Gujarat, and with smaller villages in Karnataka. These coefficients suggest that the initiatives at decentralised water supply in Karnataka have been more effective in small villages.

**Table 6.5**

*Satisfaction Estimates for the Quantity of Water: Public Tap*

| *Variables* | *Assam* | | *Gujarat* | | *Karnataka* | | *All India* | |
|---|---|---|---|---|---|---|---|---|
| | *β* | *Sig.* | *β* | *Sig.* | *β* | *Sig.* | *β* | *Sig.* |
| Village Class | 1.015 | 0.008 | 0.547 | 0.022 | -0.252 | 0.085 | -0.044 | 0.280 |
| Caste | -0.678 | 0.067 | -0.312 | 0.150 | -0.159 | 0.244 | -0.014 | 0.714 |
| Distance | 0.001 | 0.265 | 0.000 | 0.764 | 0.001 | 0.409 | -0.000 | 0.058 |
| Frequency | 0.247 | 0.021 | 0.169 | 0.051 | 0.076 | 0.244 | 0.162 | 0.000 |
| Duration | 0.009 | 0.711 | 0.022 | 0.079 | 0.083 | 0.000 | 0.026 | 0.000 |
| Break Down | -0.047 | 0.177 | -0.039 | 0.208 | 0.027 | 0.369 | -0.005 | 0.319 |
| Down Time | 0.014 | 0.442 | -0.008 | 0.708 | -0.023 | 0.047 | 0.003 | 0.379 |
| Quality | 1.969 | 0.000 | 1.421 | 0.000 | 2.131 | 0.000 | 0.852 | 0.000 |
| $\mu_0$ | 2.047 | 0.013 | 1.571 | 0.029 | 2.023 | 0.000 | 0.962 | 0.000 |
| $\mu_1$ | 4.429 | 0.000 | 3.277 | 0.000 | - | - | 2.551 | 0.000 |
| Sample | 84 | | 133 | | 557 | | 3929 | |
| Model Chi-square (8df) | 49.47 | | 36.39 | | 318.90 | | 332.68 | |

### *Hand Pump*

The profile of satisfaction with quantity of water from hand pump among user rural households is presented in Table 6.6, for the five states and all India. The table shows that the largest percentage of households strongly satisfied with the quantity of water from hand pump is in Gujarat (30.2 per cent) followed by Karnataka (25.5 per cent). The number of households reporting use of hand pump is negligible in Assam. Hence, the analysis of satisfaction from quantity of water from hand pump is carried out for the states of Bihar, Gujarat, Karnataka, Madhya Pradesh and all India.

**Table 6.6**

*Satisfaction Levels with the Quantity of Water: Hand Pump*

| *States* | *Strongly Dissatisfied* | *Dissatisfied* | *Satisfied* | *Strongly Satisfied* | *Total* |
|---|---|---|---|---|---|
| Assam | 6 (23.1) | 8 (30.8) | 9 (34.6) | 3 (11.5) | 26 (100.0) |
| Bihar | 5 (2.1) | 3 (1.3) | 198 (83.5) | 31 (13.1) | 237 (100.0) |
| Gujarat | 19 (8.1) | 63 (26.8) | 82 (34.9) | 71 (30.2) | 235 (100.0) |
| Karnataka | 13 (4.1) | 59 (18.6) | 165 (51.9) | 81 (25.5) | 318 (100.0) |
| Madhya Pradesh | 46 (3.6) | 167 (13.0) | 850 (66.4) | 217 (17.0) | 1280 (100.0) |
| **All India** | 227 (3.6) | 1033 (16.4) | 3623 (57.5) | 1421 (22.5) | 6304 (100.0) |

*Note:* Figures in the parenthesis are the percentages.

The service quality variables that are relevant for hand pump are distance, frequency of break down, downtime to repair the service and quality of water. Table 6.7 presents the results of ordered probit estimations for Bihar, Gujarat,

**Table 6.7**

*Satisfaction Estimates for the Quantity of Water: Hand Pump*

| *Variables* | *Bihar* | | *Gujarat* | | *Karnataka* | | *Madhya Pradesh* | | *All India* | |
|---|---|---|---|---|---|---|---|---|---|---|
| | $\beta$ | *Sig.* | $\beta$ | *Sig.* | $\beta$ | *Sig.* | $\beta$ | *Sig.* | $\beta$ | *Sig.* |
| Village class | 1.101 | 0.027 | -0.061 | 0.715 | 0.001 | 0.997 | 0.030 | 0.662 | 0.037 | 0.240 |
| Caste | -0.660 | 0.136 | -0.106 | 0.532 | -0.558 | 0.001 | 0.068 | 0.309 | 0.110 | 0.000 |
| Distance | -0.001 | 0.810 | -0.001 | 0.146 | -0.001 | 0.127 | -0.000 | 0.017 | -0.001 | 0.000 |
| Break down | 0.011 | 0.854 | -0.021 | 0.514 | -0.0384 | 0.273 | -0.001 | 0.696 | -0.039 | 0.000 |
| Down time | -0.149 | 0.010 | -0.013 | 0.044 | -0.0263 | 0.004 | -0.010 | 0.003 | -0.003 | 0.073 |
| Quality | 3.788 | 0.000 | 2.079 | 0.000 | 0.810 | 0.001 | 2.117 | 0.000 | 1.954 | 0.000 |
| $\mu_0$ | 2.987 | 0.000 | 0.755 | 0.007 | 0.540 | 0.065 | 0.834 | 0.000 | 0.629 | 0.000 |
| $\mu_1$ | - | - | 1.984 | 0.000 | - | - | 2.913 | 0.000 | 2.480 | 0.000 |
| Sample | 237 | | 235 | | 318 | | 1280 | | 6304 | |
| Model chi-square (6df) | 131.054 | | 112.128 | | 49.337 | | 202.571 | | 1672.8 | |

Karnataka, Madhya Pradesh and all India. The model is significant for the four states and all India. The threshold parameters are significant, positive and ordered for three categories for satisfaction for Gujarat, Madhya Pradesh and all India and for two categories for Bihar and Karnataka. The coefficient for distance is significant and has a negative sign in Madhya Pradesh and for the country taken as a whole, while the sign is negative and the coefficients are not significant in the states of Bihar, Gujarat and Karnataka. The negative sign can be taken as an indicative measure that satisfaction is associated with the access.

The service quality variables that are statistically significant at all India for hand pump are frequency of breakdown, downtime and quality of water. The sign of the coefficients is negative for breakdown and downtime and is positive for water quality. The negative coefficients for the two variables reflect the positive association between better reliability (lower frequency of breakdown) and satisfaction, and better maintenance (lower downtime) and satisfaction. Though, the coefficients of frequency of breakdown for Gujarat, Karnataka and Madhya Pradesh have negative signs, they are not significant. The statewise data on breakdown reveals that the frequency of breakdown is generally low; the reported frequency of breakdown is mostly one or two times in a year. The low variability in the frequency of break down might have made the variable not significant in the regression. But it is to be recognised that the reliability of the service seems to be relatively high. The coefficients for downtime are negative and significant in all the four states. These results show that when reliability of the service is high, satisfaction from the service depends on the maintenance of the service.

Village class is not significant at all India level and also in the states of Gujarat, Karnataka, and Madhya Pradesh. There appears to be no significant difference between small and big villages in the quality of service in water supply through hand pumps. In Bihar, the coefficient for village class is positive and significant. This implies that hand pumps are providing better service to households in big villages rather than in small villages.

In Karnataka deliberate attempt was made to provide drinking water to most of the hamlets, particularly to those inhabited by the SC and ST communities. This could be the reason for significant and negative coefficient for caste variable in Karnataka. The negative coefficient for the caste denotes that SC and ST households have reported better satisfaction rating for the quantity of hand pump water compared to other castes.

**Health Care:** State governments provide health care to the rural households through district hospitals, *taluk* hospitals, health centres and sub-centres. Depending on the nature of illness, health care is provided in out-patient and in-patient ward. The period of treatment as well as nature of interaction between patients and doctors and paramedical staff, differ substantially across out-patient and in-patient treatment—hence, they are to be taken separately for analysis, particularly on satisfaction with the service. In the sample households for the major states, 9270 households reported use of government health facilities for out-patient treatment and 1585 households for inpatient treatment. As the use of out-patient treatment is much higher than that of in-patient treatment and the ordered probit analysis requires relatively large number of observations, the analysis was carried out for the out-patient sample only.

The analysis explored satisfaction of the households with the quality of out-patient treatment in government health care facilities through the following seven variables. The variables that directly relate with the quality of treatment are waiting time, behaviour of doctor, behaviour of paramedical staff and the quality of medicines as judged by the respondents. The type of explanatory variables and their specifications are also given below in Table 6.8.

**Table 6.8**

*Specifications of Variables for Health Care*

| *Explanatory Variables* | *Type of Variables* | *Specification of Variables* |
|---|---|---|
| Village class | Dummy | 0–Small villages (less than 500 population)<br>1-Other villages |
| Caste | Dummy | 0–SC/ST community<br>1–Other communities |
| Distance from the health facility | Continuous | Number of kilometres |
| Waiting time | Continuous | Number of minutes |
| Behaviour of doctor | Dummy | 0–Bad, Average 1–Good |
| Behaviour of paramedical staff | Dummy | 0–Bad, Average 1–Good |
| Quality of Medicine | Dummy | 0–Dissatisfaction<br>1–Satisfaction |

The satisfaction rating of the user rural households of government health facilities for outpatient treatment is presented in Table 6.9 for the five states and all India. The table shows that the percentage of households strongly satisfied with treatment is highest in Gujarat (29.9 per cent) followed by Karnataka (28.1 per cent). The number of households reporting use of government health facility is very low (59 households) in Bihar. Hence, Bihar is excluded from the analysis for out-patient treatment and the analysis is carried out for the states of Assam, Gujarat, Karnataka, Madhya Pradesh, and all India.

## Table 6.9

*Satisfaction Levels with the Out-patient Treatment*

| *States* | *Strongly Dissatisfied* | *Dissatisfied* | *Satisfied* | *Strongly Satisfied* | *Total* |
|---|---|---|---|---|---|
| Assam | 7 (1.7) | 60 (14.3) | 334 (79.7) | 18 (4.3) | 419 (100.0) |
| Bihar | 5 (8.5) | 3 (5.1) | 51 (86.4) | 0 (0.0) | 59 (100.0) |
| Gujarat | 6 (1.1) | 10 (1.8) | 370 (67.2) | 165 (29.9) | 551 (100.0) |
| Karnataka | 43 (7.0) | 72 (11.7) | 328 (53.2) | 173 (28.1) | 616 (100.0) |
| Madhya Pradesh | 26 (2.5) | 38 (3.6) | 928 (87.5) | 69 (6.5) | 1061 (100.0) |
| **All India** | 219 (2.4) | 252 (2.7) | 7485 (80.7) | 1216 (13.1) | 9270 (100.0) |

*Note:* Figures in the parenthesis are the percentages.

Table 6.10 presents the results of ordered probit estimates for Assam, Gujarat, Karnataka, Madhya Pradesh, and all India. The model is significant for

## Table 6.10

*Satisfaction Estimates for Out-patient Treatment*

| *Variables* | *Assam* | | *Gujarat* | | *Karnataka* | | *Madhya Pradesh* | | *All India* | |
|---|---|---|---|---|---|---|---|---|---|---|
| | $\beta$ | *Sig.* | $\beta$ | *Sig.* | $\beta$ | *Sig.* | $\beta$ | *Sig.* | $\beta$ | *Sig.* |
| Village Class | -0.451 | 0.082 | -0.110 | 0.485 | 0.216 | 0.156 | 0.290 | 0.075 | -0.034 | 0.411 |
| Caste | -0.299 | 0.324 | -0.073 | 0.522 | 0.122 | 0.349 | -0.168 | 0.178 | 0.045 | 0.198 |
| Distance | -0.194 | 0.043 | 0.033 | 0.420 | 0.006 | 0.882 | -0.009 | 0.831 | -0.030 | 0.007 |
| Waiting time | 0.0182 | 0.000 | 0.040 | 0.017 | -0.007 | 0.007 | 0.000 | 0.868 | 0.001 | 0.191 |
| Behaviour of Doctors | 0.800 | 0.569 | 0.878 | 0.019 | 1.469 | 0.000 | -0.203 | 0.438 | 0.420 | 0.000 |
| Behaviour of paramedical staff | 0.132 | 0.925 | -0.259 | 0.415 | -0.087 | 0.747 | 0.838 | 0.002 | 0.268 | 0.000 |
| Quality of medicine | -0.088 | 0.733 | 3.197 | 0.000 | 1.677 | 0.000 | -0.266 | 0.042 | 0.505 | 0.000 |
| $\mu_0$ | 1.770 | 0.000 | 1.061 | 0.013 | 3.052 | 0.000 | 1.877 | 0.000 | 2.024 | 0.000 |
| $\mu_1$ | - | - | 4.343 | 0.000 | - | - | - | - | - | - |
| Sample | 419 | | 551 | | 616 | | 1061 | | 9270 | |
| Model Chi-square (7df) | 28.837 | | 116.518 | | 202.069 | | 33.714 | | 413.243 | |

the four states and all India. The threshold parameters are significant, positive and ordered for three categories for satisfaction only in Gujarat and for two categories for Assam, Karnataka, Madhya Pradesh, and all India. The coefficients for distance are significant and negative in Assam and in all India, and are not significant in Gujarat, Karnataka, and Madhya Pradesh. The non-significance of the distance variable in Gujarat, and Karnataka (the two states with relatively high percentage of strongly satisfied households) probably implies that distance is not a significant variable in explaining the satisfaction rating of households on health care.

The service quality variables that are statistically significant in all India for out-patient treatment are behaviour of doctors, behaviour of paramedical staff and the quality of medicine as perceived by respondents. Behaviour of doctors is also significant in Gujarat, and Karnataka. Behaviour of paramedical staff is significant in Madhya Pradesh. Quality of medicines is significant and has a proper (positive) sign in Gujarat, and Karnataka. An apparently anomalous result was observed in relation to Madhya Pradesh where the coefficient has a significant but negative sign on quality of medicines, indicating that those who mentioned that quality of medicine was not good were more satisfied. The waiting time for treatment is not significant for all India and Madhya Pradesh. While it is significant for Assam, Gujarat, and Karnataka, it has the appropriate sign only in Karnataka. This implies that patients are less sensitive to time delays if they are satisfied with the treatment. Coming to the village class variable, it is not significant for all India and for the states of Gujarat and Karnataka. The variable is significant for Assam and Madhya Pradesh; while the coefficient is negative for Assam and positive for Madhya Pradesh. In other words, households in small villages have a higher rating of satisfaction in Assam, while in Madhya Pradesh households in bigger villages have a higher rating of satisfaction. These results on the whole suggest that village size is not a significant variable to explain satisfaction with treatment.

It is interesting to observe that in Assam, the variables representing the quality of service *viz.*, behaviour of doctor, behaviour of paramedical staff and the quality of medicine are not significant. The variables that are significant are the access variables *viz.*, village class and distance, and the waiting time variable (positive coefficient—higher waiting time). All these variables along with only 4.3 per cent strongly satisfied households for out-patient treatment indicates the poor quality of health care facilities in Assam.

In Madhya Pradesh, some variables that represent the quality of service *viz.*, waiting time and behaviour of doctors are not significant. The only significant variable with an appropriate sign is the behaviour of paramedical staff. It is interesting to observe that the satisfaction rating is explained by behaviour of paramedical staff and not by the behaviour of doctors. Further, satisfaction with the service is also related with the dissatisfaction with the quality of medicine. This leads to an interesting conjecture that the paramedical staff has an important role in dealing (and possibly treating) the patients and the satisfaction rating with treatment (strongly satisfied are only 6.5 per cent) is related to the treatment given by the paramedical staff.

Among the four states, Gujarat and Karnataka have comparatively higher percentage households strongly satisfied with the outpatient treatment and in these two states satisfaction is well explained by the behaviour of doctors and quality of medicines—the two important variables that represent the quality of health care service.

**Table 6.11**

*Specification of Variables for Public Distribution System*

| *Explanatory Variables* | *Type of Variables* | *Specification of Variables* |
|---|---|---|
| Village class | Dummy | 0–Small village (< 500 population)<br>1–Other villages |
| Caste | Dummy | 0–SC/ST community<br>1–Other communities |
| Distance of ration shop | Continuous | Number of meters |
| Availability of rice | Dummy | 0–Never, Sometimes<br>1–Always |
| Availability of sugar | Dummy | 0–Never, Sometimes<br>1–Always |
| Availability of wheat | Dummy | 0–Never, Sometimes<br>1–Always |
| Availability of kerosene | Dummy | 0–Never, Sometimes<br>1–Always |
| Display price list | Dummy | 0–Never, Sometimes<br>1–Always |
| Quantity of item | Dummy | 0–Dissatisfaction<br>1–Satisfaction |
| Quality of item | Dummy | 0–Dissatisfaction<br>1–Satisfaction |
| Fairness of shopkeeper | Dummy | 0–Dissatisfaction<br>1–Satisfaction |

**Public Distribution System:** To serve as a major safety net for the poor, PDS is expected to make available basic foodgrains to households at regular time intervals. The survey shows that about 80 per cent of rural households from the major 16 states have drawn ration from fair price shops at least once. Among these users about 80 per cent have drawn ration at least once in two months. The user households report that the main items available at PDS outlets are rice, wheat, sugar and kerosene. As the performance of PDS is mainly dependent on the availability of items, the present analysis attempts to explain the satisfaction of the households with the overall availability of items in PDS outlets through the following eleven variables.

The variables that directly relate to satisfaction with the overall availability of items are the availability of the individual items *viz.*, rice, wheat, sugar and kerosene, display of prices, quantity and quality of items and the fairness of the shopkeeper. The type of explanatory variables and their specifications are presented above.

The satisfaction rating of the user rural households of public distribution for availability of items is presented in Table 6.12 for the five states and all India. The table shows that the percentage of households strongly satisfied with availability of items is highest in Gujarat (17 per cent) followed by Karnataka (16.7 per cent) and lowest in Bihar (2.3 per cent). The strongly satisfied households are only 7.4 per cent in all India. The dissatisfaction with the service is highest in Assam (60.9 per cent) followed by Bihar (55.7 per cent).

**Table 6.12**

*Satisfaction Levels for Availability of Items*

| *States* | *Dissatisfied* | *Satisfied* | *Strongly Satisfied* | *Total* |
|---|---|---|---|---|
| Assam | 449 (60.9) | 255 (34.6) | 33 (4.5) | 737 (100.0) |
| Bihar | 619 (55.7) | 467 (42.0) | 25 (2.3) | 1111 (100.0) |
| Gujarat | 178 (14.7) | 830 (68.3) | 207 (17.0) | 1215 (100.0) |
| Karnataka | 417 (36.8) | 531 (46.8) | 189 (16.7) | 1134 (100.0) |
| Madhya Pradesh | 804 (43.1) | 958 (51.4) | 102 (5.5) | 1864 (100.0) |
| **All India** | 7128 (39.0) | 9804 (53.6) | 1356 (7.4) | 18288 (100.0) |

*Note:* Figures in the parenthesis are the percentages.

## Table 6.13

*Satisfaction Estimates for the Availability of Items in PDS*

| *Variables* | *Assam* | | *Bihar* | | *Gujarat* | | *Karnataka* | | *Madhya Pradesh* | | *All India* | |
|---|---|---|---|---|---|---|---|---|---|---|---|---|
| | *β* | *Sig.* | *β* | *Sig.* | *β* | *Sig.* | *β* | *Sig.* | *β* | *Sig.* | *β* | *Sig.* |
| Village class | 0.214 | 0.049 | 0.155 | 0.082 | -0.234 | 0.209 | -0.103 | 0.229 | 0.009 | 0.895 | -0.017 | 0.427 |
| Caste group | -0.236 | 0.032 | 0.153 | 0.052 | 0.102 | 0.519 | 0.182 | 0.016 | 0.083 | 0.163 | 0.059 | 0.002 |
| Distance | -0.000 | 0.378 | -0.000 | 0.373 | -0.000 | 0.647 | 0.000 | 0.245 | 0.000 | 0.171 | -0.000 | 0.000 |
| Availability of rice | 0.155 | 0.287 | -0.135 | 0.794 | -0.471 | 0.134 | 0.561 | 0.000 | -0.022 | 0.803 | 0.095 | 0.001 |
| Availability of sugar | 0.719 | 0.000 | -0.019 | 0.957 | 0.396 | 0.072 | 0.210 | 0.151 | 0.230 | 0.001 | 0.362 | 0.000 |
| Availability of wheat | * | * | 0.326 | 0.487 | 0.485 | 0.087 | 0.049 | 0.733 | 0.678 | 0.000 | 0.207 | 0.000 |
| Availability of kerosene | 0.094 | 0.450 | 0.718 | 0.000 | -0.208 | 0.297 | 0.280 | 0.009 | 0.283 | 0.000 | 0.397 | 0.000 |
| Display price list | 0.087 | 0.397 | 0.250 | 0.001 | 0.193 | 0.369 | 0.127 | 0.100 | 0.411 | 0.000 | 0.407 | 0.000 |
| Quantity of items | 0.273 | 0.564 | 0.811 | 0.001 | 1.635 | 0.000 | 0.925 | 0.000 | 1.450 | 0.000 | 1.335 | 0.000 |
| Quality of items | 1.733 | 0.000 | -0.206 | 0.156 | 1.661 | 0.000 | 1.556 | 0.000 | 0.239 | 0.082 | 0.332 | 0.000 |
| Fairness of shopkeeper | 0.429 | 0.053 | -0.084 | 0.661 | 2.037 | 0.000 | 0.496 | 0.000 | 0.649 | 0.000 | 0.641 | 0.000 |
| $\mu_0$ | 0.644 | 0.000 | 0.962 | 0.000 | 2.191 | 0.000 | 0.547 | 0.000 | 0.684 | 0.000 | 0.439 | 0.000 |
| $\mu_1$ | 2.515 | 0.000 | 2.944 | 0.000 | - | - | 2.515 | 0.000 | 3.003 | 0.000 | 2.698 | 0.000 |
| Sample | 737 | | 1111 | | 1215 | | 1134 | | 1864 | | 18288 | |
| Model Chi-square (11df) | 199.359 | | 127.352 | | 772.019 | | 648.586 | | 579.072 | | 6249.395 | |

*Note:* * Availability is not reported

Table 6.13 presents the results of ordered probit estimates for PDS for the five states and all India. The model is significant for the five states and all India. The threshold parameters are significant, positive and ordered for three categories for satisfaction for Assam, Bihar, Karnataka, Madhya Pradesh and all India and for two categories for Gujarat.

Distance is not significant for all the five states taken one at a time, but is significant for all India. Whereas village class is not significant for all India, it is significant with a positive coefficient in the states of Assam and Bihar signifying that households in bigger villages have better rating for availability of items compared to small villages in the two states.

The coefficients for availability of the four items *viz.*, rice, sugar, wheat and kerosene are significant in all India. Display of prices, quality and quantity of items and fairness of shopkeeper are also significant in all India. This shows that all the variables representing the quality of service are significant in all India. In other words, the satisfaction of the households with the availability of items is explained by the variables that explain the quality of service in all India. Coming to the states, availability of rice is significant only in Karnataka while that of wheat is significant in Gujarat and Madhya Pradesh, which is the staple food in these states. Hence, we can see the relationship between staple foodgrain availability and satisfaction in clear terms.

Availability of sugar has a positive impact on level of satisfaction and is significant in Assam, Gujarat and Madhya Pradesh. Availability of kerosene is significant in Bihar, Karnataka and Madhya Pradesh. Display of prices is also significant in Bihar, Karnataka and Madhya Pradesh. Quantity of items is significant in all the states except in Assam. Quality of items and fairness of shopkeeper are significant in all the states except in Bihar. Kerosene is the only item that explains the satisfaction in Bihar. In all, the rating of satisfaction is explained by the quality of service in all the states. The satisfaction rating in general is highly associated with the availability of items in the states.

## Conclusion

This study attempted to empirically assess the satisfaction of the households with the service through the quality of service provision. The study used ordered probit analysis to explain the satisfaction. The model and the threshold parameters are significant and ordered at three-point scale for the states and all India for most of the services. It appears that respondent ratings of satisfaction tend to be more pointed for three categories *viz.*, dissatisfaction, satisfaction and strong satisfaction rather than for four categories.

For piped water supply, frequency of water supply, duration of water supply and the quality of water supply are significant in explaining satisfaction with the quantity of water in the states of Gujarat, Karnataka, Madhya Pradesh and all India (except frequency of water supply in Gujarat). In Gujarat, households in small villages and SC/ST community also contributed to the satisfaction level. Deliberate policy measures might have been initiated to provide piped water supply to the small villages and to the SC/ST community in Gujarat. Such a relationship between SC/ST and satisfaction level also exists at all India level.

For public tap, frequency of water supply, duration and quality of water are the significant variables in all India in explaining satisfaction with the quantity of water. Quality of water is significant in all the three states. Frequency of water supply is significant in Assam and Gujarat, while duration of water supply is significant in Gujarat and Karnataka. In all, the satisfaction with the quantity of public tap is explained by the quality of service variables.

For hand pump, the service quality variables that are significant to explain satisfaction in all India are frequency of breakdown, downtime and quality of water. Lower frequency of breakdown reflects the reliability of service and lower down time shows the quality of maintenance of service.

The frequency of breakdown is not significant for Gujarat, Karnataka and Madhya Pradesh and the downtime is significant in all the four states. The state-wise data on breakdown reveals that the frequency and the variability of breakdown are generally low; the frequency of breakdown is mostly one or two times in a year. These results show that maintenance of hand pump appears to be a much more important variable of service quality than the frequency of breakdown. Among the states the satisfaction rating is explained by SC and ST households in Karnataka, which denote that SC and ST households have reported better satisfaction rating for the quantity of hand pump water compared to other castes. This could be due to the deliberate attempt made by Karnataka to provide drinking water to most of the hamlets particularly to the hamlets inhabited by the SC and ST communities.

The variable considered for satisfaction from health care is out-patient treatment. The service quality variables that are significant in all India for out-patient treatment are behaviour of doctors, behaviour of paramedical staff and the quality of medicine. Behaviour of doctors is also significant in Gujarat and Karnataka. Behaviour of paramedical staff is significant in Madhya Pradesh. Quality of medicines is significant in Gujarat and Karnataka. The waiting time for treatment is not significant in all India and Madhya Pradesh and do not have appropriate sign in Assam, Gujarat. This implies that waiting time is not a significant variable in explaining satisfaction for health care.

Among the four states, Gujarat and Karnataka have high percentage households strongly satisfied with the out-patient treatment and in these two states satisfaction is well explained by the behaviour of doctors and quality of medicines, the two important variables representing quality of health care service.

Satisfaction from the availability of items for PDS is explained by the availability of rice, sugar, wheat and kerosene in the all India analysis. Display of prices, quality and quantity of items and fairness of shopkeeper are also significant in all India. This shows the extent to which satisfaction of the households with the availability of items is explained by the service variables in all India. The relevance of staple foodgrain supply is evident in the state level analysis, which shows availability of rice is significant in Karnataka and that of wheat is significant in Gujarat and Madhya Pradesh. Availability of sugar is significant in Assam, Gujarat and Madhya Pradesh. Availability of kerosene is significant in Bihar, Karnataka and Madhya Pradesh. Display of prices is also significant in Bihar, Karnataka and Madhya Pradesh. Quantity of items is significant in all the states except Assam. Quality of items and fairness of shopkeeper are significant in all the states except Bihar. In all, the rating of satisfaction seems to be well explained by the relevant quality of service.

The above findings, thus, bring out that the quality variables of public services mainly explain the satisfaction rating of the households with the services. The findings clearly demonstrate that an ordinary person takes most of the relevant quality factors into account while rating the satisfaction from public services. The findings disprove the doubts raised by some sections that satisfaction measures are arbitrary and subjective and strengthens the general view that feedback on user satisfaction is an important component of the assessment of public services.

# 7

# Conclusions and Policy Implications

The uniqueness of this study lies in its adoption of the user perspective in its assessment of public service delivery in the states of India. By seeking citizen feedback on each service against attributes such as access, usage, reliability and satisfaction, we have given due importance to the concerns of its users and gathered information on matters that they can readily respond to. It could be argued that a full evaluation of public services will call for much more information than what user feedback can provide. There is much truth in this statement. On the other hand, if service delivery is the focus of the assessment, there is considerable merit in seeking information of the kind that has been gathered and analysed in earlier chapters. When periodic surveys are undertaken along these lines, benchmarking service performance over time also becomes possible. If governments and service providers are receptive to such feedback, they will not only be able to improve the productivity and quality of services, but also contribute more effectively to the long term outcomes expected of their services.

Let us now sum up the findings of study and examine their policy implications. We present below the major conclusions on the five services. The service benchmarks summarised below pertain to the national level. Benchmarks at the state level can be found in the preceding chapters, but will not be repeated here. Their implications for policy and action are summarised in the final section.

1. Drinking water is accessible to 55 per cent of the Indian households within a distance of 100 meters from home. A relaxation of this rather strict norm will increase this proportion. Still, a quarter of all households depend on unprotected sources of drinking water. One-fourth of the users of public sources of water have reported frequent breakdowns of supply. Access to reliable drinking water supply is, thus, a problem for a significant proportion of the households.
2. Public health facilities are accessible to over 40 per cent of the households within a distance of one kilometer. The presence of private health facilities makes up for this limited access to some extent. Of the

households that use health facilities, a larger proportion uses public health services rather than private facilities. The presence of doctors at the public health facilities (a measure of quality and supervision) leaves much to be desired. One-third of the patients did not find a doctor present, during their visits.

3. Absence of *pucca* roads in their village, was reported by nearly 60 per cent of all households. Both public and private buses are available in many states, though, in some states there is a domination of either government or private bus transport. Government buses are rated quite low on punctuality and frequency.
4. PDS has wide coverage across the country, with over 80 per cent of the households owning ration cards and 72 per cent using fair price shops at least once every two months. But only one-fourth of the card holders reported regular availability of foodgrains in the shops. Display of prices was reported by less than 50 per cent. While the reach of the PDS network is wide, its effectiveness is greatly hurt by the high degree of unreliability and non-transparency associated with the service.
5. Government owned or supported primary schools are available to nearly 80 per cent of the households within one kilometre of their homes. The dependence on government schools is significantly high, especially in rural areas. Awareness about the mid-day meal programme is high among the households and most are beneficiaries of the scheme. *Anganwadis* (childcare) are accessible to over two-thirds of the eligible households, but only 30 per cent are regular users of this service. A major reason for the low use is the time and cost of transporting children back and forth to avail of the service.

## An Inter-service Comparison

The user feedback analysed above has some strong messages for policy-makers. Even when people give high marks for the access to a service, they signal that reliability and public satisfaction leave much to be desired. Nearly three-fourths of the households consider PDS unreliable and their full satisfaction rating for this important service is indeed low. One-third of people attest to the irregular availability of the doctors in public health care facilities. Other services do not fare much better. It is clear that access alone does not bring satisfaction to the users of services. People want effective services with some assurance of quality. Reliability, a key attribute of quality, is a major problem area in public services. This study clearly brings out the fact that this is a systemic issue across all the services. The benchmarks we have created through this survey offer a basis for judging governmental performance in this regard over time.

Comparison of different public services in a large and diverse country is a risky undertaking. The criteria for defining standards and measures, access, usage, etc., may vary from one service to another. There cannot be a uniform measure of reliability for all the services.

But satisfaction is one dimension to which these limitations do not apply to the same degree. It reflects the subjective assessment of a service by the people based on their recent experience. And it is the same set of people (more or less) who have rated their satisfaction with the different services. In an earlier chapter, a detailed analysis of the data on satisfaction has shown that it does reflect important dimensions of service delivery. Satisfaction seems to measure the overall assessment of a service by the users. Judged by measures such as reliability and full satisfaction, it is clear that there is vast scope for reform and improvement in all the five services. We refer to some services and states as better performers only in a relative sense. Though, levels of full satisfaction with all services are rather low, it is notable that, of the five public services, drinking water has done better than all others in terms of user satisfaction. PDS and primary education, on the other hand, rank the lowest in terms of satisfaction, though in terms of the access measures used in the study, they have done better than others. For the country as a whole, one could hazard a guess that drinking water is a better managed service while PDS and primary education have much scope for improvement.

Comparison of the services across the states may also suffer from some limitations. States differ in terms of resources and geographical and demographic features. Ranking the states with respect to each service, for example, is not to ignore the fact that differential performance may have been caused by some of these factors. Despite these limitations, an aggregation of the ranks they obtain for the different services provides a rough indication of how these states perform when all the services are taken together. The states are grouped into three categories. Of the 16 major states, the better performers are the southern and western states of Tamil Nadu, Maharashtra, Karnataka, Gujarat, Andhra Pradesh, and Kerala. That these states are doing better than other states on several counts have been noted by outside observers. But now we are getting a reaffirmation of this from the ordinary people who live in these states. At the other end of the spectrum are Assam, West Bengal, Orissa, Rajasthan and Bihar. In between are the remaining states, Haryana, Himachal Pradesh, Punjab, Madhya Pradesh and Uttar Pradesh. While many factors have contributed to the positioning of the states in the three categories, the distinguishing feature of the first set is that by and large these states have relatively high ratings in terms of both access and reliability in all the services. The opposite is true of four out of five of the states in the bottom category. The middle set includes states that for the most part are high on one attribute but low on the other.

## Service Delivery and the Poor

Whether public services are reaching the poor and other disadvantaged groups is a matter of great concern to most policymakers. Here again, one sees a mixed picture. Primary education and drinking water are two services that have done reasonably well in terms of access for the poor. The poor are worse-off in terms of access with respect to the other three services. Despite the barriers to access, a larger proportion of the poor use most of the services than the rest of the households, the singular exception being public transport. In terms of reliability and satisfaction, the poor give lower ratings to almost all the services across the country compared to the non-poor households.

Village size also makes a difference when it comes to access to services. Residents of the larger villages (A and B class) invariably report greater ease of access to all the five services. Drinking water shows the least disparity in terms of access. Use patterns, on the other hand, are more similar which means that the poor walk long distances to avail of the services. Clearly, longer distances mean that those living in the smaller villages and the poor (ICD) incur additional costs that hurt their ability to earn a livelihood.

A comparison of the higher and lower performers among the major states in terms of the five services yields some striking patterns. A major conclusion is that the gap between the two sets of states is much larger than the gap between the poor and the non-poor households within any state (with respect to the five services). The disparities between the top six and the bottom five states in the matter of access to the five services are enormous. Whether poor or non-poor, people in the bottom states have only about half the level of access to drinking water compared to those in the top six states. Access to health services is only slightly better for the bottom states while the disparity is even wider with respect to public transport. The access gap is much narrower in primary education and PDS. The use of services is also less widespread in the bottom states though the disparities are not as large as in access. Reliability also is of a lower order in the bottom five states, with the disparity being the widest in PDS despite its better showing on access. Full satisfaction levels for all the services are much lower in the bottom states compared to the top six states. Even more striking is the finding that the poor in the top six states are better served than even the non-poor in the bottom states in the five areas! That such wide disparities in public services persist between states despite over a half century of development programmes and subsidies is indeed a matter for serious introspection. It is sad that issues of this kind are seldom debated in our elections and are rarely pursued by the political parties.

## Policy Implications

India is a large and diverse country. Given the focus of the study on the states of the country, the policy implications of the study findings need to be probed in the context of each state. This can indeed be a mammoth exercise and will not be attempted in this chapter. It will call for a substantial amount of detailed work at the state level and can be time consuming. To a limited extent, seminars held by the authors in selected states have attempted to explore the policy implications of the findings pertinent to them. A careful assessment of the current policies governing public services and the constraints of the government in service delivery in a given state must precede the design of its new policies, given the varying political and socio-economic contexts of the states.

The analysis and conclusions presented above have implications that go well beyond the design and delivery of the individual services covered by the study. The broad picture that emerges from our analysis of the public feedback on services is that the quality of governance in most Indian states leaves much to be desired. Conventional technocratic answers for improving service delivery or a call to allocate more financial resources may not be an adequate response to this problem. The range of reforms required may cover a wide spectrum—from political leadership and administrative structures and incentives to service specific changes including alternative delivery options.

The striking inter-state disparities in the basic services discussed above clearly call for important policy reforms and actions. It is well known that the per capita expenditure on the social sector is lower in the bottom five states than in the top six. Whether this means that resource constraints are behind their poor record in the five services is not clear. If access and use of services are lower in these states, the funds they require will also be smaller. The question is whether their ability to expand and improve the services has been limited by their inability to mobilise the needed resources. One possibility is that resources are available, but their ability and will to plan and utilise them properly leave much to be desired. It is also possible that increased financial allocations have been made to the bottom five states, but diversion of resources to meet other priorities or leakages have made it difficult for them to productively use the resources. Where the state is ineffective or non-responsive, civil society efforts could have played a key role in demanding better performance and accountability from the service providers. In the better performing states, there is much greater civil society involvement in service provision and increasing evidence of alternative models of service delivery that have an influence on the responsiveness of public service providers. It is possible that people's ability to articulate 'voice' of this type is also absent in the weaker states. If such support and technical assistance are urgently needed by the weaker states in addition to funds, ways must be found to generate strategies to meet these needs.

There are some policy implications of a more specific nature that need to be highlighted in this concluding section. While the suggestions below may apply to all the states, they may well be more pertinent to the weaker performers among the states and the poorly performing service providers.

The causal factors behind the achievements and problems highlighted by the study findings can be divided into two categories. Some can be attributed to the success or failure of public policy. Others can be traced back to the design and management of service delivery mechanisms. To illustrate, central programmes tend to have uniform and rather inflexible designs that cannot be effectively implemented in all states or districts. Service delivery may suffer solely because of this constraint. Rethinking this policy should then be on the reform agenda.

Drinking water is an example of a policy that seems to be working, though ease of access is still a problem in many states. On the other hand, we have the case of PDS where the problems cannot be laid at the door of the delivery mechanisms alone. Here is an essential service with the most widespread network of shops in the country. Ration cards are available to a sizeable majority of households including the poor even in remote areas. But this advantage has been negated by what appears to be a failure of policy. We have mounting food reserves in the country on one hand, and irregularity of food supplies at the village level, on the other. The pricing and distribution policies as well as the incentive systems of state governments need to be reassessed in this case.

Every public service needs to be assessed from both points of view, namely, the extent to which policy constraints are at work and the degree to which flaws in the delivery systems are major hurdles. If policies are at fault, tinkering with delivery mechanisms alone will not solve the problem. Conflicts and contradictions of this nature would be better resolved through dialogue between governments and civil society institutions including the media, independent research and advocacy groups and NGOs.

*1. Adopt a Focussed Approach to Service Delivery in Remote Areas*

The study clearly shows that there are weaker states with poorly performing geographical areas within them. Remote villages and small communities are a case in point. Tribal districts and *taluks* also fall into the same category. Governments have been directly delivering services to the people in these difficult areas. There are many constraints that limit governments' ability to do this job effectively. Personnel problems, procedural rigidities, difficulties in monitoring and supervision in remote areas, and resource constraints are among these barriers. Civil servants assigned to difficult locations do no stay on the job for long, nor do they evince a strong motivation to perform their tasks. Lack of continuity and weak incentives to perform make the existing public institutions non-responsive to the needs of the people. Limited supervision of what goes on in the field implies that corrective actions may not be taken or even considered. The local adaptations needed to provide effective service delivery may not be feasible because rigid rules and procedures in government do not permit them. These problems and limitations are well known to many in government too. The question is whether, given this reality, there are other options that governments need to consider.

One option that has some promise is the adoption of a partnership mode by government in the delivery of specific services in select locations. Partners tend to bring different, but complementary capabilities that can enhance task performance. Non-governmental organisations (NGOs) are already engaged in such operations in several states, though not perhaps in the weakest and most remote locations. Their main constraint is in scaling up their activities. There are also cases where NGOs have performed poorly, thus casting doubts on their intent and capabilities. But no one will dispute that their form, flexible style of functioning and values are tailor made to minimise the kind of constraints that bureaucratic governments and their agencies suffer from. There are also private or corporate enterprises that possess similar strengths though their primary commitment is to earn profits and promote their commercial activities. But the more enlightened among them engage in community initiatives as a part of their concern for society. Today their social or community oriented activities are disparate and widely scattered for understandable reasons. Governments need to test the feasibility of getting some of them to be partners in service delivery in selected districts or *taluks* where such interventions could add value. The corporates in turn may bring in NGOs or other agents with field level expertise and oversee their activities. This approach is more likely to work when the corporates and NGOs have a special interest in the selected regions and communities. Partnership with them is not primarily to attract more funds, but rather to bring on board new and innovative ideas and practices and longer term commitment to ensure the effectiveness of service delivery to the poor. The proposal is that partnerships should be sought and promoted in a limited number of remote areas. If successful, more such areas could included under this approach in the next phase.

Such partnerships are already at work on a limited scale in several parts of the country. The Azim Premji Foundation is partnering the Government of Karnataka in primary education in some of its backward districts. Pradham, another voluntary body is engaged in primary education reform in a similar fashion in Maharashtra. Many NGOs are partners with governments and banks in the delivery of micro credit to the poor in several districts. Health for rural communities is another sector in which NGOs and corporates are active. The question is whether governments can learn from this experience and scale up the partnership efforts with a strong focus on service delivery in the more remote and backward areas that are poorly served. That governments face serious constraints in being effective in these difficult areas is undisputed. The remedy is not merely to pump in more money (though it may be needed), but to generate new ideas and strategies that fit the local context. Alternative options such as new partnerships and strategies to operationalise them need to be explored in earnest to break the vicious cycle of poor service performance.

*2. Enhance the Effectiveness and Quality of Service*

On the whole, the Government of India and the state governments seem to have done more in extending people's access to basic services than to improving the effectiveness and quality of the services. The pressure to extend access to services probably reflects the compulsions of a democratic system of government. Though, there are variations across services and states in this regard, service infrastructure and delivery mechanisms are available to a fair proportion of people even in the less developed states. Services such as protected drinking water supply, fair price shops and primary schools have wider reach while public transport and healthcare are somewhat more limited in terms of physical access. Similarly, there are regions within some states that need to achieve greater access to some of the services.

For the country as a whole, however, it is in ensuring effectiveness and quality in the delivery of the services that the state's role needs much greater attention. There is strong evidence to show that the satisfaction scores given to the different services by the people reflect this concern. The overall satisfaction scores of the services are more closely related to the reliability (quality) of the service than to its ease of physical access or usage.

### *3. Improve the Management Systems in Services that Require more Human Interaction*

Extending access to a service requires the building of physical infrastructure and investment of funds on a large scale. Upgrading quality and effectiveness, on the other hand, calls for much greater attention to management systems, responsiveness to solving the problems of citizens and communities, and unconventional monitoring mechanisms to track the progress of decentralised operations. Infrastructure building can be easily programmed, technology is easily determined and the process is simple to measure and monitor. Increased effectiveness and quality, on the other hand, calls for a willingness to tolerate greater ambiguity in the work environment, the use of people friendly practices and partnerships to achieve goals, and the ability to learn and adapt in light of the feedback from the field. The problem is often aggravated by the government's failure to allocate adequate funds in the budget for the operation and maintenance of services. It is also possible that funds were available, but the management and supervision of service providers left much to be desired. The government needs to shift gears to address these problems, and search for new ways to enhance the effectiveness and quality of its services to the people.

A good example of what new approaches can do comes from Kerala where local communities play an active role in the maintenance of public taps and hand pumps. The breakdown rates for drinking water facilities reported by these users are significantly lower than those users who do not play such a role in community maintenance. It is new practices of this kind that will eventually improve the quality and reliability of services. Attitudes and practices that were appropriate to the infrastructure-building phase may not always fit the requirements of the emerging tasks mentioned above.

### *4. Involve Local Groups and Institutions*

There is also evidence that the involvement of Panchayati Raj Institutions/local government institutions help to improve the quality and effectiveness of services. In Karnataka, for example, citizens rate drinking water service higher than other services. A good proportion of the people, who have rated drinking water service as better, are from areas where this service is maintained by the local government. This has important implications for other services, which are vertically managed and not accountable to local people.

### *5. Competition is Necessary but not Sufficient to Stimulate Public Sector Reforms*

Private provision of public services is very much in evidence in this study. Health care, primary education, public transport and drinking water are being provided through private sources also in a number of states. Advocates of liberalisation will predict that the pressure of competition will force public providers to improve their services. But the study findings do not support this theory. In fact, the competitive environment created by private providers has not made any positive difference to the conduct and performance of the public providers in most states. This is a finding of some significance and needs to be probed further.

Competition works in the marketplace because a firm that ignores it stands to lose its business to others. Its employees will lose their jobs and the firm may be forced to close down. But in a public hospital, even if the doctor is unavailable to the patients and the treatment is flawed, neither the doctor nor the hospital is made to pay for the poor service and neglect of duty. If their careers are unaffected and their budgets are not cut, they have no reason to change their behaviour. The lesson to be learnt is that unless competition provokes action by the public authorities to penalise poor performance and encourage better services, private provision by itself will not produce greater efficiency and responsiveness in the competing public agencies. The same is true for public schools and transport. The implications are clear. Opening up the public service arena to private competition is not enough. The government must restructure itself to effectively evaluate the performance of its agencies and create the right incentives for its personnel to deliver public services more efficiently.

### *6. Transfer Knowledge and Best Practices from the Better States to the Rest*

The ranking of the states according to their service performance does not necessarily follow the income or growth rankings of the states. The richer states, for example are not necessarily the ones to attain higher levels of service quality. It is important to look more closely at other factors present in the states that perform better. Most likely, political leadership, stability of regimes, discipline in the bureaucracy and a more active 'local voice' are responsible for this outcome. Some things like leadership and political culture cannot be easily replicated. But to the extent that better systems and practices are responsible for improved governance, there is a case for stimulating the transfer of knowledge and best practices from the better states to the low performers. It will call for more focused studies and documentation of these practices and a strategy to facilitate learning by the lagging states. Donor supported projects is another route to achieve this objective, but it is not clear how successful they are in this regard or whether the new practices introduced through such projects get replicated in a sustainable fashion.

Transfer of knowledge of good practices seems like a good idea, but in practice, it is not easy to implement unless deliberate strategies are designed and pursued. Those who innovate and implement new practices are busy people and often not good at writing and spreading their ideas in other regions and states. There are very few fora, including magazines and websites that are dedicated to this task. Government's training academies could have played a key role in this endeavour. But lack of stability in terms of leadership and the low priority attached to training and research in government have meant that the resources and skills required for this purpose are seldom assured. It is not surprising, therefore, that innovating practices in one state may not be known even in the neighbouring states. This gap in the documentation and dissemination of best practices can be remedied to a great extent if the suggestions offered above are adopted.

# References


Census of India (1991). "Housing and Amenities," Paper 2, Registrar General of India, 1993.

Central Statistical Organisation (1991). *Selected Socio-Economic Statistics, India,* Department of Statistics, Government of India, New Delhi.

———. (1999). *Statistical Abstract of India,* Ministry of Statistics and Programme Implementation, Government of India, New Delhi.

———. (2000). *Selected Socio-Economic Statistics, India,* Ministry of Statistics and Programme Implementation, Government of India, New Delhi.

Centre for Symbiosis of Technology, Environment & Management-CSTE&M (2001). *National Survey of Rural Community Water Supplies* (Sponsored by UNICEF, New Delhi), Bangalore.

CMIE (1994). *Basic Statistics,* Vol. 2, September.

Deichmann, Uwe and Somik V. Lall (2003). "Are You Satisfied? Citizen Feedback and Delivery of Urban Services", *Policy Research Working Paper* No. 3070, Development Research Group, Infrastructure and Environment, World Bank, Washington DC.

Diener, E., Suh, R. Lucas and H. Smith (1999). "Subjective Well-being: Three Decades of Progress," *Psychological Bulletin,* 125, pp. 276-302.

Department of Family Welfare (1999). *National Family Health Survey 1998-99 (NFHS 2),* Government of India.

Dev, S. Mahendra and Jos Mooij (2002). "Social Sector Expenditures in the 1990's: Analysis of Central and State Budgets," *Economic and Political Weekly,* March 2, 2002. Vol XXXVII No. 9, pp. 853-866

Dreze, Jean and Amartya Sen (1989). *Hunger and Public Action,* World Institute for Development Economic Research, Studies in Development Economics, Clarendon Press, Oxford.

———. (1995). *Economic Development and Social Opportunities,* Oxford University Press, New Delhi.

Driver, C. (2002). *The Nature of Service Quality,* mimeo, University of Plymouth Business School, Plymouth.

Frank, R.H. (1997). "The Frame of Reference as a Public Good," *Economic Journal,* 107, pp. 1832-1847.

George, P.S. (1996). "Public Distribution System, Food Subsidy and Production Incentives," *Economic and Political Weekly,* Vol. 31 (39). September 28.

Goetz, A.M. and J Gaventa (2001). *Bringing Citizen Voice and Client Focus into Service Delivery,* IDS Working Paper 138, Institute of Development Studies, Brighton.

Gomez-Ibanez, J.A. and J.R. Meyer (1993). *Going Private: The International Experience with Transport Privatization,* Brookings Instituion, 1-9; 145-163, Washington DC.

Government of India (2002). *National Human Development Report–2001,* Oxford University Press, New Delhi.

Greene, W.H. (2000) *Econometric Analysis,* (4th ed.), Englewood Cliffs, Prentice Hall. New Jersey.

International Institute of Population Sciences (2000). *National Family Health Survey, 1998-99, All India,* Mumbai.

Liao, Tim Futing (1994). *Interpreting Probability Model – Logit, Probit, and Other Generalized Linear Models,* Sage University Paper, Sage Publications.

Little, I.M.D. (2002). *Ethics, Economics and Politics,* Oxford University Press, London.

Maddala, G.S. (1983). *Limited Dependent and Qualitative Variables in Econometrics,* Cambridge University Press, Cambridge.

Ministry of Finance (2003). *Economic Survey 2002-2003,* Government of India, New Delhi.

Ministry of Health & Family Affairs (2002). *National Health Policy 2002,* Government of India, New Delhi.

Ministry of Information and Broadcasting (2001). *India 2001–A Reference Annual*, compiled and edited by Research, Reference and Training Division, Government of India, New Delhi.

Mooij, Jos E. (1994). "Public Distribution as Safety Net: Who is Saved?," *Economic and Political Weekly*, 29(3), pp. 119-126.

Narayan, Deepa, R. Patel, K. Schafft, A. Rademacher and S. Koch-Schulte (1999). "Can Anyone Hear Us? Voices from 47 Countries," *Voices of the Poor*, Vol. 1 Poverty Group, PREM, World Bank, Washington DC.

Narayan D., *et al.* (2000). *Voices of the Poor: Crying Out for Change* Oxford University Press, New York.

National Sample Survey Organisation (1999). *Drinking Water, Sanitation and Hygiene in India*. 54th Round (January-June 1998), Report No. 449. Department of Statistics, New Delhi.

Parikh, Kirit. S. (1994). "Who Gets How much from PDS: How Effectively Does It Reach the Poor?" *Sarvekshana*, Vol. 17, No.3.

Paul, Samuel (1995). *A Report Card on Public Services in Indian Cities: A View from Below*, Public Affairs Centre, Bangalore.

———. (2002). *Holding the State to Account – Citizen Monitoring in Action*, Books for Change, Bangalore.

Paul, Samuel, Suresh Balakrishnan, K. Gopakumar, Sita Sekhar and M. Vivekananda (2004). "State of India's Public Services – Benchmarks for the States," *Economic and Political Weekly*, February 28, Vol. 39 No. 9 pp. 920-933.

Planning Commission (1995). *Eighth Five Year Plan, 1992-97*, Government of India, New Delhi.

———. (1996). "Working Group for the Formulation of the Ninth Five-year Plan," *Ninth Plan Report*, Government of India, New Delhi.

———. (2002). *Tenth Five Year Plan, 2002-07*, Government of India, New Delhi.

PROBE Team (1999). *Public Report on Basic Education in India*, Oxford University Press, New Delhi.

Radhakrishna R., K. Subba Rao, S. Indrakant and C. Ravi (1997). "India's Public Distribution System: A National and International Perspective," *World Bank Discussion Paper* No. 380.

Radhakrishna R., Venkata Reddy K. (2002). "Food Security and Nutrition: Vision 2020," in *Report of the Committee on India Vision 2020*, December, Planning Commission, Government of India, New Delhi.

Ramanathan, R. (1997). "Transport–A Crucial Infrastructure" in Kirit Parikh (ed.) *India Development Report 1997*, Oxford University Press, Mumbai.

Reserve Bank of India (2000). *State Finances–A Study of Budgets of 2000-2001*, December, Mumbai.

Samuels, M. (1998). *Towards Best Practice: An Evaluation of the First Two Years of the Public Sector Benchmarking Project 1996-98*, U.K. Cabinet Office (Office of Public Service), London.

Sasser, W.E., R.P. Olsen, and D.D. Wyckoff (1978). *Management of Service Operations*, Allyn and Bacon, Boston, MA.

Shariff, Abusaleh (1999). *India Human Development Report*, National Council of Applied Economic Research, Oxford University Press, New Delhi.

Shariff, Abusaleh and Prabir Ghosh (2002). "State-Adjusted Public Expenditure on Social Sector and Poverty Alleviation Programmes," *Economic and Political Weekly*, Vol XXXVII No. 8, February 23.

Sriraman S. (1998). "Road Transport Development in India," *Current Science*, Vol.75, No.8, October 25.

UNESCO (2003). *World Water Development Report: Water for People, Water for Life*, July 11, United Nations.

United Nations Development Programme-UNDP (2002). *Human Development Report 2002*, Oxford University Press, New York.

Upp, Stephanie (1995). "Making the Grade–A Guide for Implementing the Report Card Methodology," *Working Paper* 101, Public Affairs Centre, Bangalore.

World Bank (1999). *Rural Water Supply and Sanitation*, Allied Publisher, New Delhi.

———. (2003). *World Development Report (2003)*, Washington DC.

———. (2004). *World Development Report (2004)*, Washington DC.

# Annexures

# ANNEXURE I

*Demographic Profile of Respondents—All India*

| *Profile* | | *Percentage Respondents* | | |
|---|---|---|---|---|
| | | *Rural* | *Urban* | *Total* |
| Dwelling Place | *Kutcha* | 40.2 | 17.7 | 34.2 |
| | Semi-*Pucca* | 38.3 | 37.3 | 38.1 |
| | *Pucca* | 21.5 | 45.0 | 27.7 |
| Occupation (Chief Wage Earner) | Cultivator | 37.4 | 4.1 | 28.6 |
| | Unskilled Workers | 22.8 | 16.0 | 21.0 |
| | Skilled Workers | 8.5 | 10.8 | 9.1 |
| | Seasonal Worker | 1.9 | 1.9 | 1.9 |
| | Petty Business | 8.2 | 17.4 | 10.6 |
| | Service (Govt.) | 11.0 | 26.6 | 15.2 |
| | Service (Pvt.) | 5.2 | 13.5 | 7.4 |
| | Self-employed | 2.8 | 6.1 | 3.7 |
| | Professional | 0.5 | 1.0 | 0.6 |
| | Retired | 1.7 | 2.6 | 2.0 |
| Annual Income | Up to 13,000/- | 14.4 | 7.0 | 12.5 |
| | 13,001 to 20,000/- | 23.3 | 13.9 | 20.8 |
| | 20,001 to 36,000/- | 28.2 | 23.9 | 27.1 |
| | Above 36,000/- | 34.0 | 23.9 | 39.7 |
| Education (Chief Wage Earner) | Illiterate | 30.9 | 15.2 | 26.7 |
| | NFE Educated | 5.1 | 3.9 | 4.8 |
| | Primary | 16.8 | 11.5 | 15.4 |
| | Middle | 15.8 | 15.2 | 15.6 |
| | Secondary | 16.3 | 19.7 | 17.2 |
| | Higher Secondary | 8.8 | 14.3 | 10.3 |
| | Graduate | 4.9 | 15.6 | 7.8 |
| | Post-graduate and above | 1.4 | 4.6 | 2.3 |
| Age (Chief Wage Earner) | 15–25 | 7.9 | 6.5 | 7.5 |
| | 26–35 | 28.7 | 28.3 | 28.6 |
| | 36–45 | 29.9 | 31.2 | 30.3 |
| | >45 | 33.5 | 33.9 | 33.6 |

*Note*: NFE—Non-Formal Education

# ANNEXURE II
## *Indicators for the Services*

### Table AII.1
*Access and Usage of Drinking Water Facilities*

*(per cent of households)*

| Sl. No. | States | Use of Public Protected Source | | | Use of Private Protected Source | | | Public Protected Source within 100 metres (access) | | |
|---|---|---|---|---|---|---|---|---|---|---|
| | | Rural | Urban | State | Rural | Urban | State | Rural | Urban | State |
| 1 | Andhra Pradesh | 80 | 86 | 82 | 4 | 4 | 4 | 67 | 75 | 69 |
| 2 | Arunachal Pradesh | 90 | 80 | 87 | 3 | 1 | 2 | 82 | 79 | 81 |
| 3 | Assam | 10 | 10 | 10 | 42 | 52 | 42 | 9 | 9 | 9 |
| 4 | Bihar | 18 | 19 | 18 | 66 | 75 | 68 | 15 | 19 | 16 |
| 5 | Gujarat | 70 | 89 | 75 | 4 | 1 | 4 | 63 | 88 | 70 |
| 6 | Haryana | 47 | 57 | 50 | 31 | 35 | 33 | 37 | 51 | 42 |
| 7 | Himachal Pradesh | 81 | 93 | 84 | 3 | 0 | 3 | 75 | 93 | 80 |
| 8 | Karnataka | 77 | 81 | 79 | 3 | 3 | 3 | 71 | 70 | 71 |
| 9 | Kerala | 22 | 42 | 30 | 6 | 10 | 7 | 19 | 42 | 28 |
| 10 | Madhya Pradesh | 71 | 92 | 75 | 4 | 6 | 4 | 55 | 86 | 61 |
| 11 | Maharashtra | 76 | 95 | 79 | 2 | 2 | 2 | 74 | 95 | 77 |
| 12 | Meghalaya | 63 | 95 | 77 | 5 | 5 | 5 | 52 | 91 | 69 |
| 13 | Mizoram | 77 | 63 | 72 | - | - | - | 71 | 62 | 68 |
| 14 | Nagaland | 14 | 31 | 20 | 0 | 0 | 0 | 14 | 30 | 19 |
| 15 | Orissa | 78 | 83 | 80 | 7 | 7 | 7 | 49 | 69 | 56 |
| 16 | Punjab | 15 | 67 | 31 | 79 | 32 | 65 | 15 | 67 | 30 |
| 17 | Rajasthan | 68 | 92 | 75 | 5 | 2 | 5 | 47 | 81 | 56 |
| 18 | Sikkim | 85 | 100 | 90 | 2 | 0 | 1 | 85 | 100 | 90 |
| 19 | Tamil Nadu | 90 | 90 | 90 | 2 | 2 | 2 | 81 | 89 | 83 |
| 20 | Tripura | 60 | 71 | 63 | 22 | 30 | 25 | 41 | 68 | 49 |
| 21 | Uttar Pradesh | 37 | 52 | 39 | 49 | 45 | 49 | 33 | 50 | 36 |
| 22 | West Bengal | 80 | 81 | 81 | 14 | 8 | 12 | 56 | 71 | 61 |
| | National Average | 58 | 72 | 62 | 18 | 16 | 18 | 50 | 68 | 55 |

## Table AII.2

*Maintenance and Willingness to Pay for Drinking Water*

*(per cent of households)*

| Sl. No. | States | Breakdown of Public Taps within 3 Months | | | Breakdown of Public Hand Pumps within 3 Months | | | Households Involved in Maintenance | | | Willingness to Pay More | | |
|---|---|---|---|---|---|---|---|---|---|---|---|---|---|
| | | Rural | Urban | State | Rural | Urban | State | Rural | Urban | State | Rural | Urban | State |
| 1 | Andhra Pradesh | 19 | 36 | 24 | 21 | 56 | 27 | 21 | 12 | 18 | 44 | 64 | 50 |
| 2 | Arunachal Pradesh | 18 | 12 | 17 | - | - | - | 23 | 58 | 29 | 19 | 56 | 29 |
| 3 | Assam | 37 | Ns | 30 | Ns | Ns | Ns | 13 | Ns | 11 | 22 | 49 | 30 |
| 4 | Bihar | 38 | 25 | 33 | 34 | Ns | 34 | 43 | Ns | 46 | 47 | 58 | 50 |
| 5 | Gujarat | 34 | 15 | 27 | 20 | Ns | 21 | 28 | 19 | 26 | 31 | 30 | 31 |
| 6 | Haryana | 21 | 34 | 23 | 27 | 38 | 33 | 36 | 9 | 30 | 46 | 41 | 44 |
| 7 | Himachal Pradesh | 22 | 0 | 20 | Ns | Ns | Ns | 8 | 17 | 9 | 43 | 45 | 44 |
| 8 | Karnataka | 21 | 14 | 19 | 21 | 26 | 22 | 25 | 18 | 23 | 55 | 62 | 57 |
| 9 | Kerala | 24 | 10 | 17 | - | - | - | 57 | 73 | 65 | 12 | 22 | 17 |
| 10 | Madhya Pradesh | 21 | 0 | 12 | 20 | 9 | 20 | 13 | 20 | 14 | 36 | 46 | 38 |
| 11 | Maharashtra | 10 | 16 | 11 | 10 | Ns | 11 | 28 | 46 | 29 | 47 | 27 | 43 |
| 12 | Meghalaya | 27 | 0 | 22 | - | - | - | 10 | 12 | 10 | 15 | 28 | 22 |
| 13 | Mizoram | 32 | 42 | 33 | Ns | Ns | Ns | 23 | Ns | 24 | 41 | 36 | 39 |
| 14 | Nagaland | 28 | Ns | 29 | - | Ns | Ns | 25 | Ns | 22 | 38 | 23 | 30 |
| 15 | Orissa | 0 | 18 | 12 | 14 | 22 | 16 | 8 | 5 | 7 | 31 | 43 | 35 |
| 16 | Punjab | Ns | 28 | 21 | Ns | Ns | Ns | 14 | Ns | 11 | 46 | 21 | 30 |
| 17 | Rajasthan | 47 | Ns | 45 | 58 | 67 | 60 | 50 | 55 | 51 | 70 | 85 | 75 |
| 18 | Sikkim | - | - | - | - | - | - | - | - | - | - | - | - |
| 19 | Tamil Nadu | 46 | 18 | 40 | 67 | Ns | 68 | 16 | 25 | 17 | 23 | 7 | 18 |
| 20 | Tripura | 40 | 58 | 46 | 39 | Ns | 37 | 19 | 2 | 16 | 36 | 55 | 36 |
| 21 | Uttar Pradesh | 52 | Ns | 52 | 16 | 12 | 16 | 40 | 39 | 40 | 76 | 59 | 63 |
| 22 | West Bengal | 2 | 10 | 8 | 20 | 13 | 20 | 4 | 4 | 4 | 18 | 25 | 21 |
| | National Average | 27 | 18 | 25 | 24 | 31 | 24 | 23 | 22 | 23 | 40 | 40 | 40 |

Ns: Percentage is not computed when the number of sample users is less than 30.

## Table AII.3

### *Full Satisfaction with Public Drinking Water Facilities*

*(per cent of households)*

| Sl. No. | States | Piped Supply | | | | | | Other Protected Sources | | | | | |
|---|---|---|---|---|---|---|---|---|---|---|---|---|---|
| | | Adequacy of Supply | | | Quality of Water | | | Adequacy of Supply | | | Quality of Water | | |
| | | Rural | Urban | State | Rural | Urban | State | Rural | Urban | State | Rural | Urban | State |
| 1 | Andhra Pradesh | 24 | 26 | 25 | 26 | 28 | 27 | 27 | 38 | 30 | 27 | 42 | 31 |
| 2 | Arunachal Pradesh | 3 | 2 | 3 | 4 | 3 | 4 | 16 | 2 | 13 | 26 | 2 | 21 |
| 3 | Assam | Ns | Ns | 25 | Ns | Ns | 33 | 19 | Ns | 17 | 33 | Ns | 29 |
| 4 | Bihar | Ns | 18 | 17 | Ns | 20 | 18 | 20 | 18 | 19 | 28 | 28 | 28 |
| 5 | Gujarat | 48 | 41 | 46 | 62 | 60 | 61 | 33 | 30 | 33 | 49 | 38 | 47 |
| 6 | Haryana | 17 | 51 | 27 | 31 | 58 | 39 | 34 | 20 | 31 | 44 | 33 | 41 |
| 7 | Himachal Pradesh | 10 | 15 | 12 | 17 | 18 | 18 | 22 | 58 | 26 | 41 | 58 | 43 |
| 8 | Karnataka | 41 | 23 | 35 | 52 | 32 | 45 | 38 | 22 | 34 | 47 | 39 | 45 |
| 9 | Kerala | 19 | 14 | 16 | 19 | 23 | 22 | 16 | 7 | 12 | 17 | 9 | 13 |
| 10 | Madhya Pradesh | 23 | 34 | 30 | 43 | 50 | 47 | 18 | 19 | 18 | 36 | 31 | 35 |
| 11 | Maharashtra | 7 | 20 | 11 | 8 | 23 | 13 | 17 | 39 | 19 | 18 | 45 | 20 |
| 12 | Meghalaya | Ns | 14 | 14 | Ns | 10 | 9 | 5 | 10 | 6 | 6 | 14 | 7 |
| 13 | Mizoram | 0 | 3 | 1 | 5 | 13 | 9 | 6 | 0 | 5 | 28 | 31 | 28 |
| 14 | Nagaland | Ns | 0 | 0 | Ns | 0 | 0 | 3 | 0 | 3 | 0 | 0 | 0 |
| 15 | Orissa | Ns | 12 | 11 | Ns | 18 | 17 | 5 | 5 | 5 | 8 | 11 | 9 |
| 16 | Punjab | 7 | 0 | 2 | 8 | 1 | 3 | 4 | Ns | 3 | 8 | Ns | 7 |
| 17 | Rajasthan | 9 | 9 | 9 | 31 | 16 | 23 | 7 | 4 | 6 | 28 | 28 | 28 |
| 18 | Sikkim | 20 | 12 | 17 | 23 | 28 | 25 | - | - | - | - | - | - |
| 19 | Tamil Nadu | 54 | 51 | 52 | 59 | 60 | 60 | 38 | 55 | 41 | 50 | 65 | 53 |
| 20 | Tripura | 0 | 10 | 7 | 0 | 11 | 8 | 1 | 0 | 1 | 3 | 0 | 3 |
| 21 | Uttar Pradesh | 49 | 54 | 50 | 45 | 51 | 46 | 48 | 54 | 49 | 52 | 55 | 54 |
| 22 | West Bengal | Ns | 14 | 14 | Ns | 15 | 15 | 22 | 32 | 25 | 23 | 35 | 27 |
| | National Average | 21 | 19 | 20 | 29 | 26 | 27 | 24 | 26 | 24 | 32 | 34 | 32 |

Ns: Percentage is not computed when the number of sample users is less than 30.

# Table AII.4

*Access and Usage of Health Care Facilities*

*(per cent of households)*

| Sl. No. | States | Health Facility within 1 km. | | Dependence for Minor Ailments | | | | | |
|---|---|---|---|---|---|---|---|---|---|
| | | | | Govt. Facility | | | Pvt. Hospitals | | |
| | | Rural | Urban | Rural | Urban | State | Rural | Urban | State |
| 1 | Andhra Pradesh | 36 | 55 | 51 | 67 | 55 | 20 | 28 | 22 |
| 2 | Arunachal Pradesh | 36 | 72 | 93 | 97 | 95 | 3 | 0 | 2 |
| 3 | Assam | 38 | 49 | 75 | 48 | 68 | 12 | 18 | 14 |
| 4 | Bihar | 21 | 17 | 5 | 15 | 7 | 10 | 23 | 14 |
| 5 | Gujarat | 36 | 43 | 45 | 38 | 43 | 14 | 9 | 13 |
| 6 | Haryana | 35 | 21 | 20 | 28 | 23 | 3 | 11 | 5 |
| 7 | Himachal Pradesh | 53 | 59 | 45 | 66 | 51 | 2 | 10 | 4 |
| 8 | Karnataka | 26 | 46 | 49 | 45 | 48 | 13 | 16 | 14 |
| 9 | Kerala | 57 | 59 | 62 | 58 | 60 | 35 | 39 | 37 |
| 10 | Madhya Pradesh | 44 | 53 | 53 | 31 | 49 | 12 | 31 | 16 |
| 11 | Maharashtra | 51 | 38 | 55 | 25 | 50 | 9 | 10 | 9 |
| 12 | Meghalaya | 23 | 15 | 63 | 16 | 38 | 7 | 36 | 22 |
| 13 | Mizoram | 82 | 64 | 100 | 53 | 84 | 0 | 15 | 5 |
| 14 | Nagaland | 12 | 23 | 52 | 25 | 44 | 24 | 44 | 30 |
| 15 | Orissa | 28 | 73 | 90 | 70 | 83 | 2 | 10 | 4 |
| 16 | Punjab | 62 | 24 | 23 | 26 | 24 | 13 | 11 | 12 |
| 17 | Rajasthan | 52 | 65 | 79 | 60 | 74 | 5 | 5 | 5 |
| 18 | Sikkim | 97 | 45 | 93 | 89 | 92 | 1 | 2 | 2 |
| 19 | Tamil Nadu | 44 | 42 | 60 | 35 | 53 | 24 | 27 | 24 |
| 20 | Tripura | 53 | 34 | 80 | 19 | 59 | 1 | 14 | 6 |
| 21 | Uttar Pradesh | 34 | 23 | 21 | 11 | 19 | 5 | 2 | 4 |
| 22 | West Bengal | 33 | 57 | 54 | 35 | 47 | 2 | 7 | 3 |
| | National Average | 40 | 41 | 48 | 38 | 45 | 11 | 16 | 12 |

## Table AII.5

### *Dependency for Major Ailments and Reliability of Government Health Care*

*(per cent of households)*

| Sl. No. | States | Dependence for Major Ailments | | | | | | Presence in Government Health Facilities of | | | | | |
|---|---|---|---|---|---|---|---|---|---|---|---|---|---|
| | | Govt. Facility | | | Pvt. Hospitals | | | Doctors | | | Paramedics | | |
| | | Rural | Urban | State | Rural | Urban | State | Rural | Urban | State | Rural | Urban | State |
| 1 | Andhra Pradesh | 50 | 42 | 48 | 33 | 34 | 33 | 20 | 43 | 28 | 60 | 55 | 59 |
| 2 | Arunachal Pradesh | 85 | 62 | 76 | 7 | 10 | 8 | 45 | 89 | 64 | 48 | 88 | 65 |
| 3 | Assam | 74 | 53 | 68 | 21 | 39 | 26 | 68 | 88 | 72 | 81 | 92 | 84 |
| 4 | Bihar | 10 | 21 | 13 | 53 | 39 | 49 | Ns | Ns | 79 | Ns | Ns | 89 |
| 5 | Gujarat | 59 | 54 | 58 | 38 | 45 | 40 | 94 | 98 | 95 | 95 | 99 | 96 |
| 6 | Haryana | 29 | 27 | 28 | 50 | 59 | 53 | 69 | 84 | 75 | 81 | 86 | 83 |
| 7 | Himachal Pradesh | 51 | 76 | 58 | 44 | 14 | 36 | 76 | 90 | 80 | 94 | 97 | 95 |
| 8 | Karnataka | 50 | 47 | 49 | 46 | 48 | 46 | 70 | 87 | 74 | 91 | 99 | 93 |
| 9 | Kerala | 40 | 56 | 46 | 57 | 43 | 52 | 48 | 76 | 58 | 86 | 94 | 89 |
| 10 | Madhya Pradesh | 68 | 53 | 65 | 20 | 36 | 23 | 59 | 87 | 63 | 77 | 87 | 78 |
| 11 | Maharashtra | 71 | 58 | 69 | 21 | 32 | 23 | 88 | 96 | 88 | 92 | 96 | 93 |
| 12 | Meghalaya | 56 | 21 | 38 | 25 | 66 | 47 | 57 | 80 | 64 | 59 | 72 | 63 |
| 13 | Mizoram | 100 | 82 | 94 | 0 | 12 | 4 | 44 | 77 | 54 | 77 | 71 | 75 |
| 14 | Nagaland | 26 | 20 | 24 | 68 | 68 | 68 | 64 | Ns | 68 | 79 | Ns | 78 |
| 15 | Orissa | 96 | 83 | 92 | 3 | 11 | 6 | 75 | 87 | 79 | 87 | 92 | 89 |
| 16 | Punjab | 45 | 33 | 42 | 48 | 61 | 52 | 82 | 97 | 85 | 81 | 97 | 85 |
| 17 | Rajasthan | 89 | 81 | 87 | 6 | 14 | 8 | 57 | 64 | 59 | 73 | 71 | 73 |
| 18 | Sikkim | 98 | 95 | 97 | 0 | 3 | 1 | 72 | 84 | 77 | 96 | 89 | 94 |
| 19 | Tamil Nadu | 64 | 50 | 60 | 33 | 39 | 33 | 70 | 74 | 71 | 90 | 90 | 90 |
| 20 | Tripura | 86 | 44 | 72 | 3 | 30 | 13 | 34 | Ns | 39 | 44 | Ns | 47 |
| 21 | Uttar Pradesh | 42 | 37 | 41 | 34 | 47 | 37 | 72 | 73 | 72 | 76 | 78 | 76 |
| 22 | West Bengal | 92 | 79 | 88 | 4 | 11 | 6 | 60 | 72 | 63 | 75 | 83 | 77 |
| | National Average | 57 | 51 | 55 | 31 | 38 | 33 | 67 | 79 | 70 | 82 | 86 | 83 |

Ns: Percentage is not computed when the number of sample users is less than 30.

## Table AII.6

*Full Satisfaction with Government Health Care*

*(per cent of households)*

| Sl. No. | States | Paid for Medical Services Availed (Out-patients) | | | Full Satisfaction of Out-patients with Behaviour of | | | | | |
|---|---|---|---|---|---|---|---|---|---|---|
| | | | | | Doctors | | | Paramedics | | |
| | | Rural | Urban | State | Rural | Urban | State | Rural | Urban | State |
| 1 | Andhra Pradesh | 7 | 13 | 9 | 3 | 12 | 6 | 4 | 13 | 7 |
| 2 | Arunachal Pradesh | 8 | 13 | 11 | 1 | 1 | 1 | 0 | 0 | 0 |
| 3 | Assam | 16 | 13 | 15 | 5 | 4 | 5 | 4 | 6 | 5 |
| 4 | Bihar | Ns | Ns | 13 | Ns | Ns | 8 | Ns | Ns | 5 |
| 5 | Gujarat | 25 | 22 | 24 | 31 | 28 | 30 | 27 | 25 | 27 |
| 6 | Haryana | 16 | 10 | 14 | 15 | 11 | 14 | 13 | 11 | 12 |
| 7 | Himachal Pradesh | 11 | 19 | 14 | 10 | 9 | 10 | 8 | 6 | 8 |
| 8 | Karnataka | 20 | 17 | 19 | 30 | 33 | 31 | 26 | 30 | 27 |
| 9 | Kerala | 9 | 4 | 7 | 6 | 14 | 9 | 5 | 12 | 8 |
| 10 | Madhya Pradesh | 20 | 25 | 21 | 8 | 11 | 8 | 7 | 14 | 8 |
| 11 | Maharashtra | 14 | 13 | 14 | 20 | 33 | 22 | 20 | 32 | 21 |
| 12 | Meghalaya | 10 | 8 | 9 | 16 | 12 | 15 | 16 | 12 | 15 |
| 13 | Mizoram | 6 | 7 | 6 | 1 | 7 | 2 | 1 | 3 | 1 |
| 14 | Nagaland | 44 | Ns | 46 | 1 | Ns | 1 | 1 | Ns | 1 |
| 15 | Orissa | 5 | 9 | 6 | 3 | 4 | 3 | 2 | 3 | 2 |
| 16 | Punjab | 37 | 3 | 29 | 3 | 0 | 2 | 3 | 0 | 3 |
| 17 | Rajasthan | 35 | 28 | 33 | 6 | 3 | 5 | 6 | 3 | 5 |
| 18 | Sikkim | 6 | 14 | 9 | 21 | 18 | 20 | 21 | 6 | 16 |
| 19 | Tamil Nadu | 8 | 12 | 9 | 25 | 44 | 29 | 26 | 43 | 29 |
| 20 | Tripura | 12 | Ns | 12 | 1 | Ns | 1 | 1 | Ns | 1 |
| 21 | Uttar Pradesh | 17 | 12 | 16 | 16 | 29 | 18 | 17 | 24 | 18 |
| 22 | West Bengal | 6 | 18 | 9 | 10 | 14 | 11 | 3 | 4 | 3 |
| | National Average | 16 | 15 | 16 | 13 | 15 | 14 | 12 | 14 | 12 |

Ns: Percentage is not computed when the number of sample users is less than 30.

## Table AII.7

*Access to Pucca-roads and Public Transport Facilities*

*(per cent of households)*

| *Sl. No.* | *States* | *Access to Cement/Tarred Road Rural* | *Availability of* | | | | |
|---|---|---|---|---|---|---|---|
| | | | *Bus Stop Rural* | *Public Bus* | | *Private Bus* | |
| | | | | *Rural* | *Urban* | *Rural* | *Urban* |
| 1 | Andhra Pradesh | 8 | 57 | 96 | 96 | 0 | 0 |
| 2 | Arunachal Pradesh | 8 | 24 | 23 | 12 | 6 | 6 |
| 3 | Assam | 23 | 32 | 22 | 34 | 58 | 73 |
| 4 | Bihar | 23 | 17 | 2 | 7 | 52 | 68 |
| 5 | Gujarat | 66 | 73 | 93 | 88 | 66 | 41 |
| 6 | Haryana | 82 | 39 | 58 | 59 | 61 | 65 |
| 7 | Himachal Pradesh | 47 | 45 | 76 | 86 | 77 | 88 |
| 8 | Karnataka | 47 | 65 | 91 | 100 | 16 | 33 |
| 9 | Kerala | 86 | 86 | 76 | 84 | 100 | 99 |
| 10 | Madhya Pradesh | 25 | 32 | 19 | 32 | 55 | 34 |
| 11 | Maharashtra | 47 | 67 | 88 | 86 | 77 | 39 |
| 12 | Meghalaya | 42 | 35 | 15 | 10 | 40 | 17 |
| 13 | Mizoram | 22 | 67 | 83 | 80 | 90 | 74 |
| 14 | Nagaland | 0 | 8 | 48 | 78 | 52 | 84 |
| 15 | Orissa | 22 | 27 | 10 | 38 | 45 | 61 |
| 16 | Punjab | 50 | 54 | 71 | 72 | 86 | 73 |
| 17 | Rajasthan | 42 | 38 | 46 | 66 | 75 | 80 |
| 18 | Sikkim | 28 | 35 | 69 | 51 | 59 | 62 |
| 19 | Tamil Nadu | 58 | 74 | 88 | 98 | 84 | 95 |
| 20 | Tripura | 3 | 32 | 15 | 39 | 8 | 27 |
| 21 | Uttar Pradesh | 44 | 20 | 25 | 62 | 50 | 78 |
| 22 | West Bengal | 15 | 27 | 15 | 45 | 28 | 50 |
| | National Average | 39 | 44 | 50 | 60 | 63 | 64 |

## Table AII.8

*Usage of Public Transport Facilities*

*(per cent of households)*

| Sl. No. | States | Public Bus | | | Private Bus | | |
|---|---|---|---|---|---|---|---|
| | | Rural | Urban | State | Rural | Urban | State |
| 1 | Andhra Pradesh | 93 | 99 | 95 | 0 | 0 | 0 |
| 2 | Arunachal Pradesh | 27 | 68 | 39 | 26 | 12 | 22 |
| 3 | Assam | 2 | 0 | 2 | 88 | 90 | 89 |
| 4 | Bihar | 0 | 0 | 0 | 32 | 32 | 32 |
| 5 | Gujarat | 73 | 52 | 67 | 0 | 0 | 0 |
| 6 | Haryana | 34 | 37 | 35 | 13 | 6 | 11 |
| 7 | Himachal Pradesh | 40 | 70 | 48 | 39 | 15 | 33 |
| 8 | Karnataka | 62 | 72 | 65 | 27 | 13 | 24 |
| 9 | Kerala | 16 | 7 | 13 | 79 | 78 | 79 |
| 10 | Madhya Pradesh | 3 | 29 | 8 | 82 | 52 | 76 |
| 11 | Maharashtra | 91 | 80 | 89 | 0 | 1 | 0 |
| 12 | Meghalaya | 7 | 1 | 4 | 49 | 13 | 33 |
| 13 | Mizoram | 43 | 53 | 46 | 40 | 20 | 33 |
| 14 | Nagaland | 36 | 23 | 32 | 61 | 50 | 57 |
| 15 | Orissa | 1 | 3 | 1 | 70 | 78 | 73 |
| 16 | Punjab | 15 | 34 | 20 | 65 | 62 | 64 |
| 17 | Rajasthan | 21 | 42 | 26 | 52 | 4 | 39 |
| 18 | Sikkim | 42 | 36 | 40 | 12 | 18 | 14 |
| 19 | Tamil Nadu | 73 | 75 | 73 | 18 | 16 | 17 |
| 20 | Tripura | 7 | 0 | 5 | 1 | 2 | 1 |
| 21 | Uttar Pradesh | 6 | 19 | 8 | 37 | 19 | 34 |
| 22 | West Bengal | 3 | 13 | 7 | 32 | 36 | 33 |
| | National Average | 34 | 37 | 35 | 36 | 29 | 34 |

## Table AII.9

*Full Satisfaction with Government Buses*

(per cent of households)

| Sl. No. | States | Punctuality of Govt. Buses | | | Frequency of Govt. Buses | | | Behaviour of Bus Conductors | | |
|---|---|---|---|---|---|---|---|---|---|---|
| | | Rural | Urban | State | Rural | Urban | State | Rural | Urban | State |
| 1 | Andhra Pradesh | 8 | 26 | 13 | 13 | 37 | 20 | 15 | 37 | 21 |
| 2 | Arunachal Pradesh | 4 | 0 | 2 | 4 | 1 | 3 | 2 | 0 | 1 |
| 3 | Assam | 8 | 26 | 13 | 13 | 37 | 20 | 15 | 37 | 21 |
| 4 | Bihar | Ns | Ns | Ns | Ns | Ns | Ns | Ns | Ns | Ns |
| 5 | Gujarat | 45 | 36 | 43 | 40 | 38 | 40 | 40 | 32 | 38 |
| 6 | Haryana | 18 | 25 | 21 | 17 | 25 | 20 | 19 | 28 | 22 |
| 7 | Himachal Pradesh | 13 | 20 | 15 | 8 | 21 | 12 | 13 | 14 | 14 |
| 8 | Karnataka | 20 | 26 | 22 | 19 | 25 | 21 | 21 | 28 | 23 |
| 9 | Kerala | 13 | 12 | 13 | 14 | 15 | 14 | 13 | 15 | 13 |
| 10 | Madhya Pradesh | 21 | 15 | 17 | 27 | 19 | 21 | 20 | 13 | 15 |
| 11 | Maharashtra | 14 | 20 | 15 | 14 | 23 | 15 | 16 | 17 | 16 |
| 12 | Meghalaya | 4 | Ns | 3 | 4 | Ns | 3 | 4 | Ns | 3 |
| 13 | Mizoram | 10 | 20 | 14 | 14 | 26 | 18 | 14 | 25 | 18 |
| 14 | Nagaland | 2 | 11 | 4 | 2 | 11 | 4 | 3 | 11 | 5 |
| 15 | Orissa | Ns | Ns | Ns | Ns | Ns | Ns | Ns | Ns | Ns |
| 16 | Punjab | 8 | 3 | 5 | 6 | 2 | 4 | 8 | 1 | 4 |
| 17 | Rajasthan | 11 | 7 | 9 | 12 | 7 | 10 | 12 | 7 | 10 |
| 18 | Sikkim | 15 | 9 | 13 | 15 | 7 | 13 | 14 | 6 | 12 |
| 19 | Tamil Nadu | 25 | 58 | 34 | 25 | 58 | 34 | 28 | 60 | 37 |
| 20 | Tripura | Ns | | | 6 | | 6 | 0 | | 0 |
| 21 | Uttar Pradesh | 18 | 46 | 28 | 19 | 46 | 29 | 19 | 39 | 26 |
| 22 | West Bengal | Ns | 23 | 25 | Ns | 26 | 28 | Ns | 20 | 27 |
| | National Average | 18 | 25 | 20 | 18 | 28 | 21 | 20 | 26 | 21 |

Ns: Percentage is not computed when the number of sample users is less than 30.

## Table AII.10

*Access and Use of PDS*

*(per cent of households)*

| *Sl. No.* | *States* | *PDS within 1 km.* | | *Households Possessing Own Ration Card* | | | *Use of PDS by Card Owners At Least Once in 2 Months* | | |
|---|---|---|---|---|---|---|---|---|---|
| | | *Rural* | *Urban* | *Rural* | *Urban* | *State* | *Rural* | *Urban* | *State* |
| 1 | Andhra Pradesh | 64 | 85 | 76 | 58 | 71 | 73 | 54 | 68 |
| 2 | Arunachal Pradesh | 40 | 97 | 45 | 33 | 41 | 43 | 34 | 40 |
| 3 | Assam | 72 | 89 | 60 | 53 | 58 | 99 | - | 99 |
| 4 | Bihar | 53 | 87 | 84 | 79 | 83 | 74 | 77 | 75 |
| 5 | Gujarat | 57 | 89 | 93 | 94 | 93 | 89 | 75 | 86 |
| 6 | Haryana | 53 | 92 | 96 | 94 | 95 | 84 | 87 | 85 |
| 7 | Himachal Pradesh | 47 | 83 | 98 | 86 | 95 | 86 | 70 | 82 |
| 8 | Karnataka | 67 | 81 | 83 | 69 | 79 | 96 | 81 | 93 |
| 9 | Kerala | 69 | 92 | 92 | 92 | 92 | 88 | 83 | 86 |
| 10 | Madhya Pradesh | 73 | 82 | 89 | 72 | 86 | 84 | 44 | 76 |
| 11 | Maharashtra | 84 | 96 | 84 | 87 | 85 | 62 | 30 | 56 |
| 12 | Meghalaya | 54 | 57 | 24 | 18 | 21 | 7 | 14 | 10 |
| 13 | Mizoram | 89 | 98 | 90 | 91 | 90 | 89 | 89 | 89 |
| 14 | Nagaland | 12 | 68 | 4 | 13 | 7 | 6 | 14 | 8 |
| 15 | Orissa | 58 | 94 | 94 | 90 | 93 | 99 | 98 | 99 |
| 16 | Punjab | 64 | 96 | 86 | 72 | 82 | 83 | 70 | 79 |
| 17 | Rajasthan | 46 | 90 | 97 | 97 | 97 | 84 | 81 | 83 |
| 18 | Sikkim | 93 | 98 | 84 | 78 | 82 | 84 | 79 | 82 |
| 19 | Tamil Nadu | 88 | 88 | 89 | 94 | 90 | 87 | 94 | 89 |
| 20 | Tripura | 47 | 97 | 59 | 78 | 65 | 52 | 43 | 50 |
| 21 | Uttar Pradesh | 43 | 78 | 86 | 79 | 86 | 80 | 63 | 78 |
| 22 | West Bengal | 44 | 96 | 96 | 89 | 94 | 94 | 69 | 85 |
| | National Average | 60 | 85 | 82 | 76 | 81 | 75 | 62 | 72 |

## Table AII.11

*Reliability of PDS Facilities*

*(per cent of households)*

| *Sl. No.* | *States* | *Regular Availability of Staple Foodgrain* | | | *Price Always Displayed* | | |
|---|---|---|---|---|---|---|---|
| | | *Rural* | *Urban* | *State* | *Rural* | *Urban* | *State* |
| 1 | Andhra Pradesh | 50 | 55 | 51 | 35 | 45 | 37 |
| 2 | Arunachal Pradesh | 8 | 24 | 12 | 15 | 41 | 22 |
| 3 | Assam | 12 | 4 | 10 | 35 | - | 40 |
| 4 | Bihar | 1 | 1 | 1 | 44 | 54 | 47 |
| 5 | Gujarat | 44 | 31 | 41 | 80 | 77 | 79 |
| 6 | Haryana | 2 | 2 | 2 | 19 | 25 | 21 |
| 7 | Himachal Pradesh | 11 | 11 | 11 | 54 | 76 | 58 |
| 8 | Karnataka | 51 | 31 | 47 | 33 | 46 | 36 |
| 9 | Kerala | 51 | 35 | 45 | 80 | 84 | 81 |
| 10 | Madhya Pradesh | 24 | 17 | 23 | 54 | 60 | 55 |
| 11 | Maharashtra | 39 | 31 | 38 | 55 | 75 | 57 |
| 12 | Meghalaya | 16 | 12 | 14 | 4 | 22 | 15 |
| 13 | Mizoram | 36 | 10 | 27 | 19 | 45 | 27 |
| 14 | Nagaland | Ns | Ns | 6 | Ns | Ns | 2 |
| 15 | Orissa | 10 | 9 | 10 | 35 | 64 | 44 |
| 16 | Punjab | 0 | 0 | 0 | 24 | 52 | 29 |
| 17 | Rajasthan | 7 | 4 | 6 | 40 | 60 | 45 |
| 18 | Sikkim | 42 | 18 | 34 | 70 | 85 | 75 |
| 19 | Tamil Nadu | 75 | 69 | 73 | 70 | 71 | 71 |
| 20 | Tripura | 7 | 17 | 10 | 21 | 43 | 27 |
| 21 | Uttar Pradesh | 1 | 0 | 1 | 19 | 30 | 21 |
| 22 | West Bengal | 9 | 8 | 9 | 56 | 57 | 56 |
| | National Average | 24 | 20 | 23 | 45 | 56 | 47 |

Ns: Percentage is not computed when the number of sample users is less than 30.

# Table AII.12

*Extent of Full Satisfaction with PDS*

*(per cent of households)*

| Sl. No. | States | Quantity of Supplies | | | Quality of Supplies | | | Fairness of Shopkeeper | | |
|---|---|---|---|---|---|---|---|---|---|---|
| | | Rural | Urban | State | Rural | Urban | State | Rural | Urban | State |
| 1 | Andhra Pradesh | 11 | 20 | 13 | 17 | 21 | 18 | 17 | 22 | 18 |
| 2 | Arunachal Pradesh | 1 | 0 | 0 | 1 | 0 | 0 | 1 | 0 | 0 |
| 3 | Assam | 1 | - | 2 | 5 | - | 6 | 5 | - | 7 |
| 4 | Bihar | 4 | 10 | 6 | 14 | 17 | 15 | 9 | 13 | 10 |
| 5 | Gujarat | 13 | 8 | 12 | 13 | 9 | 12 | 15 | 11 | 14 |
| 6 | Haryana | 12 | 5 | 9 | 11 | 5 | 9 | 11 | 5 | 9 |
| 7 | Himachal Pradesh | 6 | 8 | 6 | 6 | 6 | 6 | 6 | 6 | 6 |
| 8 | Karnataka | 9 | 2 | 7 | 16 | 5 | 14 | 21 | 14 | 20 |
| 9 | Kerala | 2 | 6 | 4 | 1 | 5 | 3 | 2 | 4 | 3 |
| 10 | Madhya Pradesh | 6 | 5 | 6 | 9 | 10 | 9 | 8 | 8 | 8 |
| 11 | Maharashtra | 2 | 2 | 2 | 4 | 3 | 4 | 4 | 4 | 4 |
| 12 | Meghalaya | 0 | 7 | 5 | 0 | 7 | 5 | 0 | 7 | 5 |
| 13 | Mizoram | 10 | 11 | 10 | 1 | 0 | 1 | 1 | 1 | 1 |
| 14 | Nagaland | Ns | Ns | 4 | Ns | Ns | 4 | Ns | Ns | 4 |
| 15 | Orissa | 0 | 1 | 0 | 1 | 1 | 1 | 2 | 0 | 2 |
| 16 | Punjab | 3 | 1 | 2 | 4 | 1 | 4 | 3 | 1 | 3 |
| 17 | Rajasthan | 6 | 10 | 7 | 5 | 10 | 6 | 4 | 10 | 5 |
| 18 | Sikkim | 17 | 11 | 15 | 16 | 9 | 14 | 16 | 10 | 14 |
| 19 | Tamil Nadu | 20 | 28 | 22 | 17 | 25 | 19 | 22 | 30 | 24 |
| 20 | Tripura | 15 | 20 | 16 | 14 | 20 | 16 | 2 | 0 | 1 |
| 21 | Uttar Pradesh | 12 | 16 | 13 | 14 | 19 | 15 | 14 | 16 | 14 |
| 22 | West Bengal | 2 | 2 | 2 | 2 | 1 | 1 | 2 | 4 | 2 |
| | National Average | 8 | 9 | 8 | 9 | 9 | 9 | 10 | 10 | 10 |

Ns: Percentage is not computed when the number of sample users is less than 30.

# Table AII.13

*Access and Usage of Primary Schools*

*(per cent of households)*

| Sl. No. | States | Access to a Primary Education Facility | | | | Dependence for Primary Education Facility | | | | | |
|---|---|---|---|---|---|---|---|---|---|---|---|
| | | Govt. School | | Pvt. School | | Govt. & Aided School | | | Pvt. School | | |
| | | Rural | Urban | Rural | Urban | Rural | Urban | State | Rural | Urban | State |
| 1 | Andhra Pradesh | 92 | 54 | 37 | 21 | 85 | 75 | 82 | 15 | 25 | 18 |
| 2 | Arunachal Pradesh | 23 | 37 | 9 | 3 | 96 | 87 | 93 | 4 | 13 | 7 |
| 3 | Assam | 74 | 38 | 19 | 14 | 85 | 60 | 82 | 15 | 41 | 18 |
| 4 | Bihar | 80 | 44 | 36 | 38 | 74 | 54 | 70 | 26 | 46 | 30 |
| 5 | Gujarat | 93 | 56 | 28 | 21 | 93 | 64 | 86 | 7 | 36 | 14 |
| 6 | Haryana | 81 | 32 | 46 | 52 | 63 | 38 | 56 | 37 | 62 | 44 |
| 7 | Himachal Pradesh | 75 | 38 | 22 | 31 | 86 | Ns | 83 | 14 | Ns | 17 |
| 8 | Karnataka | 82 | 53 | 26 | 15 | 85 | 70 | 80 | 16 | 30 | 20 |
| 9 | Kerala | 75 | 22 | 26 | 18 | 83 | 58 | 74 | 18 | 42 | 26 |
| 10 | Madhya Pradesh | 87 | 29 | 20 | 22 | 93 | 53 | 86 | 8 | 50 | 16 |
| 11 | Maharashtra | 83 | 53 | 17 | 18 | 96 | 71 | 93 | 4 | 29 | 7 |
| 12 | Meghalaya | 73 | 13 | 50 | 27 | 45 | 17 | 20 | 55 | Ns | 24 |
| 13 | Mizoram | 62 | 39 | 21 | 13 | 89 | Ns | 84 | 11 | Ns | 16 |
| 14 | Nagaland | 82 | 9 | 59 | 46 | 38 | 11 | 31 | 62 | 87 | 69 |
| 15 | Orissa | 89 | 54 | 20 | 8 | 97 | 83 | 93 | 3 | 17 | 7 |
| 16 | Punjab | 74 | 33 | 37 | 34 | 59 | 52 | 57 | 41 | 48 | 43 |
| 17 | Rajasthan | 85 | 51 | 36 | 36 | 80 | 59 | 75 | 20 | 41 | 25 |
| 18 | Sikkim | 52 | 17 | 7 | 39 | 84 | 33 | 63 | 16 | 67 | 37 |
| 19 | Tamil Nadu | 71 | 67 | 8 | 17 | 87 | 81 | 86 | 13 | 19 | 15 |
| 20 | Tripura | 41 | 24 | 3 | 11 | 98 | 80 | 91 | 2 | 20 | 9 |
| 21 | Uttar Pradesh | 82 | 40 | 45 | 43 | 74 | 47 | 71 | 26 | 53 | 29 |
| 22 | West Bengal | 60 | 41 | 3 | 4 | 98 | 81 | 94 | 2 | 19 | 6 |
| | National Average | 76 | 42 | 25 | 25 | 83 | 61 | 78 | 17 | 39 | 22 |

## Table AII.14

*Awareness and Use of Mid-day Meal Programme*

*(Per cent of Households)*

| *Sl. No.* | *States* | *Awareness of Mid-day Meal Scheme* | | | *Utilise Mid-day Meal (Among Aware)* | | |
|---|---|---|---|---|---|---|---|
| | | *Rural* | *Urban* | *State* | *Rural* | *Urban* | *State* |
| 1 | Andhra Pradesh | 81 | 67 | 77 | 99 | 100 | 99 |
| 2 | Arunachal Pradesh | Ns | Ns | 49 | Ns | Ns | Ns |
| 3 | Assam | 30 | - | 31 | 35 | - | 31 |
| 4 | Bihar | 38 | 37 | 38 | 54 | Ns | 54 |
| 5 | Gujarat | 94 | 83 | 92 | 88 | 84 | 87 |
| 6 | Haryana | 80 | Ns | 76 | 72 | Ns | 72 |
| 7 | Himachal Pradesh | Ns | 96 | 95 | 89 | 82 | 88 |
| 8 | Karnataka | 89 | 91 | 90 | 100 | 100 | 100 |
| 9 | Kerala | 96 | 93 | 95 | 99 | 100 | 99 |
| 10 | Madhya Pradesh | 72 | 39 | 69 | 90 | 90 | 90 |
| 11 | Maharashtra | 62 | 63 | 62 | 89 | Ns | 87 |
| 12 | Meghalaya | 0 | Ns | 0 | Ns | Ns | Ns |
| 13 | Mizoram | 31 | 33 | 32 | 79 | 67 | 75 |
| 14 | Nagaland | 11 | Ns | 12 | Ns | Ns | Ns |
| 15 | Orissa | 98 | 92 | 96 | 80 | 62 | 76 |
| 16 | Punjab | 21 | Ns | 17 | Ns | Ns | Ns |
| 17 | Rajasthan | 40 | 48 | 42 | 89 | Ns | 86 |
| 18 | Sikkim | 77 | Ns | 60 | 36 | Ns | 34 |
| 19 | Tamil Nadu | 95 | 94 | 95 | 100 | 100 | 100 |
| 20 | Tripura | 16 | 0 | 11 | Ns | Ns | Ns |
| 21 | Uttar Pradesh | 68 | 43 | 67 | 58 | Ns | 57 |
| 22 | West Bengal | 92 | 81 | 90 | 88 | 83 | 87 |
| | National Average | 69 | 65 | 68 | 83 | 82 | 83 |

Ns: Percentage is not computed when the number of sample users is less than 30.

## Table AII.15

*Full Satisfaction with Government Schools*

*(Per cent of Households)*

| Sl. No. | States | Full Satisfaction With Behaviour of Teachers in Govt. Run & Aided Primary School | | | Extent of Full Satisfaction With: Quality of School Building | | | Extent of Full Satisfaction With: Quality of Toilet | | |
|---|---|---|---|---|---|---|---|---|---|---|
| | | Rural | Urban | State | Rural | Urban | State | Rural | Urban | State |
| 1 | Andhra Pradesh | 14 | 20 | 16 | 14 | 28 | 18 | 1 | 12 | 4 |
| 2 | Arunachal Pradesh | Ns | Ns | 1 | Ns | Ns | 0 | Ns | Ns | 0 |
| 3 | Assam | 14 | - | 14 | 6 | - | 6 | 3 | - | 2 |
| 4 | Bihar | 9 | 12 | 9 | 3 | 10 | 4 | 1 | 5 | 1 |
| 5 | Gujarat | 24 | 18 | 23 | 24 | 12 | 22 | 8 | 10 | 9 |
| 6 | Haryana | 6 | Ns | 5 | 4 | Ns | 5 | 1 | Ns | 3 |
| 7 | Himachal Pradesh | 7 | 4 | 6 | 4 | 4 | 4 | 3 | 4 | 3 |
| 8 | Karnataka | 25 | 29 | 26 | 21 | 28 | 23 | 6 | 8 | 7 |
| 9 | Kerala | 16 | 19 | 17 | 15 | 16 | 16 | 8 | 15 | 10 |
| 10 | Madhya Pradesh | 19 | 18 | 20 | 13 | 16 | 13 | 2 | 9 | 3 |
| 11 | Maharashtra | 20 | 32 | 21 | 16 | 30 | 17 | 11 | 27 | 13 |
| 12 | Meghalaya | 0 | Ns | 0 | 0 | Ns | 0 | 0 | Ns | 0 |
| 13 | Mizoram | 2 | 0 | 2 | 16 | Ns | 16 | 7 | Ns | 5 |
| 14 | Nagaland | 0 | Ns | 0 | 0 | Ns | 0 | 0 | Ns | 0 |
| 15 | Orissa | 3 | 2 | 3 | 3 | 2 | 3 | 1 | 1 | 1 |
| 16 | Punjab | 1 | Ns | 1 | 1 | Ns | 1 | 2 | Ns | 1 |
| 17 | Rajasthan | 8 | 0 | 6 | 7 | 1 | 6 | 3 | 0 | 2 |
| 18 | Sikkim | 16 | Ns | 16 | 19 | Ns | 17 | 14 | Ns | 12 |
| 19 | Tamil Nadu | 36 | 44 | 38 | 27 | 36 | 30 | 13 | 30 | 18 |
| 20 | Tripura | 0 | 3 | 1 | 0 | 3 | 1 | 0 | 0 | 0 |
| 21 | Uttar Pradesh | 15 | 7 | 15 | 18 | 12 | 18 | 8 | 5 | 8 |
| 22 | West Bengal | 18 | 31 | 21 | 12 | 24 | 14 | 3 | 12 | 4 |
| | National Average | 16 | 17 | 16 | 13 | 16 | 14 | 5 | 10 | 6 |

Ns: Percentage is not computed when the number of sample users is less than 30.

# Table AII.16

## *Access, Use, Reliability and Full Satisfaction with Anganwadis*

*(per cent of rural households)*

| Sl. No. | States | Access of Anganwadis within 1 km. | Usage of Anganwadis | Regular Opening of Anganwadis | Good Behaviour of Anganwadi Workers | Reasons for Sending Children to Anganwadi | | |
|---|---|---|---|---|---|---|---|---|
| | | | | | | Pre-Facility School | Availability of Supplementary Diet | Immunisation |
| 1 | Andhra Pradesh | 49 | 31 | Ns | Ns | Ns | Ns | Ns |
| 2 | Arunachal Pradesh | 52 | Ns | Ns | Ns | Ns | Ns | Ns |
| 3 | Assam | 43 | 30 | 87 | 91 | 78 | 9 | 52 |
| 4 | Bihar | 32 | 8 | Ns | Ns | Ns | Ns | Ns |
| 5 | Gujarat | 85 | 40 | 95 | 94 | 69 | 42 | 90 |
| 6 | Haryana | 84 | 29 | 91 | 88 | 89 | 45 | 95 |
| 7 | Himachal Pradesh | 71 | 32 | Ns | Ns | Ns | Ns | Ns |
| 8 | Karnataka | 92 | 40 | 99 | 74 | 82 | 41 | 90 |
| 9 | Kerala | 71 | 29 | 96 | Ns | Ns | Ns | Ns |
| 10 | Madhya Pradesh | 87 | 26 | 83 | 68 | 70 | 51 | 77 |
| 11 | Maharashtra | 96 | 40 | 99 | 86 | 83 | 21 | 91 |
| 12 | Meghalaya | 58 | Ns | Ns | Ns | Ns | Ns | Ns |
| 13 | Mizoram | 85 | 49 | 89 | 75 | 86 | 42 | 42 |
| 14 | Nagaland | 96 | 35 | 12 | 62 | 62 | 47 | 3 |
| 15 | Orissa | 87 | 50 | 92 | 76 | 83 | 75 | 89 |
| 16 | Punjab | 70 | 15 | Ns | Ns | Ns | Ns | Ns |
| 17 | Rajasthan | 76 | 26 | 80 | 64 | 64 | 38 | 83 |
| 18 | Sikkim | 66 | Ns | Ns | Ns | Ns | Ns | Ns |
| 19 | Tamil Nadu | 82 | 33 | 99 | 75 | 87 | 24 | 92 |
| 20 | Tripura | 79 | 9 | Ns | Ns | Ns | Ns | Ns |
| 21 | Uttar Pradesh | 42 | 19 | 64 | 64 | 58 | 47 | 66 |
| 22 | West Bengal | 72 | 15 | Ns | Ns | Ns | Ns | Ns |
| | National Average | 71 | 30 | 87 | 78 | 76 | 40 | 79 |

Ns: Percentage is not computed when the number of sample users is less than 30.

## ANNEXURE III

*Detailed State Level Tables on Indicators for the Services*

The tables in this annexure present the indicators for the services for each state by the selected districts. These tables bring out the intra state variations in the indicators. As the districts within a state are selected from different socio-cultural regions and representation was given to both better and less-developed districts, the survey captured wide variations in the provision of services and consequently in the user feed back on the services. Administrators, policymakers and academicians may be interested in looking at the performance of the districts from the perspective of users of the services.

Though, the main focus of the study is on presenting reliable estimates of the different dimensions of the five services at state level, the district level figures serve the purpose of assessing the relative performance of districts. In many states the district level indicators provide a reasonable accuracy keeping the error margin of the estimates within 10 per cent at 90 per cent confidence level.

Child Care System data was presented only for rural areas.

All the estimates for the indicators are given in terms of the percentage of households except for rural access which is based on the percentage of villages.

The following symbols are used where the reporting households are less than 100.

* Indicates that the reporting households are between 60-100 in number.

** Indicates that the reporting households are between 30-60 in number.

# Indicates that the reporting households are less than 30 in number.

NA refers to cases where the indicator is not applicable.

## III.1: Andhra Pradesh

### *a. Drinking Water*

| Sl. No. | Units | Use of Public Protected Source | Use of Private Protected Source | Public Protected Source within 100 Metres | Breakdown of Public Taps within 3 Months | Breakdown of Public Handpumps within 3 Months | Households Involved in Maintenance | Willingness to Pay More | Full Satisfaction with Public Drinking Water Facilities: Piped Supply – Adequacy of Supply | Piped Supply – Quality of Water | Other Protected Public Source – Adequacy of Supply | Other Protected Public Source – Quality of Water |
|---|---|---|---|---|---|---|---|---|---|---|---|---|
| 1 | Anantapur | 98 | 0 | 77 | 11 | 4 | 11 | 64 | 28 | 28 | 33 | 33 |
| 2 | Chittoor | 84 | 8 | 66 | 4 | 34 | 57 | 17 | 30 | 30 | 19 | 19 |
| 3 | Guntur | 63 | 9 | 45 | 19 | 28 | 5 | 69 | 18 | 18 | 56 | 60 |
| 4 | Mahboobnagar | 96 | 1 | 90 | 28 | 21 | 2 | 42 | 17 | 26 | 5 | 7 |
| 5 | Nizamabad | 77 | 5 | 75 | 44 | 88 | 41 | 15 | 26 | 28 | 21 | 21 |
| 6 | Vizianagaram | 62 | 1 | 50 | 3 | 1 | 15 | 65 | | | 36 | 34 |
| 7 | Rural Average | 80 | 4 | 67 | 19 | 21 | 21 | 44 | 24 | 26 | 27 | 27 |
| 8 | Urban Average | 86 | 4 | 75 | 36 | 56 | 12 | 64 | 26 | 28 | 38 | 42 |
| 9 | State Average | 82 | 4 | 69 | 24 | 27 | 18 | 50 | 25 | 27 | 30 | 31 |

## b. Health Care

| Sl. No. | Units | Health Facility within 1 km. | Dependence for Minor Ailments | | Dependence for Major Ailments | | Presence in Government Health Facilities of | | Paid for Medical Services Availed (Out-Patients) | Full Satisfaction of Out-Patients with Behaviour of | |
|---|---|---|---|---|---|---|---|---|---|---|---|
| | | | Govt. Facility | Pvt. Hospitals | Govt. Facility | Pvt. Hospitals | Doctors | Paramedics | | Doctors | Paramedics |
| 1 | Anantapurl | 31 | 66 | 20 | 61 | 26 | 14 | 76 | 5 | 4 | 5 |
| 2 | Chittoor | 41 | 70 | 28 | 69 | 30 | 14 | 71 | 19 | 5 | 5 |
| 3 | Guntur | 19 | 64 | 21 | 40 | 27 | 20 | 27 | 13 | 3 | 3 |
| 4 | Mahboobnagar | 34 | 24 | 23 | 33 | 54 | 33 | 36 | 6 | 1 | 1 |
| 5 | Nizamabad | 47 | 53 | 21 | 58 | 39 | 23 | 60 | 2 | 1 | 1 |
| 6 | Vizianagaram | 27 | 41 | 11 | 41 | 12 | 16 | 97 | 2 | 7 | 7 |
| 7 | Rural Average | 36 | 51 | 20 | 50 | 33 | 20 | 60 | 7 | 3 | 4 |
| 8 | Urban Average | 55 | 67 | 28 | 42 | 34 | 43 | 55 | 13 | 12 | 13 |
| 9 | State Average | NA | 55 | 22 | 48 | 33 | 28 | 59 | 9 | 6 | 7 |

## *c. Road Transport*

| *Sl. No.* | *Units* | *Access to Cemen/Tarred Road* | *Availability of* | | | *Usage of Transport Facility* | | *Full Satisfaction With* | | |
|---|---|---|---|---|---|---|---|---|---|---|
| | | | *Bus Stop* | *Public Bus* | *Private Bus* | *Public Bus* | *Private Bus* | *Punctuality of Govt. Buses* | *Frequency of Govt. Buses* | *Behaviour of Bus Conductors* |
| 1 | Anantapur | 13 | 31 | 88 | 0 | 89 | 0 | 11 | 23 | 35 |
| 2 | Chittoor | 7 | 79 | 100 | 0 | 98 | 0 | 2 | 2 | 2 |
| 3 | Guntur | 8 | 73 | 93 | 0 | 99 | 0 | 14 | 19 | 16 |
| 4 | Mahboobnagar | 0 | 53 | 100 | 0 | 94 | 0 | 10 | 14 | 17 |
| 5 | Nizamabad | 11 | 61 | 100 | 0 | 100 | 0 | 6 | 9 | 8 |
| 6 | Vizianagaram | 8 | 42 | 92 | 0 | 80 | 0 | 4 | 8 | 12 |
| 7 | Rural Average | 8 | 57 | 96 | 0 | 93 | 0 | 8 | 13 | 15 |
| 8 | Urban Average | NA | NA | 96 | 0 | 99 | 0 | 26 | 37 | 37 |
| 9 | State Average | NA | NA | NA | NA | 95 | 0 | 13 | 20 | 21 |

## *d. Public Distribution System*

| Sl. No. | Units | PDS within 1 km. | Households Possessing Own Ration Card | Use of PDS by Card Owners At Least Once in 2 Months | Reliability of PDS Facilities | | Extent of Full Satisfaction With | | |
|---|---|---|---|---|---|---|---|---|---|
| | | | | | Regular Availability of Staple Foodgrain | Price Always Displayed | Quantity of Supplies | Quality of Supplies | Fairness of Shopkeeper |
| 1 | Anantapur | 88 | 80 | 80 | 53 | 31 | 13 | 26 | 25 |
| 2 | Chittoor | 50 | 70 | 68 | 55 | 52 | 14 | 13 | 11 |
| 3 | Guntur | 80 | 71 | 66 | 50 | 35 | 22 | 19 | 23 |
| 4 | Mahboobnagar | 60 | 88 | 85 | 63 | 27 | 8 | 11 | 5 |
| 5 | Nizamabad | 39 | 73 | 69 | 23 | 24 | 0 | 0 | 0 |
| 6 | Vizianagaram | 75 | 77 | 73 | 52 | 42 | 12 | 32 | 35 |
| 7 | Rural Average | 64 | 76 | 73 | 50 | 35 | 11 | 17 | 17 |
| 8 | Urban Average | 85 | 58 | 54 | 55 | 45 | 20 | 21 | 22 |
| 9 | State Average | NA | 71 | 68 | 51 | 37 | 13 | 18 | 18 |

## e. Primary School

| Sl. No. | Units | Access to a Primary Education Facility | | Dependence for Primary Education Facility | | Full Satisfaction with Behaviour of Teachers in Govt./Aided School | Awareness of Mid-Day Meal Scheme | Utilise Mid-Day Meal (Among Aware) | Extent of Full Satisfaction With | |
|---|---|---|---|---|---|---|---|---|---|---|
| | | Govt. School | Pvt. School | Govt. School | Pvt. School | | | | Quality of School Building | Quality of Toilet |
| 1 | Anantapur | 94 | 25 | 85 | 15 | 28 | 100 | 100 | 21 | 2 |
| 2 | Chittoor | 79 | 57 | 78 | 22 | 7 | 82 | 100 | 11 | 0 |
| 3 | Guntur | 93 | 47 | 83 | 17 | 10 | 49 | 100 | 21 | 0 |
| 4 | Mahboobnagar | 100 | 27 | 89 | 11 | 19 | 79 | 98 | 16 | 2 |
| 5 | Nizamabad | 100 | 39 | 86 | 14 | 0 | 75 | 96 | 0 | 0 |
| 6 | Vizianagaram | 83 | 25 | 89 | 12 | 19 | 98 | 100 | 19 | 0 |
| 7 | Rural Average | 92 | 37 | 85 | 15 | 14 | 81 | 99 | 14 | 1 |
| 8 | Urban Average | 54 | 21 | 75 | 25 | 20 | 67 | 100 | 28 | 12 |
| 9 | State Average | NA | NA | 82 | 18 | 16 | 77 | 99 | 18 | 4 |

*f. Child Care System*

| *Sl. No.* | *Units* | *Access of Anganwadis within 1 km.* | *Usage of Anganwadis* |
|---|---|---|---|
| 1 | Anantapur | 69 | 19 |
| 2 | Chittoor | 7 | 15 |
| 3 | Guntur | 60 | 0 |
| 4 | Mahboobnagar | 67 | 40 |
| 5 | Nizamabad | 44 | 64 |
| 6 | Vizianagaram | 42 | – |
| 7 | Rural Average | 49 | 31 |

## III.2: Arunachal Pradesh

### *a. Drinking Water*

| Sl No. | Units | Use of Public Protected Source | Use of Private Protected Source | Public Protected Source within 100 Metres | Breakdown of Public Taps within 3 Months | Households Involved in Maintenance | Willingness to Pay More | Full Satisfaction with Public Drinking Water Facilities: Piped Supply | | Full Satisfaction with Public Drinking Water Facilities: Other Protected Public Sources | |
|---|---|---|---|---|---|---|---|---|---|---|---|
| | | | | | | | | Adequacy of Supply | Quality of Water | Adequacy of Supply | Quality of Water |
| 1 | Changlang | 87 | 7 | 87 | 12 | 34 | 20 | 1* | 4* | 21 | 31 |
| 2 | Upper Subansiri | 94 | 0 | 94 | 33* | 27* | 35 | 6* | 6* | 3* | 2* |
| 3 | West Siang | 89 | 0 | 63 | 11** | 0* | 2 | 2* | 2* | 18* | 38* |
| 4 | Rural Average | 90 | 3 | 82 | 18 | 23 | 19 | 3 | 4 | 16 | 26 |
| 5 | Urban Average | 80 | 1 | 79 | 12** | 58** | 56 | 2 | 3 | 2** | 2** |
| 6 | State Average | 87 | 2 | 81 | 17 | 29 | 29 | 3 | 4 | 13 | 21 |

## b. Health Care

| Sl. No. | Units | Health Facility within 1 km. | Dependence for Minor Ailments | | Dependence for Major Ailments | | Presence in Government Health Facilities of | | Paid for Medical Services Availed (Out-Patients) | Full Satisfaction of Out-Patients with Behaviour of | |
|---|---|---|---|---|---|---|---|---|---|---|---|
| | | | Govt. Facility | Pvt. Hospitals | Govt. Facility | Pvt. Hospitals | Doctors | Paramedics | | Doctors | Paramedics |
| 1 | Changlang | 50 | 98 | 0 | 86 | 11 | 78* | 72* | 9* | 2* | 1* |
| 2 | Upper Subansiri | 0 | 85* | 8* | 75* | 4* | 2** | 21** | 12** | 0** | 0** |
| 3 | West Siang | 56 | 97** | 0** | 100** | 0** | # | # | # | # | # |
| 4 | Rural Average | 36 | 93 | 3 | 85 | 7 | 45 | 48 | 8 | 1 | 0 |
| 5 | Urban Average | 72 | 97 | 0 | 62 | 10 | 89 | 88 | 13 | 1 | 0 |
| 6 | State Average | NA | 95 | 2 | 76 | 8 | 64 | 65 | 11 | 1 | 0 |

## c. Road Transport

| Sl. No. | Units | Access to Cement/Tarred Road | Availability of | | | Usage of Transport Facility | | Full Satisfaction with | | |
|---|---|---|---|---|---|---|---|---|---|---|
| | | | Bus Stops | Public Bus | Private Bus | Public Bus | Private Bus | Punctuality of Govt. Buses | Frequency of Govt. Buses | Behaviour of Bus Conductors |
| 1 | Changlang | 13 | 50 | 7 | 0 | 47 | 24 | 6 | 6 | 3 |
| 2 | Upper Subansiri | 0 | 57 | 50 | 20 | 24 | 13 | 0** | 0** | 0** |
| 3 | West Siang | 11 | 6 | 18 | 0 | 0 | 41 | | | |
| 4 | Rural Average | 8 | 24 | 23 | 6 | 27 | 26 | 4 | 4 | 2 |
| 5 | Urban Average | - | - | 12 | 6 | 68 | 12 | 0 | 1 | 0 |
| 6 | State Average | NA | NA | NA | NA | 39 | 22 | 2 | 3 | 1 |

## d. Public Distribution System

| Sl. No. | Units | PDS within 1 km. | Households Possessing Own Ration Card | Use of PDS by Card Owners at Least Once in 2 Months | Reliability of PDS Facilities | | Extent of Full Satisfaction With | | |
|---|---|---|---|---|---|---|---|---|---|
| | | | | | Regular Availability of Staple Foodgrain | Price Always Displayed | Quantity of Supplies | Quality of Supplies | Fairness of Shopkeeper |
| 1 | Changlang | 75 | 43 | 47 | 13 | 33 | 1 | 1 | 1 |
| 2 | Upper Subansiri | 0 | 44 | 50 | 6* | 0* | 0* | 0* | 0* |
| 3 | West Siang | 44 | 47 | 31 | 0** | 0** | 0** | 0** | 0** |
| 4 | Rural Average | 40 | 45 | 43 | 8 | 15 | 1 | 1 | 1 |
| 5 | Urban Average | 97 | 33 | 34 | 24* | 41* | 0* | 0* | 0* |
| 6 | State Average | NA | 41 | 40 | 12 | 22 | 0 | 0 | 0 |

## e. Primary School

| Sl. No. | Units | Access to a Primary Education Facility | | Dependence for Primary Education Facility | | Full Satisfaction with Behaviour of Teachers in Govt./Aided School | Awareness of Mid-Day Meal Scheme | Utilise Mid-Day Meal (Among Aware) | Extent of Full Satisfaction With | |
|---|---|---|---|---|---|---|---|---|---|---|
| | | Govt. School | Pvt. School | Govt. School | Pvt. School | | | | Quality of School Building | Quality of Toilet |
| 1 | Changlang | 14 | 14 | 95* | 5* | # | # | # | # | # |
| 2 | Upper Subansiri | 40 | 0 | 96** | 4** | # | # | # | # | # |
| 3 | West Siang | 18 | 9 | 94** | 6** | # | # | # | # | # |
| 4 | Rural Average | 23 | 9 | 96 | 4** | 2** | 32** | # | 0** | 0** |
| 5 | Urban Average | 37 | 3 | 87* | 13** | # | # | # | # | # |
| 6 | State Average | NA | NA | 93 | 7** | 1* | 49* | # | 0* | 0* |

## f. Child Care System

| Sl. No. | Units | Access of Anganwadis within 1 km. | Usage of Anganwadis |
|---|---|---|---|
| 1 | Changlang | 50 | # |
| 2 | Upper Subansiri | 50 | # |
| 3 | West Siang | 56 | # |
| 4 | Rural Average | 52 | # |

## III.3: Assam

### *a. Drinking Water*

| Sl. No. | Units | Use of Public Protected Source | Use of Private Protected Source | Public Protected Source within 100 Metres | Breakdown of Public Handpump within 3 Months | Households Involved in Maintenance | Willingness to Pay More |
|---|---|---|---|---|---|---|---|
| 1 | Bongaigaon | 1 | 33 | 1 | # | # | # |
| 2 | Dhuburi | 9 | 63 | 8 | # | # | # |
| 3 | Dibrugarh | 4 | 91 | 4 | # | # | # |
| 4 | Hailakandi | 18 | 10 | 16 | # | # | # |
| 5 | Nagaon | 11 | 71 | 10 | # | # | # |
| 6 | North Cachar Hills | 21 | 10 | 21 | # | # | # |
| 7 | Sonitpur | 8 | 5 | 8 | # | # | # |
| 8 | Rural Average | 10 | 42 | 9 | 37* | 13 | 22 |
| 9 | Urban Average | 10 | 52 | 9 | # | # | 49 |
| 10 | State Average | 10 | 42 | 9 | 30 | 11 | 30 |

## b. Health Care

| Sl. No. | Units | Health Facility within 1 km. | Dependence for Minor Ailments | | Dependence for Major Ailments | | Presence in Government Health Facilities of | | Paid for Medical Services Availed (Out-Patients) | Full Satisfaction of Out-Patients with Behaviour of | |
|---|---|---|---|---|---|---|---|---|---|---|---|
| | | | Govt. Facility | Pvt. Hospitals | Govt. Facility | Pvt. Hospitals | Doctors | Paramedics | | Doctors | Paramedics |
| 1 | Bongaigaon | 44 | 81 | 3 | 73 | 13 | 73* | 84* | 5* | 0* | 0* |
| 2 | Dhuburi | 41 | 66* | 7* | 89* | 5* | # | # | # | # | # |
| 3 | Dibrugarh | 29 | 48 | 39 | 42 | 51 | 88* | 87* | 9* | 0* | 0* |
| 4 | Hailakandi | 19 | 87 | 4 | 76 | 20 | 71 | 81 | 17 | 16 | 12 |
| 5 | Nagaon | 50 | 86* | 4* | 89* | 11* | 62** | 77** | 23** | 3** | 0** |
| 6 | North Cachar Hills | 39 | 63** | 17** | 87** | 13** | # | # | # | # | # |
| 7 | Sonitpur | 47 | 87* | 13* | 86* | 13* | 58** | 79** | 26** | 0** | 0** |
| 8 | Rural Average | 38 | 75 | 12 | 74 | 21 | 68 | 81 | 16 | 5 | 4 |
| 9 | Urban Average | 49 | 48 | 18 | 53 | 39 | 88 | 92 | 13 | 4 | 6 |
| 10 | State Average | NA | 68 | 14 | 68 | 26 | 72 | 84 | 15 | 5 | 5 |

## c. Road Transport

| Sl. No. | Units | Access to Cement/Tarred Road within 1 km. | Availability within 1 km. of | | | Usage of Transport Facility | | Full Satisfaction With | | |
|---|---|---|---|---|---|---|---|---|---|---|
| | | | Bus Stops | Public Bus | Private Bus | Public Bus | Private Bus | Punctuality of Govt. Buses | Frequency of Govt. Buses | Behaviour of Bus Conductors |
| 1 | Bongaigaon | 31 | 38 | 19 | 69 | 0 | 99 | # | # | # |
| 2 | Dhuburi | 12 | 29 | 18 | 41 | 5 | 82 | # | # | # |
| 3 | Dibrugarh | 41 | 18 | 6 | 29 | 0 | 94 | # | # | # |
| 4 | Hailakandi | 29 | 38 | 0 | 50 | 0 | 96 | # | # | # |
| 5 | Nagaon | 6 | 31 | 25 | 75 | 1 | 82 | # | # | # |
| 6 | North Cachar Hills | 31 | 46 | 39 | 69 | 4 | 74 | # | # | # |
| 7 | Sonitpur | 16 | 29 | 53 | 77 | 6 | 86 | # | # | # |
| 8 | Rural Average | 23 | 32 | 22 | 58 | 2 | 88 | 8 | 13 | 15 |
| 9 | Urban Average | NA | NA | 34 | 73 | 0 | 90 | 26 | 37 | 37 |
| 10 | State Average | NA | NA | NA | NA | 2 | 89 | 13 | 20 | 21 |

### *d. Public Distribution System*

| *Sl. No.* | *Units* | *PDS Outlet within 1 km* | *Households Possessing Own Ration Card* | *Use of PDS by Card Owners at Least Once in 2 Months* | *Reliability of PDS Facilities* | | *Extent of Full Satisfaction With* | | |
|---|---|---|---|---|---|---|---|---|---|
| | | | | | *Regular Availability of Staple Foodgrain* | *Price Always Displayed* | *Quantity of Supplies* | *Quality of Supplies* | *Fairness of Shopkeeper* |
| 1 | Bongaigaon | 75 | 77 | 100 | 14 | 54 | 1 | 1 | 1 |
| 2 | Dhuburi | 65 | 59 | 100 | 4 | 19 | 4 | 20 | 7 |
| 3 | Dibrugarh | 77 | 42 | 100* | 22* | 47* | 0* | 0* | 0* |
| 4 | Hailakandi | 88 | 42 | 100* | 31* | 32* | 1* | 2* | 0* |
| 5 | Nagaon | 81 | 80 | 99 | 5 | 29 | 1 | 3 | 11 |
| 6 | North Cachar Hills | 23 | 48 | 98** | 9** | 47** | 2** | 12** | 12** |
| 7 | Sonitpur | 88 | 68 | 96 | 7 | 22 | 1 | 7 | 7 |
| 8 | Rural Average | 72 | 60 | 99 | 12 | 35 | 1 | 5 | 5 |
| 9 | Urban Average | 89 | 53 | # | 4 | # | # | # | # |
| 10 | State Average | NA | 58 | 99 | 10 | 40 | 2 | 6 | 7 |

## e. Primary School

| Sl. No. | Units | Access to a Primary Education Facility within 1 km. | | Dependence for Primary Education Facility | | Full Satisfaction with Behaviour of Teachers in Govt./Aided School | Awareness of Mid-Day Meal Scheme | Utilise Mid-Day Meal (Among Aaware) | Extent of Full Satisfaction With | |
|---|---|---|---|---|---|---|---|---|---|---|
| | | Govt. School | Pvt. School | Govt. School | Pvt. School | | | | Quality of School Building | Quality of Toilet |
| 1 | Bongaigaon | 63 | 6 | 95** | 5** | 3** | 46** | # | 5** | 3** |
| 2 | Dhuburi | 100 | 18 | 98** | 2* | 28** | 21** | # | 11** | 9** |
| 3 | Dibrugarh | 59 | 29 | 68** | 32** | # | # | # | # | # |
| 4 | Hailakandi | 81 | 0 | 100** | 0** | 0** | 35** | # | 6** | 0** |
| 5 | Nagaon | 75 | 38 | 73** | 27** | 21** | 21** | # | 3** | 3** |
| 6 | North Cachar Hills | 85 | 31 | 90** | 10** | # | # | # | # | # |
| 7 | Sonitpur | 58 | 12 | 89** | 11** | 7** | 20** | # | 3** | 0** |
| 8 | Rural Average | 74 | 19 | 85 | 15 | 14 | 30 | 35* | 6 | 3 |
| 9 | Urban Average | 38 | 14 | 60 | 41 | # | # | # | # | # |
| 10 | State Average | NA | NA | 82 | 18 | 14 | 31 | 31 | 6 | 2 |

### *f. Child Care System*

| *Sl. No.* | *Units* | *Anganwadis within 1 km.* | *Usage of Anganwadis* |
|---|---|---|---|
| 1 | Bongaigaon | 50 | # |
| 2 | Dhuburi | 24 | 11** |
| 3 | Dibrugarh | 29 | # |
| 4 | Hailakandi | 38 | # |
| 5 | Nagaon | 81 | 40* |
| 6 | North Cachar Hills | 8 | # |
| 7 | Sonitpur | 65 | 39** |
| 8 | Rural Average | 43 | 30 |

## III.4: Bihar

### a. Drinking Water

| Sl No. | Units | Use of Public Protected Source | Use of Private Protected Source | Public Protected Source within 100 Metres | Breakdown of Public Handpumps within 3 Months | Households Involved in Maintenance | Willingness to Pay More | Full Satisfaction with Public Drinking Water Facilities Other Protected Public Sources | |
|---|---|---|---|---|---|---|---|---|---|
| | | | | | | | | Adequacy of Supply | Quality of Water |
| 1 | Aurangabad | 35 | 48 | 29 | 44* | 35* | 68 | 37* | 40* |
| 2 | Jehanabad | 15 | 75 | 14 | 17** | 63** | 57 | 0** | 0** |
| 3 | Nawada | 37 | 35 | 32 | 33* | 49* | 43 | 0* | 11* |
| 4 | Saharsa | 10 | 78 | 10 | # | # | 37 | # | # |
| 5 | Samastipur | 14 | 62 | 12 | # | # | 18 | # | # |
| 6 | Saran | 7 | 83 | 6 | # | # | 31 | # | # |
| 7 | Vaishali | 5 | 82 | 5 | # | # | 20 | # | # |
| 8 | Rural Average | 18 | 66 | 15 | 34 | 43 | 47 | 20 | 28 |
| 9 | Urban Average | 19 | 75 | 19 | # | # | 58 | 18 | 28 |
| 10 | State Average | 18 | 68 | 16 | 34 | 46 | 50 | 19 | 28 |

## *b. Health Care*

| Sl. No. | Units | Health Facility within 1 km. | Dependence for Minor Ailments | | Dependence for Major Ailments | | Presence in Government Health Facilities of | | Paid for Medical Services Availed (Out-Patients) | Full Satisfaction of Out-Patients with Behaviour of | |
|---|---|---|---|---|---|---|---|---|---|---|---|
| | | | Govt. Facility | Pvt. Hospitals | Govt. Facility | Pvt. Hospitals | Doctors | Paramedics | | Doctors | Paramedics |
| 1 | Aurangabad | 6 | 1 | 5 | 3 | 82 | # | # | # | # | # |
| 2 | Jehanabad | 29 | 3 | 5 | 3 | 86 | # | # | # | # | # |
| 3 | Nawada | 35 | 7 | 0 | 23 | 25 | # | # | # | # | # |
| 4 | Saharsa | 6 | 11 | 26 | 14 | 34 | # | # | # | # | # |
| 5 | Samastipur | 17 | 2 | 5 | 13 | 61 | # | # | # | # | # |
| 6 | Saran | 31 | 1 | 11 | 11 | 46 | # | # | # | # | # |
| 7 | Vaishali | 17 | 6 | 19 | 4 | 44 | # | # | # | # | # |
| 8 | Rural Average | 21 | 5 | 10 | 10 | 53 | # | # | # | # | # |
| 9 | Urban Average | 17 | 15 | 23 | 21 | 39 | # | # | # | # | # |
| 10 | State Average | NA | 7 | 14 | 13 | 49 | 79 | 89 | 13 | 8 | 5 |

## *c. Road Transport*

| *Sl. No.* | *Units* | *Access to Cement/Tarred Road within 1 km.* | *Availability within 1 km. of* | | | *Usage of Transport Facility* | | *Full Satisfaction With* | | |
|---|---|---|---|---|---|---|---|---|---|---|
| | | | *Bus Stops* | *Public Bus* | *Private Bus* | *Public Bus* | *Private Bus* | *Punctuality of Govt. Buses* | *Frequency of Govt. Buses* | *Behaviour of Bus Conductors* |
| 1 | Aurangabad | 6 | 6 | 0 | 29 | 0 | 34 | # | # | # |
| 2 | Jehanabad | 25 | 24 | 0 | 50 | 0 | 43 | # | # | # |
| 3 | Nawada | 33 | 15 | 5 | 52 | 0 | 29 | # | # | # |
| 4 | Saharsa | 24 | 6 | 0 | 53 | 0 | 17 | # | # | # |
| 5 | Samastipur | 6 | 17 | 6 | 71 | 0 | 21 | # | # | # |
| 6 | Saran | 19 | 6 | 6 | 59 | 1 | 28 | # | # | # |
| 7 | Vaishali | 44 | 44 | 0 | 47 | 0 | 50 | # | # | # |
| 8 | Rural Average | 23 | 17 | 2 | 52 | 0 | 32 | # | # | # |
| 9 | Urban Average | - | - | 7 | 68 | 0 | 32 | # | # | # |
| 10 | State Average | NA | NA | NA | NA | 0 | 32 | # | # | # |

## *d. Public Distribution System*

| *Sl. No.* | *Units* | *PDS Outlet within 1 km.* | *Households Possessing Own Ration Card* | *Use of PDS by Card Owners at Least Once in 2 Months* | *Reliability of PDS Facilities* | | *Extent of Full Satisfaction With* | | |
|---|---|---|---|---|---|---|---|---|---|
| | | | | | *Regular Availability of Staple Foodgrain* | *Price Always Displayed* | *Quantity of Supplies* | *Quality of Supplies* | *Fairness of Shopkeepers* |
| 1 | Aurangabad | 63 | 89 | 89 | 0 | 11 | 1 | 14 | 1 |
| 2 | Jehanabad | 41 | 94 | 93 | 2 | 60 | 3 | 13 | 7 |
| 3 | Nawada | 55 | 80 | 37 | 0 | 52 | 0 | 2 | 0 |
| 4 | Saharsa | 24 | 71 | 53 | 1 | 58 | 4 | 28 | 21 |
| 5 | Samastipur | 44 | 91 | 92 | 1 | 62 | 1 | 1 | 0 |
| 6 | Saran | 63 | 86 | 76 | 0 | 32 | 7 | 19 | 16 |
| 7 | Vaishali | 78 | 79 | 78 | 4 | 37 | 16 | 22 | 16 |
| 8 | Rural Average | 53 | 84 | 74 | 1 | 44 | 4 | 14 | 9 |
| 9 | Urban Average | 87 | 79 | 77 | 1 | 54 | 10 | 17 | 13 |
| 10 | State Average | NA | 83 | 75 | 1 | 47 | 6 | 15 | 10 |

## e. Primary School

| Sl. No. | Units | Access to a Primary Education Facility | | Dependence for Education Facility | | Full Satisfaction with Behaviour of Teachers in Govt./Aided School | Awareness of Mid-Day Meal Scheme | Utilise Mid-Day Meal (Among Aware) | Extent of Full Satisfaction With | |
|---|---|---|---|---|---|---|---|---|---|---|
| | | Govt. School | Pvt. School | Govt. School | Pvt. School | | | | Quality of School Building | Quality of Toilet |
| 1 | Aurangabad | 94 | 29 | 82* | 18* | 22* | 52* | # | 8* | 0* |
| 2 | Jehanabad | 83 | 33 | 75* | 25* | 2** | # | # | 0** | 0** |
| 3 | Nawada | 76 | 38 | 61** | 39** | 3** | # | # | 0** | 0** |
| 4 | Saharsa | 77 | 29 | 84** | 16** | 9** | # | # | 0** | 0** |
| 5 | Samastipur | 82 | 41 | 95* | 25* | 4** | # | # | 4** | 4** |
| 6 | Saran | 71 | 41 | 58* | 42* | 11** | # | # | 5** | 0** |
| 7 | Vaishali | 79 | 37 | 63** | 37** | 6** | # | # | 6** | 0** |
| 8 | Rural Average | 80 | 36 | 74 | 26 | 9 | 38 | 54 | 3 | 1 |
| 9 | Urban Average | 44 | 38 | 54 | 46 | 12* | 37* | # | 10* | 5* |
| 10 | State Average | N.A | N.A | 70 | 30 | 9 | 38 | 54 | 4 | 1 |

*f. Child Care System*

| *Sl. No.* | *Units* | *Access of Anganwadis within 1 km.* | *Usage of Anganwadis* |
|---|---|---|---|
| 1 | Aurangabad | 31 | 10** |
| 2 | Jehanabad | 0 | # |
| 3 | Nawada | 60 | 6* |
| 4 | Saharsa | 29 | # |
| 5 | Samastipur | 33 | 13** |
| 6 | Saran | 13 | # |
| 7 | Vaishali | 50 | 8** |
| 8 | Rural Average | 32 | 8 |

## III.5: Gujarat

### a. Drinking Water

| Sl. No. | Units | Use of Public Protected Source | Use of Private Protected Source | Public Protected Source within 100 Metres | Breakdown of Public Handpumps within 3 Months | Households Involved in Maintenance | Willingness to Pay More | Full Satisfaction with Public Drinking Water Facilities | | | |
|---|---|---|---|---|---|---|---|---|---|---|---|
| | | | | | | | | Piped Supply | | Other Protected Public Sources | |
| | | | | | | | | Adequacy of Supply | Quality of Water | Adequacy of Supply | Quality of Water |
| 1 | Ahmedabad | 81 | 4 | 81 | # | # | 22 | 62 | 76 | # | # |
| 2 | Banaskantha | 76 | 4 | 70 | # | 37** | 29 | 50 | 52 | 32** | 39** |
| 3 | Bhavnagar | 42 | 10 | 27 | # | 25* | 47 | # | # | 22* | 40* |
| 4 | Kutchh | 60 | 3 | 57 | # | 27** | 42 | 35* | 51* | 23** | 42** |
| 5 | Sabarkantha | 71 | 4 | 62 | 23* | 31* | 36 | 56* | 66* | 37* | 53* |
| 6 | Vadodara | 89 | 1 | 82 | 16* | 26 | 24 | 31 | 52 | 40 | 55 |
| 7 | Rural Average | 70 | 4 | 63 | 20 | 28 | 31 | 48 | 62 | 33 | 49 |
| 8 | Urban Average | 89 | 1 | 88 | # | 19* | 30 | 41 | 60 | 30* | 38* |
| 9 | State Average | 75 | 4 | 70 | 21 | 26 | 31 | 46 | 61 | 33 | 47 |

## *b. Health Care*

| Sl. No. | Units | Health Facility within 1 km. | Dependence for Minor Ailments | | Dependence for Major Ailments | | Presence in Government Health Facilities of | | Paid for Medical Services Availed (Out-Patients) | Full Satisfaction of Out-Patients with Behaviour of | |
|---|---|---|---|---|---|---|---|---|---|---|---|
| | | | Govt. Facility | Pvt. Hospitals | Govt. Facility | Pvt. Hospitals | Doctors | Paramedics | | Doctors | Paramedics |
| 1 | Ahmedabad | 47 | 38 | 12 | 55 | 44 | 97* | 99* | 9* | 23* | 21* |
| 2 | Banaskantha | 24 | 48 | 15 | 56 | 40 | 97* | 96* | 40* | 33* | 32* |
| 3 | Bhavnagar | 35 | 42 | 12 | 61 | 38 | 90* | 95* | 28* | 29* | 22* |
| 4 | Kutchh | 33 | 52 | 14 | 61 | 38 | 96 | 95 | 20 | 39 | 30 |
| 5 | Sabarkantha | 29 | 50 | 13 | 56 | 41 | 95 | 95 | 26 | 30 | 30 |
| 6 | Vadodara | 47 | 40 | 17 | 68 | 27 | 89* | 91* | 27* | 32* | 27* |
| 7 | Rural Average | 36 | 45 | 14 | 59 | 38 | 94 | 95 | 25 | 31 | 27 |
| 8 | Urban Average | 43 | 38 | 9 | 54 | 45 | 98 | 99 | 22 | 28 | 25 |
| 9 | State Average | N.A | 43 | 13 | 58 | 40 | 95 | 96 | 24 | 30 | 27 |

## c. Road Transport

| Sl. No. | Units | Access to Cement/Tarred Road within 1 km. | Availability within 1 km. of | | | Usage of Transport Facility | | Full Satisfaction With | | |
|---|---|---|---|---|---|---|---|---|---|---|
| | | | Bus Stops | Public Bus | Private Bus | Public Bus | Private Bus | Punctuality of Govt. Buses | Frequency of Govt. Buses | Behaviour of Bus Conductors |
| 1 | Ahmedabad | 71 | 65 | 82 | 35 | 81 | 0 | 50 | 49 | 44 |
| 2 | Banaskantha | 82 | 94 | 94 | 88 | 66 | 0 | 40 | 35 | 40 |
| 3 | Bhavnagar | 65 | 65 | 100 | 65 | 66 | 0 | 41 | 37 | 35 |
| 4 | Kutchh | 50 | 78 | 94 | 56 | 84 | 0 | 45 | 38 | 38 |
| 5 | Sabarkantha | 65 | 53 | 95 | 95 | 80 | 0 | 43 | 42 | 39 |
| 6 | Vadodara | 65 | 82 | 94 | 88 | 60 | 0 | 46 | 40 | 44 |
| 7 | Rural Average | 66 | 73 | 93 | 66 | 73 | 0 | 45 | 40 | 40 |
| 8 | Urban Average | NA | NA | 88 | 41 | 52 | 0 | 36 | 38 | 32 |
| 9 | State Average | NA | NA | NA | NA | 67 | 0 | 43 | 40 | 38 |

## *d. Public Distribution System*

| Sl. No. | Units | PDS Outlet within 1 km. | Households Possessing Own Ration Card | Use of PDS by Card Owners at Least Once in 2 Months | Reliability of PDS Facilities | | Extent of Full Satisfaction With | | |
|---|---|---|---|---|---|---|---|---|---|
| | | | | | Regular Availability of Staple Foodgrain | Price Always Displayed | Quantity of Supplies | Quality of Supplies | Fairness of Shopkeeper |
| 1 | Ahmedabad | 65 | 92 | 88 | 35 | 81 | 11 | 11 | 11 |
| 2 | Banaskantha | 47 | 93 | 83 | 45 | 88 | 22 | 23 | 28 |
| 3 | Bhavnagar | 59 | 94 | 92 | 40 | 76 | 10 | 9 | 10 |
| 4 | Kutchh | 44 | 96 | 96 | 58 | 77 | 9 | 11 | 15 |
| 5 | Sabarkantha | 65 | 94 | 91 | 42 | 90 | 17 | 16 | 16 |
| 6 | Vadodara | 65 | 91 | 87 | 38 | 66 | 9 | 9 | 13 |
| 7 | Rural Average | 57 | 93 | 89 | 44 | 80 | 13 | 13 | 15 |
| 8 | Urban Average | 89 | 94 | 75 | 31 | 77 | 8 | 9 | 11 |
| 9 | State Average | NA | 93 | 86 | 41 | 79 | 12 | 12 | 14 |

## *e. Primary School*

| Sl. No. | Units | Access to a Primary Education Facility | | Dependence for Education Facility | | Full Satisfaction with Behaviour of Teachers in Govt./Aided School | Awareness of Mid-Day Meal Scheme | Utilise Mid-Day Meal (Among Aware) | Extent of Full Satisfaction With | |
|---|---|---|---|---|---|---|---|---|---|---|
| | | Govt. School | Pvt. School | Govt. School | Pvt. School | | | | Quality of School Building | Quality of Toilet |
| 1 | Ahmedabad | 96 | 24 | 96* | 5* | 20* | 100* | 94* | 19* | 9* |
| 2 | Banaskantha | 97 | 29 | 97* | 3* | 28* | 96* | 86* | 28* | 14* |
| 3 | Bhavnagar | 94 | 29 | 94* | 6* | 20* | 96* | 82* | 23* | 4* |
| 4 | Kutchh | 89 | 33 | 89* | 11* | 17* | 95* | 84** | 9* | 2* |
| 5 | Sabarkantha | 95 | 28 | 95* | 5* | 21** | 95** | 89** | 34** | 7** |
| 6 | Vadodara | 87 | 25 | 87* | 13* | 40** | 83** | 93** | 37** | 14** |
| 7 | Rural Average | 93 | 28 | 93 | 7 | 24 | 94 | 88 | 24 | 8 |
| 8 | Urban Average | 56 | 21 | 64 | 36 | 18* | 83* | 84* | 12* | 10* |
| 9 | State Average | NA | NA | 86 | 14 | 23 | 92 | 87 | 22 | 9 |

*f. Anganwadi*

| *Sl. No.* | *Units* | *Access of Anganwadis within 1 km.* | *Usage of Anganwadis* |
|---|---|---|---|
| 1 | Ahmedabad | 94 | 46 |
| 2 | Banaskantha | 82 | 16 |
| 3 | Bhavnagar | 77 | 54 |
| 4 | Kutchh | 83 | 41 |
| 5 | Sabarkantha | 88 | 42 |
| 6 | Vadodara | 88 | 41 |
| 7 | Rural Average | 85 | 40 |

## III.6: Haryana

### *a. Drinking Water*

| *Sl No.* | *Units* | *Use of Public Protected Source* | *Use of Private Protected Source* | *Public Protected Source within 100 Metres* | *Breakdown of Public Handpumps within 3 Months* | *Households Involved in Maintenance* | *Willingness to Pay More* | *Full Satisfaction with Public Drinking Water Facilities Other Protected Public Sources* | |
|---|---|---|---|---|---|---|---|---|---|
| | | | | | | | | *Adequacy of Supply* | *Quality of Water* |
| 1 | Sonipat | 41 | 45 | 34 | # | 25** | 27 | 48** | 50** |
| 2 | Mahendragarh | 63 | 12 | 32 | 10* | 16* | 80 | 22* | 31* |
| 3 | Hisar | 66 | 17 | 57 | 9** | 47* | 36 | 42* | 44* |
| 4 | Yamunanagar | 31 | 59 | 29 | 24** | 50** | 24 | 25** | 46** |
| 5 | Panipat | 41 | 41 | 39 | 41** | 47** | 24 | 39** | 56** |
| 6 | Gurgaon | 37 | 17 | 30 | 35** | 37** | 68 | 27** | 41** |
| 7 | Rural Average | 47 | 31 | 37 | 21 | 36 | 46 | 34 | 44 |
| 8 | Urban Average | 57 | 35 | 51 | 34* | 9 | 41 | 20 | 33 |
| 9 | State Average | 50 | 33 | 42 | 23 | 30 | 44 | 31 | 41 |

## b. Health Care

| Sl. No. | Units | Health Facility within 1 km. | Dependence for Minor Ailments | | Dependence for Major Ailments | | Presence in Government Health Facilities of | | Paid for Medical Services Availed (Out-Patients) | Full Satisfaction of Out-Patients with Behaviour of | |
|---|---|---|---|---|---|---|---|---|---|---|---|
| | | | Govt. Facility | Pvt. Hospitals | Govt. Facility | Pvt. Hospitals | Doctors | Paramedics | | Doctors | Paramedics |
| 1 | Sonipat | 50 | 15 | 6 | 33 | 31 | # | # | # | # | # |
| 2 | Mahendragarh | 32 | 6 | 4 | 10 | 62 | # | # | # | # | # |
| 3 | Hisar | 33 | 27 | 3 | 53 | 45 | 85** | 100** | 13** | 4** | 7** |
| 4 | Yamunanagar | 38 | 33 | 1 | 31 | 59 | 71** | 78** | 61** | 12** | 12** |
| 5 | Panipat | 35 | 33 | 3 | 39 | 59 | 53** | 76** | 18** | 25** | 25** |
| 6 | Gurgaon | 19 | 7 | 1 | 7 | 42 | # | # | # | # | # |
| 7 | Rural Average | 35 | 20 | 3 | 29 | 50 | 69 | 81 | 16 | 15 | 13 |
| 8 | Urban Average | 21 | 28 | 11 | 27 | 59 | 84 | 86 | 10 | 11 | 11 |
| 9 | State Average | NA | 23 | 5 | 28 | 53 | 75 | 83 | 14 | 14 | 12 |

## c. Road Transport

| Sl. No. | Units | Access to Cement/Tarred Road within 1 km. | Availability within 1 km. of | | | Usage of Transport Facility | | Full Satisfaction with | | |
|---|---|---|---|---|---|---|---|---|---|---|
| | | | Bus Stops | Public Bus | Private Bus | Public Bus | Private Bus | Punctuality of Govt. Buses | Frequency of Govt. Buses | Behaviour of Bus Conductors |
| 1 | Sonipat | 75 | 50 | 57 | 50 | 56 | 6 | 40* | 35* | 40* |
| 2 | Mahendragarh | 92 | 37 | 56 | 63 | 16 | 6 | # | # | # |
| 3 | Hisar | 87 | 50 | 80 | 80 | 42 | 29 | 13* | 12* | 15* |
| 4 | Yamunanagar | 67 | 38 | 55 | 45 | 22 | 23 | 0** | 0** | 6** |
| 5 | Panipat | 87 | 35 | 67 | 75 | 44 | 9 | 13* | 14* | 13* |
| 6 | Gurgaon | 100 | 25 | 20 | 80 | 21 | 7 | 9** | 9** | 9** |
| 7 | Rural Average | 82 | 39 | 58 | 61 | 34 | 13 | 18 | 17 | 19 |
| 8 | Urban Average | NA | NA | 59 | 65 | 37 | 6 | 25 | 25 | 28 |
| 9 | State Average | NA | NA | NA | NA | 35 | 11 | 21 | 20 | 22 |

## *d. Public Distribution System*

| *Sl. No.* | *Units* | *PDS Outlet within 1 km.* | *Households Possessing Own Ration Card* | *Use of PDS by Card Owners at Least Once in 2 Months* | *Reliability of PDS Facilities* | | *Extent of Full Satisfaction With* | | |
|---|---|---|---|---|---|---|---|---|---|
| | | | | | *Regular Availability of Staple Foodgrain* | *Price Always Displayed* | *Quantity of Supplies* | *Quality of Supplies* | *Fairness of Shopkeeper* |
| 1 | Sonipat | 75 | 99 | 84 | 1 | 24 | 16 | 17 | 14 |
| 2 | Mahendragarh | 42 | 98 | 90 | 0 | 9 | 13 | 13 | 13 |
| 3 | Hisar | 50 | 98 | 97 | 2 | 29 | 9 | 8 | 8 |
| 4 | Yamunanagar | 47 | 100 | 74 | 2 | 26 | 4 | 3 | 3 |
| 5 | Panipat | 53 | 93 | 87 | 4 | 22 | 24 | 24 | 23 |
| 6 | Gurgaon | 56 | 91 | 73 | 0 | 6 | 1 | 1 | 1 |
| 7 | Rural Average | 53 | 96 | 84 | 2 | 19 | 12 | 11 | 11 |
| 8 | Urban Average | 92 | 94 | 87 | 2 | 25 | 5 | 5 | 5 |
| 9 | State Average | NA | 95 | 85 | 2 | 21 | 9 | 9 | 9 |

## *e. Primary School*

| Sl. No. | Units | *Access to a Primary Education Facility* | | *Dependence for Education Facility* | | *Full Satisfaction with Behaviour of Teachers in Govt./Aided School* | *Awareness of Mid-Day Meal Scheme* | *Utilise Mid-Day Meal (Among Aware)* | *Extent of Full Satisfaction With* | |
|---|---|---|---|---|---|---|---|---|---|---|
| | | *Govt. School* | *Pvt. School* | *Govt. School* | *Pvt. School* | | | | *Quality of School Building* | *Quality of Toilet* |
| 1 | Sonipat | 71 | 71 | 49** | 51** | # | # | # | # | # |
| 2 | Mahendragarh | 75 | 44 | 57** | 43** | # | # | # | # | # |
| 3 | Hisar | 100 | 40 | 66** | 34*** | 3** | # | # | 6** | 3** |
| 4 | Yamunanagar | 90 | 35 | 73** | 27** | # | # | # | # | # |
| 5 | Panipat | 75 | 50 | 58*** | 42** | # | # | # | # | # |
| 6 | Gurgaon | 60 | 20 | 76** | 24** | # | # | # | # | # |
| 7 | Rural Average | 81 | 46 | 63 | 37 | 6 | 80 | 72 | 4 | 1 |
| 8 | Urban Average | 32 | 52 | 38 | 62 | # | # | # | # | # |
| 9 | State Average | NA | NA | 56 | 44 | 5 | 76 | 72 | 5 | 3 |

## *f. Anganwadi*

| *Sl. No.* | *Units* | *Access of Anganwadis within 1 km..* | *Usage of Anganwadis* |
|---|---|---|---|
| 1 | Sonipat | 81 | 23** |
| 2 | Mahendragarh | 77 | 14** |
| 3 | Hisar | 94 | 41* |
| 4 | Yamunanagar | 84 | 47** |
| 5 | Panipat | 100 | 44* |
| 6 | Gurgaon | 63 | 6* |
| 7 | Rural Average | 84 | 29 |

## III.7: Himachal Pradesh

### a. Drinking Water

| Sl. No. | Units | Use of Public Protected Source | Use of Private Protected Source | Public Protected Source within 100 Metres | Breakdown of Public Handpumps within 3 Months | Households Involved in Maintenance | Willingness to Pay More | Full Satisfaction With Public Drinking Water Facilities | | | |
|---|---|---|---|---|---|---|---|---|---|---|---|
| | | | | | | | | Piped Supply | | Other Protected Public Sources | |
| | | | | | | | | Adequacy of Supply | Quality of Water | Adequacy of Supply | Quality of Water |
| 1 | Sirmaur | 89 | 0 | 87 | 9* | 26* | 44 | 31** | 33** | 34* | 44* |
| 2 | Kangra | 79 | 2 | 70 | 35* | 7* | 66 | 2** | 16** | 19* | 42* |
| 3 | Chamba | 72 | 3 | 59 | 35* | 1* | 41 | # | # | 34* | 71* |
| 4 | Hamirpur | 86 | 8 | 85 | 10* | 1* | 29 | 2* | 3* | 1* | 3* |
| 5 | Rural Average | 81 | 3 | 75 | 22 | 8 | 43 | 10 | 17 | 22 | 41 |
| 6 | Urban Average | 93 | 0 | 93 | 0 | 17 | 45 | 15 | 18 | 58 | 58 |
| 7 | State Average | 84 | 3 | 80 | 20 | 9 | 44 | 12 | 18 | 26 | 43 |

## b. Health Care

| Sl. No. | Units | Health Facility within 1 km. | Dependence for Minor Ailments | | Dependence for Major Ailments | | Presence in Government Health Facilities of | | Paid for Medical Services Availed (Out-Patients) | Full Satisfaction of Out-Patients with Behaviour of | |
|---|---|---|---|---|---|---|---|---|---|---|---|
| | | | Govt. Facility | Pvt. Hospitals | Govt. Facility | Pvt. Hospitals | Doctors | Paramedics | | Doctors | Paramedics |
| 1 | Sirmaur | 60 | 63 | 1 | 80 | 20 | 58* | 92* | 26 | 5* | 7* |
| 2 | Kangra | 47 | 21 | 1 | 27 | 63 | 91** | 85** | 9 | 30** | 24** |
| 3 | Chamba | 60 | 35 | 3 | 38 | 53 | 54** | 94** | 2 | 13** | 11** |
| 4 | Hamirpur | 46 | 66 | 1 | 66 | 33 | 99* | 100* | 5 | 5* | 2* |
| 5 | Rural Average | 53 | 45 | 2 | 51 | 44 | 76 | 94 | 11 | 10 | 8 |
| 6 | Urban Average | 59 | 66 | 10 | 76 | 14 | 90 | 97 | 19 | 9 | 6 |
| 7 | State Average | NA | 51 | 4 | 58 | 36 | 80 | 95 | 14 | 10 | 8 |

## *c. Road Transport*

| *Sl. No.* | *Units* | *Access to Cement/Tarred Road within 1 km.* | *Availability within 1 km. of* | | | *Usage of Transport Facility* | | *Full Satisfaction With* | | |
|---|---|---|---|---|---|---|---|---|---|---|
| | | | *Bus Stops* | *Public Bus* | *Private Bus* | *Public Bus* | *Private Bus* | *Punctuality of Govt. Buses* | *Frequency of Govt. Buses* | *Behaviour of Bus Conductors* |
| 1 | Sirmaur | 60 | 60 | 85 | 75 | 73 | 13 | 7* | 4* | 5* |
| 2 | Kangra | 33 | 53 | 62 | 62 | 29 | 33 | 22** | 4** | 24** |
| 3 | Chamba | 27 | 33 | 69 | 75 | 46 | 30 | 19* | 18* | 22* |
| 4 | Hamirpur | 82 | 36 | 88 | 95 | 21 | 74 | 0** | 0** | 3** |
| 5 | Rural Average | 47 | 45 | 76 | 77 | 40 | 39 | 13 | 8 | 13 |
| 6 | Urban Average | NA | NA | 86 | 88 | 70 | 15 | 20 | 21 | 14 |
| 7 | State Average | NA | NA | NA | NA | 48 | 33 | 15 | 12 | 14 |

### *d. Public Distribution System*

| Sl. No. | Units | PDS Outlet within 1 km. | Households Possessing Own Ration Card | Use of PDS by Card Owners at Least Once in 2 Months | Reliability of PDS Facilities | | Extent of Full Satisfaction With | | |
|---|---|---|---|---|---|---|---|---|---|
| | | | | | Regular Availability of Staple Foodgrain | Price Always Displayed | Quantity of Supplies | Quality of Supplies | Fairness of Shopkeeper |
| 1 | Sirmaur | 40 | 99 | 85 | 21 | 73 | 8 | 8 | 9 |
| 2 | Kangra | 47 | 96 | 76 | 2 | 23 | 11 | 11 | 11 |
| 3 | Chamba | 53 | 98 | 83 | 1 | 30 | 5 | 6 | 6 |
| 4 | Hamirpur | 46 | 99 | 99 | 19 | 83 | 0 | 1 | 1 |
| 5 | Rural Average | 47 | 98 | 86 | 11 | 54 | 6 | 6 | 6 |
| 6 | Urban Average | 83 | 86 | 70 | 11 | 76 | 8 | 6 | 6 |
| 7 | State Average | NA | 95 | 82 | 11 | 58 | 6 | 6 | 6 |

## *e. Primary School*

| Sl. No. | Units | Access to a Primary Education Facility | | Dependence for Education Facility | | Full Satisfaction with Behaviour of Teachers in Govt./Aided School | Awareness of Mid-Day Meal Scheme | Utilise Mid-Day Meal (Among Aware) | Extent of Full Satisfaction With | |
|---|---|---|---|---|---|---|---|---|---|---|
| | | Govt. School | Pvt. School | Govt. School | Pvt. School | | | | Quality of School Building | Quality of Toilet |
| 1 | Sirmaur | 60 | 10 | 90** | 10** | 13** | 97** | # | 10** | 10** |
| 2 | Kangra | 83 | 17 | 74** | 26** | # | # | # | # | # |
| 3 | Chamba | 86 | 14 | 93** | 7** | 8** | 100** | 93** | 3** | 0** |
| 4 | Hamirpur | 71 | 33 | 76** | 24** | # | # | # | # | # |
| 5 | Rural Average | 75 | 22 | 86 | 14 | 7 | # | 89* | 4 | 3 |
| 6 | Urban Average | 38 | 31 | 55** | 45** | 4 | 96 | 82 | 4 | 4 |
| 7 | State Average | NA | NA | 83 | 17 | 6 | 95 | 88 | 4 | 3 |

## *f. Child Care System*

| Sl. No. | Units | Access of Anganwadis within 1 km. | Usage of Anganwadis |
|---|---|---|---|
| 1 | Sirmaur | 70 | 41** |
| 2 | Kangra | 80 | # |
| 3 | Chamba | 60 | 39** |
| 4 | Hamirpur | 73 | 30** |
| 5 | Rural Average | 71 | 32 |

## III.8: Karnataka

### *a. Drinking Water*

| Sl. No. | Units | Use of Public Protected Source | Use of Private Protected Source | Public Protected Source within 100 Metres | Breakdown of Public Taps within 3 Months | Breakdown of Public Handpumps within 3 Months | Households Involved in Maintenance | Willingness to Pay More | Full Satisfaction with Public Drinking Water Facilities: Piped Supply | | Full Satisfaction with Public Drinking Water Facilities: Other Protected Public Source | |
|---|---|---|---|---|---|---|---|---|---|---|---|---|
| | | | | | | | | | Adequacy of Supply | Quality of Water | Adequacy of Supply | Quality of Water |
| 1 | Belgaum | 65 | 2 | 49 | 34 | 16 | 4 | 41 | 12 | 24 | 25 | 29 |
| 2 | Bijapur | 74 | 1 | 64 | 16 | 13 | 13 | 60 | 25 | 25 | 13 | 18 |
| 3 | Bellary | 81 | 6 | 75 | 14 | 58 | 40 | 44 | 63 | 67 | 53 | 65 |
| 4 | Gulbarga | 77 | 2 | 70 | 37 | 15 | 36 | 62 | 33 | 37 | 40 | 36 |
| 5 | Chikkamaglur | 86 | 2 | 85 | 13 | 14 | 6 | 44 | 68 | 68 | 35 | 43 |
| 6 | Kodagu | 50 | 4 | 50 | 21 | 7 | 32 | 74 | 47 | 53 | 62 | 68 |
| 7 | Bangalore | 84 | 9 | 79 | 16 | 40 | 32 | 51 | 28 | 36 | 36 | 50 |
| 8 | Mandya | 94 | 2 | 92 | 32 | 35 | 33 | 66 | 46 | 71 | 54 | 67 |
| 9 | Rural Average | 77 | 3 | 71 | 21 | 21 | 25 | 55 | 41 | 52 | 38 | 47 |
| 10 | Urban Average | 81 | 3 | 70 | 14 | 26 | 18 | 62 | 23 | 32 | 22 | 39 |
| 11 | State Average | 79 | 3 | 71 | 19 | 22 | 23 | 57 | 35 | 45 | 34 | 45 |

## *b. Health Care*

| Sl. No. | Units | Health Facility within 1 km. | Dependence for Minor Ailments | | Dependence for Major Ailments | | Presence in Government Health Facilities of | | Paid for Medical Services Availed (Out-Patients) | Full Satisfaction of Out-Patients with Behaviour of | |
|---|---|---|---|---|---|---|---|---|---|---|---|
| | | | Govt. Facility | Pvt. Hospitals | Govt. Facility | Pvt. Hospitals | Doctors | Paramedics | | Doctors | Paramedics |
| 1 | Belgaum | 29 | 33 | 22 | 42 | 54 | 74 | 100 | 28 | 4 | 11 |
| 2 | Bijapur | 18 | 28 | 12 | 33 | 58 | 78 | 98 | 28 | 9 | 7 |
| 3 | Bellary | 13 | 52 | 7 | 52 | 39 | 67 | 76 | 27 | 54 | 27 |
| 4 | Gulbarga | 41 | 53 | 5 | 62 | 35 | 26 | 95 | 7 | 2 | 0 |
| 5 | Chikkamaglur | 21 | 51 | 9 | 56 | 42 | 84 | 96 | 16 | 20 | 16 |
| 6 | Kodagu | 13 | 65 | 16 | 61 | 36 | 70 | 79 | 21 | 52 | 43 |
| 7 | Bangalore | 25 | 45 | 19 | 39 | 37 | 71 | 97 | 19 | 26 | 19 |
| 8 | Mandya | 44 | 68 | 15 | 53 | 44 | 88 | 92 | 21 | 44 | 41 |
| 9 | Rural Average | 26 | 49 | 13 | 50 | 46 | 70 | 91 | 20 | 30 | 26 |
| 10 | Urban Average | 46 | 45 | 16 | 47 | 48 | 87 | 99 | 17 | 33 | 30 |
| 11 | State Average | NA | 48 | 14 | 49 | 46 | 74 | 93 | 19 | 31 | 27 |

## *c. Road Transport*

| *Sl. No.* | *Units* | *Access to Cement/Tarred Road within 1 km.* | *Availability within 1 km. of* | | | *Usage of Transport Facility* | | *Full Satisfaction With* | | |
|---|---|---|---|---|---|---|---|---|---|---|
| | | | *Bus Stops* | *Public Bus* | *Private Bus* | *Public Bus* | *Private Bus* | *Punctuality of Govt. Buses* | *Frequency of Govt. Buses* | *Behaviour of Bus Conductors* |
| 1 | Belgaum | 29 | 71 | 94 | 6 | 60 | 6 | 11 | 9 | 9 |
| 2 | Bijapur | 71 | 71 | 94 | 12 | 82 | 2 | 16 | 13 | 18 |
| 3 | Bellary | 31 | 38 | 94 | 6 | 76 | 19 | 25 | 23 | 31 |
| 4 | Gulbarga | 24 | 59 | 100 | - | 100 | 0 | 21 | 23 | 16 |
| 5 | Chikkamaglur | 50 | 79 | 79 | 57 | 32 | 59 | 11 | 5 | 27 |
| 6 | Kodagu | 46 | 47 | 67 | 47 | 11 | 74 | 7 | 7 | 0 |
| 7 | Bangalore | 75 | 81 | 100 | - | 98 | 1 | 27 | 29 | 28 |
| 8 | Mandya | 50 | 77 | 94 | 6 | 22 | 71 | 17 | 20 | 22 |
| 9 | Rural Average | 47 | 65 | 91 | 16 | 62 | 27 | 20 | 19 | 21 |
| 10 | Urban Average | NA | NA | 100 | 33 | 72 | 13 | 26 | 25 | 28 |
| 11 | State Average | NA | NA | 91 | 16 | 65 | 24 | 22 | 21 | 23 |

## *d. Public Distribution System*

| Sl. No. | Units | PDS Outlet within 1 km. | Households Possessing Own Ration Card | Use of PDS by Card Owners at Least Once in 2 Months | Reliability of PDS Facilities | | Extent of Full Satisfaction With | | |
|---|---|---|---|---|---|---|---|---|---|
| | | | | | Regular Availability of Staple Foodgrain | Price Always Displayed | Quantity of Supplies | Quality of Supplies | Fairness of Shopkeeper |
| 1 | Belgaum | 59 | 94 | 98 | 59 | 23 | 0 | 6 | 8 |
| 2 | Bijapur | 88 | 78 | 88 | 62 | 16 | 4 | 9 | 13 |
| 3 | Bellary | 50 | 70 | 96 | 16 | 15 | 2 | 13 | 15 |
| 4 | Gulbarga | 82 | 82 | 91 | 55 | 14 | 23 | 23 | 23 |
| 5 | Chikkamaglur | 43 | 88 | 99 | 54 | 43 | 1 | 5 | 12 |
| 6 | Kodagu | 47 | 80 | 97 | 36 | 53 | 6 | 36 | 47 |
| 7 | Bangalore | 88 | 83 | 97 | 61 | 60 | 16 | 17 | 27 |
| 8 | Mandya | 75 | 90 | 99 | 54 | 40 | 14 | 24 | 31 |
| 9 | Rural Average | 67 | 83 | 96 | 51 | 33 | 9 | 16 | 21 |
| 10 | Urban Average | 81 | 69 | 81 | 31 | 46 | 2 | 5 | 14 |
| 11 | State Average | NA | 79 | 93 | 47 | 36 | 7 | 14 | 20 |

## e. Primary School

| Sl. No. | Units | Access to a Primary Education Facility | | Dependence for Education Facility | | Full Satisfaction with Behaviour of Teachers in Govt./Aided School | Awareness of Mid-Day Meal Scheme | Utilise Mid-Day Meal (Among Aware) | Extent of Full Satisfaction With | |
|---|---|---|---|---|---|---|---|---|---|---|
| | | Govt. School | Pvt. School | Govt. School | Pvt. School | | | | Quality of School Building | Quality of Toilet |
| 1 | Belgaum | 94 | 18 | 94 | 6 | 9 | 91 | 100 | 13 | 2 |
| 2 | Bijapur | 94 | 12 | 95 | 5 | 9 | 95 | 100 | 7 | 0 |
| 3 | Bellary | 94 | 6 | 95 | 5 | 33 | 98 | 100 | 35 | 2 |
| 4 | Gulbarga | 88 | 35 | 88 | 12 | 14 | 56 | # | 17 | 0 |
| 5 | Chikkamaglur | 79 | 14 | 93 | 7 | 25 | 97 | 100 | 10 | 10 |
| 6 | Kodagu | 60 | 13 | 90 | 10 | 67 | 97 | # | 50 | 27 |
| 7 | Bangalore | 69 | 50 | 48 | 52 | 20 | # | # | # | # |
| 8 | Mandya | 77 | 59 | 65 | 35 | 44 | 91 | # | 34 | 13 |
| 9 | Rural Average | 82 | 26 | 85 | 16 | 25 | 89 | 100 | 21 | 6 |
| 10 | Urban Average | 53 | 15 | 70 | 30 | 29 | 91 | 100 | 28 | 8 |
| 11 | State Average | NA | NA | 80 | 20 | 26 | 90 | 100 | 23 | 7 |

### *f. Child Care System*

| *Sl. No.* | *Units* | *Access of Anganwadis within 1 km.* | *Usage of Anganwadis* |
|---|---|---|---|
| 1 | Belgaum | 88 | 63 |
| 2 | Bijapur | 94 | 56 |
| 3 | Bellary | 100 | 39 |
| 4 | Gulbarga | 100 | 12 |
| 5 | Chikkamaglur | 64 | 56 |
| 6 | Kodagu | 94 | 53 |
| 7 | Bangalore | 93 | 23 |
| 8 | Mandya | 100 | 36 |
| 9 | Rural Average | 92 | 40 |

## III.9: Kerala

### a. Drinking Water

| Sl. No. | Units | Use of Public Protected Source | Use of Private Protected Source | Public Protected Source within 100 Metres | Breakdown of Public Handpumps within 3 Months | Households Involved in Maintenance | Willingness to Pay More | Full Satisfaction With Public Drinking Water Facilities | | | |
|---|---|---|---|---|---|---|---|---|---|---|---|
| | | | | | | | | Piped Supply | | Other Protected Public Sources | |
| | | | | | | | | Adequacy of Supply | Quality of Water | Adequacy of Supply | Quality of Water |
| 1 | Idukki | 27 | 14 | 24 | # | # | 14 | # | # | # | # |
| 2 | Kannur | 3* | 1* | 3* | # | # | 0* | # | # | # | # |
| 3 | Kasargod | 5 | 3 | 2 | # | # | 13 | # | # | # | # |
| 4 | Palakkad | 54 | 4 | 44 | 23* | 66* | 9 | # | # | 5* | 9* |
| 5 | Pathanamthitta | 8 | 1 | 8 | # | # | 38 | # | # | # | # |
| 6 | Thiruvananthapuram | 19 | 7 | 19 | # | # | 10 | # | # | # | # |
| 7 | Rural Average | 22 | 6 | 19 | 24 | 57 | 12 | 19** | 19** | 16 | 17 |
| 8 | Urban Average | 42 | 10 | 42 | 10 | 73 | 22 | 14 | 23 | 7 | 9 |
| 9 | State Average | 30 | 7 | 28 | 17 | 65 | 17 | 16 | 22 | 12 | 13 |

## b. Health Care

| Sl. No. | Units | Health Facility within 1 km. | Dependence for Minor Ailments | | Dependence for Major Ailments | | Presence in Government Health Facilities of | | Paid for Medical Services Availed (Out-Patients) | Full Satisfaction of Out-Patients with Behaviour of | |
|---|---|---|---|---|---|---|---|---|---|---|---|
| | | | Govt. Facility | Pvt. Hospitals | Govt. Facility | Pvt. Hospitals | Doctors | Paramedics | | Doctors | Paramedics |
| 1 | Idukki | 44 | 33 | 63 | 21 | 76 | 43** | 87** | 23** | 9** | 9** |
| 2 | Kannur | 75 | 92* | 8* | 63* | 35* | 41** | 96** | 2** | 4** | 6** |
| 3 | Kasargod | 67 | 86 | 11 | 28 | 70 | 41 | 83 | 1 | 3 | 2 |
| 4 | Palakkad | 50 | 76 | 19 | 56 | 40 | 40 | 82 | 15 | 0 | 0 |
| 5 | Pathanamthitta | 60 | 39* | 60* | 35* | 64* | 76** | 98** | 14** | 19** | 19** |
| 6 | Thiruvananthapuram | 60 | 44 | 56 | 53 | 46 | 79** | 79** | 3** | 18** | 12** |
| 7 | Rural Average | 57 | 62 | 35 | 40 | 57 | 48 | 86 | 9 | 6 | 5 |
| 8 | Urban Average | 59 | 58 | 39 | 56 | 43 | 76 | 94 | 4 | 14 | 12 |
| 9 | State Average | NA | 60 | 37 | 46 | 52 | 58 | 89 | 7 | 9 | 8 |

## c. Road Transport

| Sl. No. | Units | Access to Cement/Tarred Road within 1 km. | Availability within 1 km. of | | | Usage of Transport Facility | | Full Satisfaction with | | |
|---|---|---|---|---|---|---|---|---|---|---|
| | | | Bus Stops | Public Bus | Private Bus | Public Bus | Private Bus | Punctuality of Govt. Buses | Frequency of Govt. Buses | Behaviour of Bus Conductors |
| 1 | Idukki | 89 | 78 | 67 | 100 | 3 | 89 | # | # | # |
| 2 | Kannur | 100 | 100 | 75 | 100 | 3 | 98 | # | # | # |
| 3 | Kasargod | 78 | 100 | 67 | 100 | 25 | 74 | 11** | 14** | 11** |
| 4 | Palakkad | 70 | 90 | 70 | 100 | 4 | 96 | # | # | # |
| 5 | Pathanamthitta | 100 | 60 | 100 | 100 | 12 | 82 | # | # | # |
| 6 | Thiruvananthapuram | 100 | 80 | 100 | 100 | 56 | 30 | 8* | 8* | 7* |
| 7 | Rural Average | 86 | 86 | 76 | 100 | 16 | 79 | 13 | 14 | 13 |
| 8 | Urban Average | NA | NA | 84 | 99 | 7 | 78 | 12 | 15 | 15 |
| 9 | State Average | NA | NA | NA | NA | 13 | 79 | 13 | 14 | 13 |

## d. Public Distribution System

| Sl. No. | Units | PDS Outlet within 1 km. | Households Possessing Own Ration Card | Use of PDS by Card Owners at Least Once in 2 Months | Reliability of PDS Facilities | | Extent of Full Satisfaction With | | |
|---|---|---|---|---|---|---|---|---|---|
| | | | | | Regular Availability of Staple Foodgrain | Price Always Displayed | Quantity of Supplies | Quality of Supplies | Fairness of Shopkeeper |
| 1 | Idukki | 67 | 80 | 79 | 53 | 75 | 3 | 2 | 4 |
| 2 | Kannur | 50 | 100* | 99* | 46* | 76* | 3* | 1* | 1* |
| 3 | Kasargod | 67 | 93 | 92 | 74 | 90 | 2 | 2 | 1 |
| 4 | Palakkad | 90 | 94 | 91 | 45 | 70 | 1 | 0 | 1 |
| 5 | Pathanamthitta | 60 | 95 | 87 | 28* | 81* | 4* | 3* | 2* |
| 6 | Thiruvananthapuram | 60 | 94 | 81 | 46* | 87* | 1* | 0* | 1* |
| 7 | Rural Average | 69 | 92 | 88 | 51 | 80 | 2 | 1 | 2 |
| 8 | Urban Average | 92 | 92 | 83 | 35 | 84 | 6 | 5 | 4 |
| 9 | State Average | | 92 | 86 | 45 | 81 | 4 | 3 | 3 |

### e. Primary School

| Sl. No. | Units | Access to a Primary Education Facility | | Dependence for Education Facility | | Full Satisfaction with Behaviour of Teachers in Govt./Aided School | Awareness of Mid-Day Meal Scheme | Utilise Mid-Day Meal (Among Aware) | Extent of Full Satisfaction With | |
|---|---|---|---|---|---|---|---|---|---|---|
| | | *Govt. School* | *Pvt. School* | *Govt. School* | *Pvt. School* | | | | *Quality of School Building* | *Quality of Toilet* |
| 1 | Idukki | 33 | 0 | 77 | 23 | 32** | 94** | # | 39** | 19** |
| 2 | Kannur | 75 | 25 | 88 | 12 | # | # | # | # | # |
| 3 | Kasargod | 100 | 33 | 87 | 13 | 11** | 98** | 100** | 11** | 6** |
| 4 | Palakkad | 70 | 30 | 81 | 19 | 2** | 100** | 98** | 5** | 0** |
| 5 | Pathanamthitta | 80 | 60 | 58 | 42 | # | # | # | # | # |
| 6 | Thiruvananthapuram | 100 | 20 | 89 | 11 | 32** | 94** | # | 23** | 16** |
| 7 | Rural Average | 75 | 26 | 83 | 18 | 16 | 96 | 99 | 15 | 8 |
| 8 | Urban Average | 22 | 18 | 58 | 42 | 19 | 93 | 100 | 16 | 15 |
| 9 | State Average | NA | NA | 74 | 26 | 17 | 95 | 99 | 16 | 10 |

## f. *Child Care System*

| *Sl. No.* | *Units* | *Access of Anganwadis within 1 km.* | *Usage of Anganwadis* |
|---|---|---|---|
| 1 | Idukki | 89 | 32** |
| 2 | Kannur | 50 | # |
| 3 | Kasargod | 67 | 30** |
| 4 | Palakkad | 70 | # |
| 5 | Pathanamthitta | 60 | # |
| 6 | Thiruvananthapuram | 80 | 39** |
| 9 | Rural Average | 71 | 29 |

## III.10: Madhya Pradesh

### *a. Drinking Water*

| Sl. No. | Units | Use of Public Protected Source | Use of Private Protected Source | Public Protected Source within 100 Metres | Breakdown of Public Taps within 3 Months | Breakdown of Public Handpumps within 3 Months | Households Involved in Maintenance | Willingness to Pay More | Full Satisfaction With Public Drinking Water Facilities | | | |
|---|---|---|---|---|---|---|---|---|---|---|---|---|
| | | | | | | | | | Piped Supply | | Other Protected Public Source | |
| | | | | | | | | | Adequacy of Supply | Quality of Water | Adequacy of Supply | Quality of Water |
| 1 | Balaghat | 81 | 2 | 75 | # | 3 | 0 | 41 | # | # | 16 | 18 |
| 2 | Betul | 60 | 9 | 54 | # | 24* | 10* | 59 | # | # | 28* | 36* |
| 3 | Datia | 63 | 3 | 39 | # | 26 | 3* | 24 | # | # | 6* | 39* |
| 4 | Dewas | 74 | 6 | 61 | # | 13* | 17 | 49 | # | # | 2 | 12 |
| 5 | East Nimar | 100 | 0 | 94 | # | 27 | 2 | 8 | 10** | 72** | 1 | 60 |
| 6 | Jabalpur | 87 | 2 | 84 | # | 4 | 2 | 20 | 7** | 10** | 1 | 6 |
| 7 | Mandsaur | 66 | 4 | 50 | # | 14* | 21 | 40 | # | # | 30 | 31 |
| 8 | Rajgarh | 64 | 1 | 31 | # | 6* | 0* | 15* | # | # | 26* | 49* |
| 9 | Ratlam | 79 | 7 | 50 | # | 25* | 26* | 19 | # | # | 16* | 42* |
| 10 | Satna | 77 | 2 | 34 | # | 18* | 34* | 18 | # | # | 26 | 46 |
| 11 | Shahdol | 55 | 1 | 49 | # | 27* | 8* | 47* | # | # | 11* | 39* |
| 12 | Shivpuri | 63 | 3 | 49 | # | 54* | 24* | 72 | # | # | 58* | 66* |
| 13 | Ujjain | 54 | 12 | 37 | # | 44 | 21 | 86* | # | # | 28* | 33* |
| 14 | Rural Average | 71 | 4 | 55 | 21 | 20 | 13 | 36 | 23 | 43 | 18 | 36 |
| 15 | Urban Average | 92 | 6 | 86 | 0 | 9 | 20 | 46 | 34 | 50 | 19 | 31 |
| 16 | State Average | 75 | 4 | 61 | 12 | 20 | 14 | 38 | 30 | 47 | 18 | 35 |

## b. Health Care

| Sl. No. | Units | Health Facility within 1 km. | Dependence for Minor Ailments | | Dependence for Major Ailments | | Presence in Government Health Facilities of | | Paid for Medical Services Availed (Out-Patients) | Full Satisfaction of Out-Patients with Behaviour of | |
|---|---|---|---|---|---|---|---|---|---|---|---|
| | | | Govt. Facility | Pvt. Hospitals | Govt. Facility | Pvt. Hospitals | Doctors | Paramedics | | Doctors | Paramedics |
| 1 | Balaghat | 31 | 38* | 9 | 80* | 10* | 55** | 68** | 24** | 11** | 8** |
| 2 | Betul | 59 | 63 | 10 | 70 | 20 | 52 | 76 | 5 | 14 | 18 |
| 3 | Datia | 80 | 80 | 8 | 86 | 11 | 73 | 72 | 6 | 1 | 1 |
| 4 | Dewas | 38 | 70 | 8 | 82 | 17 | 52* | 75* | 34* | 0* | 0* |
| 5 | East Nimar | 53 | 83 | 0 | 96 | 1 | 22 | 83 | 20 | 1 | 4 |
| 6 | Jabalpur | 50 | 68 | 10 | 67 | 25 | 44* | 94* | 33* | 3* | 1* |
| 7 | Mandsaur | 47 | 34 | 27 | 42 | 56 | 76** | 89** | 13** | 20** | 24** |
| 8 | Rajgarh | 57 | 62 | 16 | 52 | 30 | 36* | 56* | 8* | 13* | 15* |
| 9 | Ratlam | 21 | 19 | 5 | 53 | 28 | 80** | 77** | 51** | 0** | 0** |
| 10 | Satna | 31 | 24 | 14 | 71 | 9 | 84* | 94* | 21* | 0* | 0* |
| 11 | Shahdol | 25 | 78 | 4 | 80 | 8 | 74 | 64 | 16 | 3 | 4 |
| 12 | Shivpuri | 44 | 28 | 35 | 59 | 31 | 72* | 85* | 43* | 15* | 15* |
| 13 | Ujjain | 41 | 41 | 12 | 42 | 15 | 69* | 62* | 16* | 34* | 15* |
| 14 | Rural Average | 44 | 53 | 12 | 68 | 20 | 59 | 77 | 20 | 8 | 7 |
| 15 | Urban Average | 53 | 31 | 31 | 53 | 36 | 87 | 87 | 25 | 11 | 14 |
| 16 | State Average | NA | 49 | 16 | 65 | 23 | 63 | 78 | 21 | 8 | 8 |

### c. Road Transport

| Sl. No. | Units | Access to Cement/Tarred Road within 1 km. | Availability within 1 km. of | | | Usage of Transport Facility | | Full Satisfaction With | | |
|---|---|---|---|---|---|---|---|---|---|---|
| | | | Bus Stops | Public Bus | Private Bus | Public Bus | Private Bus | Punctuality of Govt. Buses | Frequency of Govt. Buses | Behaviour of Bus Conductors |
| 1 | Balaghat | 31 | 25 | 31 | 63 | 1 | 85 | # | # | # |
| 2 | Betul | 12 | 41 | 6 | 53 | 0 | 95 | # | # | # |
| 3 | Datia | 33 | 27 | 0 | 40 | 1 | 93 | # | # | # |
| 4 | Dewas | 19 | 25 | 25 | 75 | 0 | 86 | # | # | # |
| 5 | East Nimar | 18 | 24 | 24 | 24 | 13 | 85 | # | # | # |
| 6 | Jabalpur | 35 | 50 | 6 | 75 | 0 | 79 | # | # | # |
| 7 | Mandsaur | 53 | 59 | 24 | 82 | 0 | 98 | # | # | # |
| 8 | Rajgarh | 20 | 14 | 14 | 50 | 9 | 70 | # | # | # |
| 9 | Ratlam | 36 | 36 | 21 | 64 | 1 | 91 | # | # | # |
| 10 | Satna | 24 | 19 | 13 | 31 | 0 | 63 | # | # | # |
| 11 | Shahdol | 13 | 25 | 13 | 38 | 0 | 76 | # | # | # |
| 12 | Shivpuri | 13 | 38 | 38 | 63 | 13 | 71 | # | # | # |
| 13 | Ujjain | 18 | 29 | 29 | 59 | 3 | 73 | # | # | # |
| 14 | Rural Average | 25 | 32 | 19 | 55 | 3 | 82 | 21* | 27* | 20* |
| 15 | Urban Average | NA | | 32 | 34 | 29 | 52 | 15 | 19 | 13 |
| 16 | State Average | NA | NA | NA | NA | 8 | 76 | 17 | 21 | 15 |

## d. Public Distribution System

| Sl. No. | Units | PDS Outlet within 1 km. | Households Possessing Own Ration Card | Use of PDS by Card Owners at Least Once in 2 Months | Reliability of PDS Facilities | | Extent of Full Satisfaction With | | |
|---|---|---|---|---|---|---|---|---|---|
| | | | | | Regular Availability of Staple Foodgrain | Price Always Displayed | Quantity of Supplies | Quality of Supplies | Fairness of Shopkeeper |
| 1 | Balaghat | 63 | 94 | 94 | 31 | 34 | 7 | 8 | 8 |
| 2 | Betul | 77 | 86 | 83 | 32 | 90 | 11 | 12 | 15 |
| 3 | Datia | 80 | 97 | 91 | 10 | 40 | 5 | 2 | 2 |
| 4 | Dewas | 38 | 92 | 92 | 11 | 43 | 0 | 0 | 0 |
| 5 | East Nimar | 47 | 93 | 94 | 57 | 40 | 1 | 2 | 1 |
| 6 | Jabalpur | 56 | 85 | 80 | 41 | 42 | 0 | 2 | 1 |
| 7 | Mandsaur | 59 | 92 | 91 | 34 | 72 | 8 | 14 | 14 |
| 8 | Rajgarh | 64 | 71 | 66 | 30 | 49 | 9 | 6 | 3 |
| 9 | Ratlam | 43 | 96 | 96 | 5 | 57 | 18 | 19 | 25 |
| 10 | Satna | 13 | 85 | 67 | 12 | 49 | 2 | 3 | 4 |
| 11 | Shahdol | 56 | 90 | 78 | 9 | 37 | 1 | 3 | 2 |
| 12 | Shivpuri | 44 | 74 | 74 | 6 | 70 | 5 | 7 | 8 |
| 13 | Ujjain | 59 | 97 | 89 | 23 | 74 | 7 | 37 | 23 |
| 14 | Rural Average | 73 | 89 | 84 | 24 | 54 | 6 | 9 | 8 |
| 15 | Urban Average | 82 | 72 | 44 | 17 | 60 | 5 | 10 | 8 |
| 16 | State Average | NA | 86 | 76 | 23 | 55 | 6 | 9 | 8 |

## *e. Primary School*

| Sl. No. | Units | Access to a Primary Education Facility | | Dependence for Education Facility | | Full Satisfaction with Behaviour of Teachers in Govt./Aided School | Awareness of Mid-Day Meal Scheme | Utilise Mid-Day Meal (Among Aware) | Extent of Full Satisfaction With | |
|---|---|---|---|---|---|---|---|---|---|---|
| | | Govt. School | Pvt. School | Govt. School | Pvt. School | | | | Quality of School Building | Quality of Toilet |
| 1 | Balaghat | 81 | 19 | 94** | 6** | 6** | 78** | 72** | 2** | 0** |
| 2 | Betul | 77 | 18 | 95* | 5* | 12** | 85** | 96** | 7** | 2** |
| 3 | Datia | 93 | 13 | 100* | 0* | 47* | 49* | 90** | 47* | 7* |
| 4 | Dewas | 88 | 13 | 98** | 2** | 12** | 65** | # | 14** | 0** |
| 5 | East Nimar | 88 | 12 | 97** | 3** | 13** | 84** | 91** | 0** | 0** |
| 6 | Jabalpur | 75 | 38 | 81** | 19** | 0** | 89** | 94** | 0** | 0** |
| 7 | Mandsaur | 77 | 29 | 88** | 12** | 22** | 100** | 84** | 16** | 2** |
| 8 | Rajgarh | 93 | 7 | 96* | 4* | 28* | 71* | 98** | 15* | 0* |
| 9 | Ratlam | 100 | 29 | 80** | 20** | 30** | 60** | # | 22** | 3** |
| 10 | Satna | 94 | 25 | 92* | 8* | 4* | 74* | 100** | 4* | 0* |
| 11 | Shahdol | 81 | 13 | 94* | 6* | 12* | 77* | 92** | 8* | 0* |
| 12 | Shivpuri | 100 | 25 | 87* | 13* | 22** | 56** | 97** | 16** | 6** |
| 13 | Ujjain | 94 | 18 | 96* | 4* | 25* | 68* | 77** | 3* | 3* |
| 14 | Rural Average | 87 | 20 | 93 | 8 | 19 | 72 | 90 | 13 | 2 |
| 15 | Urban Average | 29 | 22 | 53 | 50 | 18 | 39 | 90 | 16 | 9 |
| 16 | State Average | NA | NA | 86 | 16 | 20 | 69 | 90 | 13 | 3 |

## *f. Child Care System*

| *Sl. No.* | *Units* | *Access of Anganwadis within 1 km.* | *Usage of Anganwadis* |
|---|---|---|---|
| 1 | Balaghat | 75 | 44** |
| 2 | Betul | 94 | 26** |
| 3 | Datia | 100 | 49* |
| 4 | Dewas | 81 | 19* |
| 5 | East Nimar | 94 | 12* |
| 6 | Jabalpur | 81 | 12* |
| 7 | Mandsaur | 71 | 38** |
| 8 | Rajgarh | 71 | 6** |
| 9 | Ratlam | 71 | 27** |
| 10 | Satna | 56 | 9** |
| 11 | Shahdol | 100 | 36* |
| 12 | Shivpuri | 94 | 26* |
| 13 | Ujjain | 82 | 34* |
| 14 | Rural Average | 87 | 26 |

## III.11: Maharashtra

### *a. Drinking Water*

| Sl. No. | Units | Use of Public Protected Source | Use of Private Protected Source | Public Protected Source within 100 Metres | Breakdown of Public Taps within 3 Months | Breakdown of Public Handpumps within 3 Months | Households Involved in Maintenance | Willingness to Pay More | Full Satisfaction with Public Drinking Water Facilities | | | |
|---|---|---|---|---|---|---|---|---|---|---|---|---|
| | | | | | | | | | Piped Supply | | Other Protected Public Source | |
| | | | | | | | | | Adequacy of Supply | Quality of Water | Adequacy of Supply | Quality of Water |
| 1 | Aurangabad | 83 | 1 | 79 | 15* | 5** | 26 | 19 | 1 | 2 | 4 | 3 |
| 2 | Buldhana | 73 | 1 | 72 | 1 | 7* | 60 | 48 | 21** | 21** | 15 | 15 |
| 3 | Chandrapur | 51 | 4 | 50 | # | 7* | 48 | 16 | 35** | 37** | 44 | 44 |
| 4 | Dhule | 95 | 1 | 94 | 21 | # | 0 | 69 | 1 | 2 | 0 | 2 |
| 5 | Jalgaon | 97 | 1 | 94 | 6 | - | 9 | 64 | 2 | 2 | 2 | 2 |
| 6 | Nashik | 80 | 2 | 77 | 23** | 20 | 8 | 51 | 0 | 0 | 0 | 2 |
| 7 | Parbhani | 87 | 0 | 84 | # | 7 | 32 | 46 | 61** | 61** | 50 | 50 |
| 8 | Ratnagiri | 45 | 0 | 44 | 5** | # | 17** | 32 | 13* | 15* | 0** | 14* |
| 9 | Solapur | 81 | 2 | 81 | 0** | # | 23* | 58 | 0* | 5* | 0* | 14* |
| 10 | Thane | 42 | 11 | 38 | # | # | # | 43 | 0** | 6** | # | # |
| 11 | Rural Average | 76 | 2 | 74 | 10 | 10 | 28 | 47 | 7 | 8 | 17 | 18 |
| 12 | Urban Average | 95 | 2 | 95 | 16* | # | 46 | 27 | 20 | 23 | 39 | 45 |
| 13 | State Average | 79 | 2 | 77 | 11 | 11 | 29 | 43 | 11 | 13 | 19 | 20 |

## b. Health Care

| Sl. No. | Units | Health Facility within 1 km. | Dependence for Minor Ailments | | Dependence for Major Ailments | | Presence in Government Health Facilities of | | Paid for Medical Services Availed (Out-Patients) | Full Satisfaction of Out-Patients with Behaviour of | |
|---|---|---|---|---|---|---|---|---|---|---|---|
| | | | Govt. Facility | Pvt. Hospitals | Govt. Facility | Pvt. Hospitals | Doctors | Paramedics | | Doctors | Paramedics |
| 1 | Aurangabad | 66 | 60 | 0 | 84 | 2 | 88 | 89 | 24 | 2 | 0 |
| 2 | Buldhana | 48 | 69 | 14 | 84 | 11 | 78 | 98 | 14 | 17 | 16 |
| 3 | Chandrapur | 60 | 68 | 20 | 73 | 23 | 85 | 91 | 14 | 40 | 39 |
| 4 | Dhule | 66 | 43 | 4 | 48 | 34 | 92 | 89 | 3 | 0 | 0 |
| 5 | Jalgaon | 47 | 57 | 3 | 63 | 27 | 88 | 86 | 5 | 0 | 0 |
| 6 | Nashik | 57 | 44 | 8 | 46 | 42 | 89 | 86 | 10 | 0 | 0 |
| 7 | Parbhani | 55 | 82 | 17 | 83 | 16 | 96 | 97 | 23 | 72 | 71 |
| 8 | Ratnagiri | 24 | 7 | 6 | 74 | 25 | # | # | # | # | # |
| 9 | Solapur | 25 | 41 | 0 | 98 | 1 | # | # | # | # | # |
| 10 | Thane | 36 | 28* | 3* | 70* | 25* | # | # | # | # | # |
| 11 | Rural Average | 51 | 55 | 9 | 71 | 21 | 88 | 92 | 14 | 20 | 20 |
| 12 | Urban Average | 38 | 25 | 10 | 58 | 32 | 96 | 96 | 13 | 33 | 32 |
| 13 | State Average | NA | 50 | 9 | 69 | 23 | 88 | 93 | 14 | 22 | 21 |

## c. Road Transport

| Sl. No. | Units | Access to Cement/Tarred Road within 1 km. | Availability within 1 km. of | | | Usage of Transport Facility | | Full Satisfaction With | | |
|---|---|---|---|---|---|---|---|---|---|---|
| | | | Bus Stops | Public Bus | Private Bus | Public Bus | Private Bus | Punctuality of Govt. Buses | Frequency of Govt. Buses | Behaviour of Bus Conductors |
| 1 | Aurangabad | 59 | 41 | 83 | 90 | 78 | 0 | 1 | 1 | 1 |
| 2 | Buldhana | 45 | 71 | 84 | 74 | 98 | 0 | 19 | 18 | 24 |
| 3 | Chandrapur | 43 | 63 | 77 | 70 | 94 | 1 | 32 | 34 | 34 |
| 4 | Dhule | 55 | 93 | 100 | 83 | 98 | 0 | 1 | 1 | 1 |
| 5 | Jalgaon | 50 | 74 | 94 | 79 | 97 | 0 | 1 | 2 | 3 |
| 6 | Nashik | 46 | 82 | 96 | 79 | 91 | 0 | 1 | 1 | 2 |
| 7 | Parbhani | 35 | 55 | 77 | 69 | 90 | 0 | 46 | 45 | 56 |
| 8 | Ratnagiri | 48 | 60 | 100 | 76 | 82 | 0 | 13 | 13 | 8 |
| 9 | Solapur | 31 | 69 | 81 | 81 | 80 | 1 | 13 | 10 | 12 |
| 10 | Thane | 57 | 57 | 86 | 57 | 86 | 0 | 11 | 10 | 10 |
| 11 | Rural Average | 47 | 67 | 88 | 77 | 91 | 0 | 14 | 14 | 16 |
| 12 | Urban Average | NA | NA | 86 | 39 | 80 | 1 | 20 | 23 | 17 |
| 13 | State Average | NA | NA | NA | NA | 89 | 0 | 15 | 15 | 16 |

## d. Public Distribution System

| Sl. No. | Units | PDS Outlet within 1 km. | Households Possessing Own Ration Card | Use of PDS by Card Owners At Least Once in 2 Months | Reliability of PDS Facilities | | Extent of Full Satisfaction With | | |
|---|---|---|---|---|---|---|---|---|---|
| | | | | | Regular Availability of Staple Foodgrain | Price Always Displayed | Quantity of Supplies | Quality of Supplies | Fairness of Shopkeeper |
| 1 | Aurangabad | 90 | 69 | 68 | 18 | 30 | 0 | 0 | 0 |
| 2 | Buldhana | 94 | 83 | 49 | 48 | 56 | 4 | 7 | 9 |
| 3 | Chandrapur | 77 | 89 | 50 | 60 | 56 | 4 | 18 | 15 |
| 4 | Dhule | 90 | 80 | 70 | 54 | 64 | 0 | 0 | 0 |
| 5 | Jalgaon | 82 | 83 | 59 | 65 | 71 | 1 | 1 | 1 |
| 6 | Nashik | 86 | 88 | 76 | 40 | 54 | 0 | 0 | 1 |
| 7 | Parbhani | 90 | 77 | 75 | 21 | 16 | 2 | 7 | 8 |
| 8 | Ratnagiri | 80 | 95 | 57 | 20 | 90 | 6 | 5 | 6 |
| 9 | Solapur | 81 | 96 | 50 | 20* | 92* | 3* | 3* | 2* |
| 10 | Thane | 50 | 97 | 60 | 23* | 89* | 4* | 4* | 1* |
| 11 | Rural Average | 84 | 84 | 62 | 39 | 55 | 2 | 4 | 4 |
| 12 | Urban Average | 96 | 87 | 30 | 31 | 75 | 2 | 3 | 4 |
| 13 | State Average | NA | 85 | 56 | 38 | 57 | 2 | 4 | 4 |

## *e. Primary School*

| Sl. No. | Units | Access to a Primary Education Facility | | Dependence for Education Facility | | Full Satisfaction with Behaviour of Teachers in Govt./Aided School | Awareness of Mid-Day Meal Scheme | Utilise Mid-Day Meal (Among Aware) | Extent of Full Satisfaction With | |
|---|---|---|---|---|---|---|---|---|---|---|
| | | Govt. School | Pvt. School | Govt. School | Pvt. School | | | | Quality of School Building | Quality of Toilet |
| 1 | Aurangabad | 93 | 14 | 93* | 7* | 3* | 77* | 83** | 3* | 1* |
| 2 | Buldhana | 94 | 3 | 100* | 0* | 31* | 94* | 96* | 29* | 16* |
| 3 | Chandrapur | 87 | 23 | 93* | 7* | 38* | 52* | 88** | 27* | 30* |
| 4 | Dhule | 83 | 14 | 96** | 4** | # | 31** | # | 0** | 0** |
| 5 | Jalgaon | 82 | 29 | 85** | 15** | # | 46** | # | 0** | 0** |
| 6 | Nashik | 79 | 14 | 96** | 4** | # | 25** | # | 0** | 0** |
| 7 | Parbhani | 86 | 10 | 99* | 1* | 43* | 46* | 100** | 35* | 21* |
| 8 | Ratnagiri | 76 | 20 | 90** | 10** | # | 81** | 63** | 17** | # |
| 9 | Solapur | 69 | 31 | # | # | # | # | # | # | # |
| 10 | Thane | 57 | 14 | # | # | # | # | # | # | # |
| 11 | Rural Average | 83 | 17 | 96 | 4 | 20 | 62 | 89 | 16 | 11 |
| 12 | Urban Average | 53 | 18 | 71 | 29 | 32* | 63* | # | 30* | 27* |
| 13 | State Average | NA | NA | 93 | 7 | 21 | 62 | 87 | 17 | 13 |

## *f. Child Care System*

| *Sl. No.* | *Units* | *Access of Anganwadis within 1 km.* | *Usage of Anganwadis* |
|---|---|---|---|
| 1 | Aurangabad | 97 | 67* |
| 2 | Buldhana | 97 | 31 |
| 3 | Chandrapur | 100 | 41 |
| 4 | Dhule | 97 | 21* |
| 5 | Jalgaon | 97 | 40 |
| 6 | Nashik | 96 | 43* |
| 7 | Parbhani | 93 | 47* |
| 8 | Ratnagiri | 92 | 8** |
| 9 | Solapur | 94 | 50** |
| 10 | Thane | 100 | 57** |
| 11 | Rural Average | 96 | 40 |

## III.12: Meghalaya

### a. Drinking Water

| Sl. No. | Units | Use of Public Protected Source | Use of Private Protected Source | Public Protected Source within 100 Metres | Breakdown of Public Handpumps within 3 Months | Households Involved in Maintenance | Willingness to Pay More | Full Satisfaction With Public Drinking Water Facilities: Piped Supply: Adequacy of Supply | Piped Supply: Quality of Water | Other Protected Public Sources: Adequacy of Supply | Other Protected Public Sources: Quality of Water |
|---|---|---|---|---|---|---|---|---|---|---|---|
| 1 | East Khasi Hills | 73 | 12 | 54 | 24 | 21 | 21 | # | # | 3 | 3 |
| 2 | Jaintia Hills | 29 | 1 | 23 | 5** | 0** | 0 | # | # | 25** | 25** |
| 3 | West Garo Hills | 84 | 0 | 82 | 29* | 3 | 17 | # | # | 7 | 7 |
| 4 | West Khasi Hills | 56 | 6 | 44 | 36 | 10 | 8 | # | # | 0 | 3 |
| 5 | Rural Average | 63 | 5 | 52 | 27 | 10 | 15 | # | # | 5 | 6 |
| 6 | Urban Average | 95 | 5 | 91 | 0* | 12* | 28 | 14 | 10 | 10* | 14* |
| 7 | State Average | 77 | 5 | 69 | 22 | 10 | 22 | 14 | 9 | 6 | 7 |

## b. Health Care

| Sl. No. | Units | Health Facility within 1 km. | Dependence for Minor Ailments | | Dependence for Major Ailments | | Presence in Government Health Facilities of | | Paid for Medical Services Availed (Out-Patients) | Full Satisfaction of Out-Patients with Behaviour of | |
|---|---|---|---|---|---|---|---|---|---|---|---|
| | | | Govt. Facility | Pvt. Hospitals | Govt. Facility | Pvt. Hospitals | Doctors | Paramedics | | Doctors | Paramedics |
| 1 | East Khasi Hills | 0 | 41* | 15* | 32* | 65* | # | # | # | # | # |
| 2 | Jaintia Hills | 14 | 48** | 0** | 44** | 4** | # | # | # | # | # |
| 3 | West Garo Hills | 50 | 74* | 7* | 55* | 19* | 74** | 78** | 13** | 17** | 17** |
| 4 | West Khasi Hills | 29 | 88** | 0** | 100** | 0** | 33** | 33** | 0** | 0** | 0** |
| 5 | Rural Average | 23 | 63 | 7 | 56 | 25 | 57 | 59 | 10 | 16 | 16 |
| 6 | Urban Average | 15 | 16 | 36 | 21 | 66 | 80** | 72** | 8** | 12** | 12** |
| 7 | State Average | NA | 38 | 22 | 38 | 47 | 64 | 63 | 9 | 15 | 15 |

## *c. Road Transport*

| Sl. No. | Units | Access to Cement/Tarred Road within 1 km. | Availability within 1 km. of | | | Usage of Transport Facility | | Full Satisfaction With | | |
|---|---|---|---|---|---|---|---|---|---|---|
| | | | Bus Stops | Public Bus | Private Bus | Public Bus | Private Bus | Punctuality of Govt. Buses | Frequency of Govt. Buses | Behaviour of Bus Conductors |
| 1 | East Khasi Hills | 67 | 50 | 14 | 43 | 6 | 36 | # | # | # |
| 2 | Jaintia Hills | 43 | 43 | 33 | 67 | 1 | 68 | # | # | # |
| 3 | West Garo Hills | 17 | 17 | 0 | 50 | 6 | 51 | # | # | # |
| 4 | West Khasi Hills | 43 | 29 | 14 | 14 | 14 | 49 | 0** | 0** | 0** |
| 5 | Rural Average | 42 | 35 | 15 | 40 | 7 | 49 | 4** | 4** | 4** |
| 6 | Urban Average | NA | NA | 10 | 17 | 1 | 13 | # | # | # |
| 7 | State Average | NA | NA | NA | NA | 4 | 33 | 3* | 3* | 3* |

## d. Public Distribution System

| Sl. No. | Units | PDS Outlet within 1 km. | Households Possessing Own Ration Card | Use of PDS by Card Owners At Least Once in 2 Months | Reliability of PDS Facilities | | Extent of Full Satisfaction With | | |
|---|---|---|---|---|---|---|---|---|---|
| | | | | | Regular Availability of Staple Foodgrain | Price Always Displayed | Quantity of Supplies | Quality of Supplies | Fairness of Shopkeeper |
| 1 | East Khasi Hills | 67 | 26 | 7 | # | # | # | # | # |
| 2 | Jaintia Hills | 71 | 36 | 6 | # | # | # | # | # |
| 3 | West Garo Hills | 17 | 17 | 10 | # | # | # | # | # |
| 4 | West Khasi Hills | 57 | 19 | 4 | # | # | # | # | # |
| 5 | Rural Average | 54 | 24 | 7 | 16** | 4** | 0** | 0** | 0** |
| 6 | Urban Average | 57 | 18 | 14 | 12* | 22* | 7* | 7* | 7* |
| 7 | State Average | NA | 21 | 10 | 14 | 15 | 5 | 5 | 5 |

## *e. Primary School*

| Sl. No. | Units | Access to a Primary Education Facility within 1 km. | | Dependence for Primary Education Facility | | Full Satisfaction with Behaviour of Teachers in Govt./Aided School | Awareness of Mid-Day Meal Scheme | Utilise Mid-Day Meal (Among Aware) | Extent of Full Satisfaction With | |
|---|---|---|---|---|---|---|---|---|---|---|
| | | Govt. School | Pvt. School | Govt. School | Pvt. School | | | | Quality of School Building | Quality of Toilet |
| 1 | East Khasi Hills | 100 | 43 | 47** | 53** | # | # | # | # | # |
| 2 | Jaintia Hills | 50 | 50 | # | # | # | # | # | # | # |
| 3 | West Garo Hills | 83 | 67 | # | # | # | # | # | # | # |
| 4 | West Khasi Hills | 57 | 43 | 65** | 35** | # | # | # | # | # |
| 5 | Rural Average | 73 | 50 | 45 | 55 | 0* | 0* | # | 0* | 0* |
| 6 | Urban Average | 13 | 27 | 17* | # | # | # | # | # | # |
| 7 | State Average | NA | NA | 20 | 24 | 0* | 0* | # | 0* | 0* |

## *f. Child Care System*

| *Sl. No.* | *Units* | *Access of Anganwadis within 1 km.* | *Usage of Anganwadis* |
|---|---|---|---|
| 1 | East Khasi Hills | 33 | # |
| 2 | Jaintia Hills | 29 | # |
| 3 | West Garo Hills | 100 | # |
| 4 | West Khasi Hills | 71 | # |
| 5 | Rural Average | 58 | # |

## III.13: Mizoram

### a. Drinking Water

| Sl. No. | Units | Use of Public Protected Source | Use of Private Protected Source | Public Protected Source within 100 Metres | Breakdown of Public Taps within 3 Months | Households Involved in Maintenance | Willingness to Pay More | Full Satisfaction With Public Drinking Water Facilities | | | |
|---|---|---|---|---|---|---|---|---|---|---|---|
| | | | | | | | | Piped Supply | | Other Protected Public Sources | |
| | | | | | | | | Adequacy of Supply | Quality of Water | Adequacy of Supply | Quality of Water |
| 1 | Aizwal | 67 | 0 | 57 | 40 | 30 | 61 | # | # | 7 | 35 |
| 2 | Lunglei | 87 | 1 | 87 | 0** | 0** | 24 | 0 | 5 | 2 | 8 |
| 3 | Rural Average | 77 | 0 | 71 | 32 | 23 | 41 | 0 | 5 | 6 | 28 |
| 4 | Urban Average | 63 | 0 | 62 | 42 | # | 36 | 3 | 13 | 0 | 31 |
| 5 | State Average | 72 | 0 | 68 | 33 | 24 | 39 | 1 | 9 | 5 | 28 |

## b. Health Care

| Sl. No. | Units | Health Facility within 1 km. | Dependence for Minor Ailments | | Dependence for Major Ailments | | Presence in Government Health Facilities of | | Paid for Medical Services Availed (Out-Patients) | Full Satisfaction of Out-Patients with Behaviour of | |
|---|---|---|---|---|---|---|---|---|---|---|---|
| | | | Govt. Facility | Pvt. Hospitals | Govt. Facility | Pvt. Hospitals | Doctors | Paramedics | | Doctors | Paramedics |
| 1 | Aizwal | 71 | 100* | 0 | 100* | 0 | 38* | 58* | # | 0* | 0* |
| 2 | Lunglei | 92 | 100* | 0 | 100* | 0 | 52 | 91 | 6** | 1 | 1 |
| 3 | Rural Average | 82 | 100 | 0 | 100 | 0 | 44 | 77 | 6* | 1 | 1 |
| 4 | Urban Average | 64 | 53 | 15 | 82 | 12 | 77* | 71* | 7* | 7* | 3* |
| 5 | State Average | NA | 84 | 5 | 94 | 4 | 54 | 75 | 6 | 2 | 1 |

## c. Road Transport

| Sl. No. | Units | Access to Cement/Tarred Road | Availability of | | | Usage of Transport Facility | | Full Satisfaction With | | |
|---|---|---|---|---|---|---|---|---|---|---|
| | | | Bus Stops | Public Bus | Private Bus | Public Bus | Private Bus | Punctuality of Govt. Buses | Frequency of Govt. Buses | Behaviour of Bus Conductors |
| 1 | Aizwal | 36 | 79 | 75 | 88 | 68 | 19 | 12 | 16 | 16 |
| 2 | Lunglei | 8 | 54 | 92 | 92 | 15 | 65 | # | # | # |
| 3 | Rural Average | 22 | 67 | 83 | 90 | 43 | 40 | 10 | 14 | 14 |
| 4 | Urban Average | NA | NA | 80 | 74 | 53 | 20 | 20 | 26 | 25 |
| 5 | State Average | NA | NA | NA | NA | 46 | 33 | 14 | 18 | 18 |

## *d. Public Distribution System*

| *Sl. No.* | *Units* | *PDS Outlet within 1 km.* | *Households Possessing Own Ration Card* | *Use of PDS by Card Owners At Least Once in 2 Months* | *Reliability of PDS Facilities* | | *Extent of Full Satisfaction With* | | |
|---|---|---|---|---|---|---|---|---|---|
| | | | | | *Regular Availability of Staple Foodgrain* | *Price Always Displayed* | *Quantity of Supplies* | *Quality of Supplies* | *Fairness of Shopkeeper* |
| 1 | Aizwal | 86 | 91 | 90 | 36 | 33 | 18 | 1 | 2 |
| 2 | Lunglei | 92 | 89 | 88 | 36 | 2 | 1 | 0 | 0 |
| 3 | Rural Average | 89 | 90 | 89 | 36 | 19 | 10 | 1 | 1 |
| 4 | Urban Average | 98 | 91 | 89 | 10 | 45 | 11 | 0 | 1 |
| 5 | State Average | N.A | 90 | 89 | 27 | 27 | 10 | 1 | 1 |

## e. Primary School

| Sl. No. | Units | Access to a Primary Education Facility | | Dependence for Education Facility | | Full Satisfaction with Behaviour of Teachers in Govt./Aided School | Awareness of Mid-Day Meal Scheme | Utilise Mid-Day Meal (Among Aware) | Extent of Full Satisfaction With | |
|---|---|---|---|---|---|---|---|---|---|---|
| | | Govt. School | Pvt. School | Govt. School | Pvt. School | | | | Quality of School Building | Quality of Toilet |
| 1 | Aizwal | 56 | 13 | # | # | # | # | # | # | # |
| 2 | Lunglei | 69 | 31 | # | # | # | # | # | # | # |
| 3 | Rural Average | 62 | 21 | 89** | 11** | 2** | 31** | 79 | 16** | 7** |
| 4 | Urban Average | 39 | 13 | # | # | # | 33 | 67 | # | # |
| 5 | State Average | NA | NA | 84* | 16* | 2* | 32* | 75 | 16* | 5* |

## f. Child Care System

| Sl. No. | Units | Access of Anganwadis within 1 km. | Usage of Anganwadis |
|---|---|---|---|
| 1 | Aizwal | 86 | 54** |
| 2 | Lunglei | 85 | # |
| 3 | Rural Average | 85 | 49* |

## III.14: Nagaland

### a. Drinking Water

| Sl. No. | Units | Use of Public Protected Source | Use of Private Protected Source | Use Unprotected Source | Public Protected Source within 100 metres | Willingness to pay more | Full Satisfaction with Public Drinking Water Facilities: Piped Supply | |
|---|---|---|---|---|---|---|---|---|
| | | | | | | | Adequacy of Supply | Quality of Water |
| 1 | Wokha | 10 | 0 | 90 | 10 | 55 | # | # |
| 2 | Zunheboto | 19 | 0 | 81 | 18 | 29 | # | # |
| 3 | Rural Average | 14 | 0 | 86 | 14 | 38 | # | # |
| 4 | Urban Average | 31 | 0 | 70 | 30 | 23 | 0** | 0** |
| 5 | State Average | 20 | 0 | 80 | 19 | 30 | 0* | 0* |

## b. Health Care

| Sl. No. | Units | Health Facility within 1 km. | Dependence for Minor Ailments | | Dependence for Major Ailments | | Presence in Government Health Facilities of | | Paid for Medical Services Availed (Out-Patients) | Full Satisfaction of Out-Patients with Behaviour of | |
|---|---|---|---|---|---|---|---|---|---|---|---|
| | | | Govt. Facility | Pvt. Hospitals | Govt. Facility | Pvt. Hospitals | Doctors | Paramedics | | Doctors | Paramedics |
| 1 | Wokha | 15 | 41 | 26 | 23 | 69 | 64** | 92** | 76** | 0** | 0** |
| 2 | Zunheboto | 8 | 65 | 21 | 28 | 67 | 64* | 69* | 16* | 2* | 2* |
| 3 | Rural Average | 12 | 52 | 24 | 26 | 68 | 64 | 79 | 44 | 1 | 1 |
| 4 | Urban Average | 23 | 25 | 44 | 20 | 68 | # | # | # | # | # |
| 5 | State Average | NA | 44 | 30 | 24 | 68 | 68 | 78 | 46 | 1 | 1 |

## c. Road Transport

| Sl. No. | Units | Access to Cement/Tarred Road | Availability of | | | Usage of Transport Facility | | Full Satisfaction with | | |
|---|---|---|---|---|---|---|---|---|---|---|
| | | | Bus Stops | Public Bus | Private Bus | Public Bus | Private Bus | Punctuality of Govt. Buses | Frequency of Govt. Buses | Behaviour of Bus Conductors |
| 1 | Wokha | 0 | 8 | 29 | 29 | 44 | 54 | 0* | 0* | 0* |
| 2 | Zunheboto | 0 | 8 | 69 | 77 | 28 | 68 | 5** | 5** | 7** |
| 3 | Rural Average | 0 | 8 | 48 | 52 | 36 | 61 | 2 | 2 | 3 |
| 4 | Urban Average | NA | NA | 78 | 84 | 23 | 50 | 11** | 11** | 11** |
| 5 | State Average | NA | NA | NA | NA | 32 | 57 | 4 | 4 | 5 |

## *d. Public Distribution System*

| Sl. No. | Units | PDS Outlet within 1 km. | Households Possessing Own Ration Card | Use of PDS by Card Owners At Least Once in 2 Months | Reliability of PDS Facilities | | Extent of Full Satisfaction With | | |
|---|---|---|---|---|---|---|---|---|---|
| | | | | | Regular Availability of Staple Foodgrain | Price Always Displayed | Quantity of Supplies | Quality of Supplies | Fairness of Shopkeeper |
| 1 | Wokha | 15 | 4 | 5 | # | # | # | # | # |
| 2 | Zunheboto | 8 | 5 | 7 | # | # | # | # | # |
| 3 | Rural Average | 12 | 4 | 6 | # | # | # | # | # |
| 4 | Urban Average | 68 | 13 | 14 | # | # | # | # | # |
| 5 | State Average | NA | 7 | 8 | 6** | 2** | 4* | 4* | 4* |

## e. Primary School

| Sl. No. | Units | Access to a Primary Education Facility | | Dependence for Primary Education Facility | | Full Satisfaction with Behaviour of Teachers in Govt./Aided School | Awareness of Mid-Day Meal Scheme | Utilise Mid-Day Meal (Among Aware) | Extent of Full Satisfaction With | |
|---|---|---|---|---|---|---|---|---|---|---|
| | | Govt. School | Pvt. School | Govt. School | Pvt. School | | | | Quality of School Building | Quality of Toilet |
| 1 | Wokha | 86 | 57 | 44** | 56** | # | # | # | # | # |
| 2 | Zunheboto | 77 | 62 | 34** | 66** | # | # | # | # | # |
| 3 | Rural Average | 82 | 59 | 38* | 62* | 0** | 11** | # | 0** | 0** |
| 4 | Urban Average | 9 | 46 | 11** | 87** | # | # | # | # | # |
| 5 | State Average | NA | NA | 31 | 69 | 0** | 12** | # | 0** | 0** |

## f. Child Care System

| Sl. No. | Units | Access of Anganwadis within 1 km. | Usage of Anganwadis |
|---|---|---|---|
| 1 | Wokha | 92 | 40** |
| 2 | Zunheboto | 100 | 31** |
| 3 | Rural Average | 96 | 35* |

## III.15: Orissa

### a. Drinking Water

| Sl. No. | Units | Use of Public Protected Source | Use of Private Protected Source | Public Protected Source within 100 Metres | Breakdown of Public Handpumps within 3 Months | Households Involved in Maintenance | Willingness to Pay More | Full Satisfaction with Public Drinking Water Facilities Other Protected Public Sources | |
|---|---|---|---|---|---|---|---|---|---|
| | | | | | | | | Adequacy of Supply | Quality of Water |
| 1 | Balangir | 92 | 0 | 47 | 10 | 2 | 43 | 1 | 1 |
| 2 | Cluster I[11] | 69 | 19 | 39 | 25 | 11 | 33 | 9 | 16 |
| 3 | Cluster II | 65 | 11 | 39 | 19 | 11 | 39 | 17 | 23 |
| 4 | Mayurbhanj | 54 | 8 | 35 | 15** | 20** | 28 | 2** | 7** |
| 5 | Cluster III | 90 | 0 | 66 | 4 | 4 | 24 | 1 | 1 |
| 6 | Sundargarh | 97 | 1 | 67 | 15 | 5 | 24 | 2 | 2 |
| 7 | Rural average | 78 | 7 | 49 | 14 | 8 | 31 | 5 | 8 |
| 8 | Urban average | 83 | 7 | 69 | 22 | 5 | 43 | 5 | 11 |
| 9 | State average | 80 | 7 | 56 | 16 | 7 | 35 | 5 | 9 |

Cluster I: Baleshwar and Bhadrak, Cluster II: Jajpur, Jagatsinghpur and Kendrapara, Cluster III: Sambalpur and Bargarh.

## b. Health Care

| Sl. No. | Units | Health Facility within 1 km. | Dependence for Minor Ailments | | Dependence for Major Ailments | | Presence in Government Health Facilities of | | Paid for Medical Services Availed (Out-Patients) | Full Satisfaction of Out-Patients with Behaviour of | |
|---|---|---|---|---|---|---|---|---|---|---|---|
| | | | Govt. Facility | Pvt. Hospitals | Govt. Facility | Pvt. Hospitals | Doctors | Paramedics | | Doctors | Paramedics |
| 1 | Balangir | 43 | 98 | 1 | 100 | 0 | 91 | 95 | 9 | 0 | 0 |
| 2 | Cluster I | 59 | 95 | 0 | 95 | 4 | 77 | 88 | 5 | 8 | 5 |
| 3 | Cluster II | 12 | 84 | 3 | 96 | 3 | 47 | 83 | 5 | 3 | 2 |
| 4 | Mayurbhanj | 8 | 73* | 2* | 95* | 2* | 76* | 86* | 2* | 7* | 3* |
| 5 | Cluster III | 18 | 90 | 1 | 95 | 2 | 87 | 89 | 4 | 0 | 0 |
| 6 | Sundargarh | 27 | 93 | 3 | 94 | 6 | 75 | 84 | 2 | 2 | 2 |
| 7 | Rural Average | 28 | 90 | 2 | 96 | 3 | 75 | 87 | 5 | 3 | 2 |
| 8 | Urban Average | 73 | 70 | 10 | 83 | 11 | 87 | 92 | 9 | 4 | 3 |
| 9 | State Average | NA | 83 | 4 | 92 | 6 | 79 | 89 | 6 | 3 | 2 |

### c. Road Transport

| Sl. No. | Units | Access to Cement/ Tarred Road | Availability of | | | Usage of Transport Facility | |
|---|---|---|---|---|---|---|---|
| | | | Bus Stops | Public Bus | Private Bus | Public Bus | Private Bus |
| 1 | Balangir | 29 | 43 | 29 | 43 | 3 | 77 |
| 2 | Cluster I | 24 | 41 | 0 | 59 | 0 | 83 |
| 3 | Cluster II | 6 | 29 | 0 | 41 | 0 | 62 |
| 4 | Mayurbhanj | 15 | 8 | 8 | 39 | 0 | 54 |
| 5 | Cluster III | 29 | 12 | 12 | 53 | 1 | 84 |
| 6 | Sundargarh | 27 | 27 | 13 | 40 | 0 | 55 |
| 7 | Rural Average | 22 | 27 | 10 | 45 | 1 | 70 |
| 8 | Urban Average | NA | NA | 38 | 61 | 3 | 78 |
| 9 | State Average | NA | NA | NA | NA | 1 | 73 |

## d. Public Distribution System

| Sl. No. | Units | PDS Outlet within 1 km. | Households Possessing Own Ration Card | Use of PDS by Card Owners At Least Once in 2 Months | Reliability of PDS Facilities | | Extent of Full Satisfaction With | | |
|---|---|---|---|---|---|---|---|---|---|
| | | | | | Regular Availability of Staple Foodgrain | Price Always Displayed | Quantity of Supplies | Quality of Supplies | Fairness of Shopkeeper |
| 1 | Balangir | 43 | 97 | 100 | 8 | 61 | 0 | 0 | 0 |
| 2 | Cluster I | 82 | 97 | 99 | 1 | 39 | 1 | 3 | 6 |
| 3 | Cluster II | 59 | 94 | 96 | 8 | 21 | 0 | 0 | 1 |
| 4 | Mayurbhanj | 46 | 91 | 99 | 17* | 34* | 2* | 2* | 2* |
| 5 | Cluster III | 53 | 91 | 100 | 12 | 39 | 0 | 0 | 3 |
| 6 | Sundargarh | 60 | 96 | 99 | 18 | 22 | 0 | 0 | 1 |
| 7 | Rural Average | 58 | 94 | 99 | 10 | 35 | 0 | 1 | 2 |
| 8 | Urban Average | 94 | 90 | 98 | 9 | 64 | 1 | 1 | 0 |
| 9 | State Average | NA | 93 | 99 | 10 | 44 | 0 | 1 | 2 |

## e. Primary School

| Sl. No. | Units | Access to a Primary Education Facility | | Dependence for Primary Education Facility | | Full Satisfaction with Behaviour of Teachers in Govt./Aided School | Awareness of Mid-Day Meal Scheme | Utilise Mid-Day Meal (Among Aware) | Extent of Full Satisfaction With | |
|---|---|---|---|---|---|---|---|---|---|---|
| | | Govt. School | Pvt. School | Govt. School | Pvt. School | | | | Quality of School Building | Quality of Toilet |
| 1 | Balangir | 93 | 29 | 95* | 5* | 0** | # | # | 0** | 0** |
| 2 | Cluster I | 82 | 35 | 92* | 8* | 13** | # | # | 9** | 4** |
| 3 | Cluster II | 82 | 24 | 88** | 12** | 6** | # | # | 0** | 0* |
| 4 | Mayurbhanj | 92 | 8 | 100** | 0** | 3** | # | # | 6** | 3** |
| 5 | Cluster III | 100 | 18 | 99* | 2* | 0* | 100* | 94* | 3* | 0* |
| 6 | Sundargarh | 87 | 8 | 93** | 7** | 0** | # | # | 0** | 0* |
| 7 | Rural Average | 89 | 20 | 97 | 3 | 3 | 98 | 80 | 3 | 1 |
| 8 | Urban Average | 54 | 8 | 83 | 17 | 2 | 92* | 62* | 2 | 1 |
| 9 | State Average | N.A | N.A | 93 | 7 | 3 | 96 | 76 | 3 | 1 |

## *f. Child Care System*

| *Sl. No.* | *Units* | *Access of Anganwadis within 1 km.* | *Usage of Anganwadis* |
|---|---|---|---|
| 1 | Balangir | 93 | 76** |
| 2 | Cluster I | 65 | 50** |
| 3 | Cluster II | 71 | 22** |
| 4 | Mayurbhanj | 100 | 61** |
| 5 | Cluster III | 100 | 56* |
| 6 | Sundargarh | 100 | 37** |
| 7 | Rural Average | 87 | 50 |

## III.16: Punjab

### a. Drinking Water

| Sl. No. | Units | Use of Public Protected Source | Use of Private Protected Source | Public Protected Source within 100 Metres | Breakdown of Public Taps within 3 Months | Households Involved in Maintenance | Willingness to Pay More | Full Satisfaction with Public Drinking Water Facilities — Piped Water Supply | |
|---|---|---|---|---|---|---|---|---|---|
| | | | | | | | | Adequacy of Supply | Quality of Water |
| 1 | Amritsar | 4 | 93 | 4 | # | # | 50 | # | # |
| 2 | Bathinda | 25 | 70 | 24 | # | # | 35 | 0** | 3** |
| 3 | Ferozepur | 10 | 83 | 9 | # | # | 63 | # | # |
| 4 | Gurdaspur | 21 | 72 | 19 | # | # | 53 | # | # |
| 5 | Ludhiana | 14 | 85 | 14 | # | # | 59 | # | # |
| 6 | Rupnagar | 19 | 75 | 17 | # | # | 33 | # | # |
| 7 | Rural Average | 15 | 79 | 15 | # | 14 | 46 | 7 | 8 |
| 8 | Urban Average | 67 | 32 | 67 | 28 | # | 21 | 0 | 1 |
| 9 | State Average | 31 | 65 | 30 | 21 | 11* | 30 | 2 | 3 |

## b. Health Care

| Sl. No. | Units | Health Facility within 1 km. | Dependence for Minor Ailments | | Dependence for Major Ailments | | Presence in Government Health Facilities of | | Paid for Medical Services Availed (Out-Patients) | Full Satisfaction of Out-Patients with Behaviour of | |
|---|---|---|---|---|---|---|---|---|---|---|---|
| | | | Govt. Facility | Pvt. Hospitals | Govt. Facility | Pvt. Hospitals | Doctors | Paramedics | | Doctors | Paramedics |
| 1 | Amritsar | 100 | 15 | 15 | 20 | 73 | # | # | # | # | # |
| 2 | Bathinda | 71 | 30 | 9 | 47 | 48 | 95* | 95* | 30* | 0* | 0* |
| 3 | Ferozepur | 44 | 14 | 25 | 47 | 46 | 95** | 76** | 15** | 2** | 2** |
| 4 | Gurdaspur | 35 | 13 | 2 | 40 | 58 | 66** | 71** | 57** | 4** | 4** |
| 5 | Ludhiana | 59 | 31 | 5 | 63 | 24 | 80* | 77* | 63* | 7* | 7* |
| 6 | Rupnagar | 67 | 37 | 21 | 53 | 42 | 72* | 82* | 32* | 1* | 4* |
| 7 | Rural Average | 62 | 23 | 13 | 45 | 48 | 82 | 81 | 37 | 3 | 3 |
| 8 | Urban Average | 24 | 26 | 11 | 33 | 61 | 97 | 97 | 3 | 0 | 0 |
| 9 | State Average | NA | 24 | 12 | 42 | 52 | 85 | 85 | 29 | 2 | 3 |

## *c. Road Transport*

| Sl. No. | Units | Access to Cement/Tarred Road | Availability of | | | Usage of Transport Facility | | Full Satisfaction With | | |
|---|---|---|---|---|---|---|---|---|---|---|
| | | | Bus Stops | Public Bus | Private Bus | Public Bus | Private Bus | Punctuality of Govt. Buses | Frequency of Govt. Buses | Behaviour of Bus Conductors |
| 1 | Amritsar | 31 | 69 | 75 | 75 | 9 | 90 | # | # | # |
| 2 | Bathinda | 57 | 86 | 57 | 71 | 8 | 86 | # | # | # |
| 3 | Ferozepur | 44 | 31 | 69 | 81 | 20 | 52 | 0** | 0** | 0** |
| 4 | Gurdaspur | 65 | 24 | 68 | 100 | 3 | 49 | # | # | # |
| 5 | Ludhiana | 35 | 53 | 65 | 77 | 3 | 66 | # | # | # |
| 6 | Rupnagar | 67 | 78 | 88 | 100 | 47 | 47 | 12* | 8* | 9* |
| 7 | Rural Average | 50 | 54 | 71 | 86 | 15 | 65 | 8 | 6 | 8 |
| 8 | Urban Average | NA | NA | 72 | 73 | 34 | 62 | 3 | 2 | 1 |
| 9 | State Average | NA | NA | NA | NA | 20 | 64 | 5 | 4 | 4 |

## *d. Public Distribution System*

| Sl. No. | Units | PDS Outlet within 1 km. | Households Possessing Own Ration Card | Use of PDS by Card Owners At Least Once in 2 Months | Reliability of PDS Facilities | | Extent of Full Satisfaction With | | |
|---|---|---|---|---|---|---|---|---|---|
| | | | | | Regular Availability of Staple Foodgrain | Price Always Displayed | Quantity of Supplies | Quality of Supplies | Fairness of Shopkeeper |
| 1 | Amritsar | 75 | 42 | 100 | 0* | 12* | 5* | 5* | 5* |
| 2 | Bathinda | 86 | 96 | 64 | 1* | 29* | 0* | 1* | 0* |
| 3 | Ferozepur | 63 | 96 | 100 | 0 | 8 | 0 | 0 | 0 |
| 4 | Gurdaspur | 59 | 87 | 64 | 1* | 21* | 5* | 3* | 5* |
| 5 | Ludhiana | 47 | 96 | 100 | 1 | 41 | 6 | 11 | 10 |
| 6 | Rupnagar | 67 | 96 | 73 | 0 | 27 | 3 | 5 | 13 |
| 7 | Rural Average | 64 | 86 | 83 | 0 | 24 | 3 | 4 | 3 |
| 8 | Urban Average | 96 | 72 | 70 | 0 | 52 | 1 | 1 | 1 |
| 9 | State Average | NA | 82 | 79 | 0 | 29 | 2 | 4 | 3 |

## *e. Primary School*

| Sl. No. | Units | Access to a Primary Education Facility | | Dependence for Education Primary Facility | | Full Satisfaction with Behaviour of Teachers in Govt./Aided School | Awareness of Mid-Day Meal Scheme | Utilise Mid-Day Meal (Among Aware) | Extent of Full Satisfaction With | |
|---|---|---|---|---|---|---|---|---|---|---|
| | | Govt. School | Pvt. School | Govt. School | Pvt. School | | | | Quality of School Building | Quality of Toilet |
| 1 | Amritsar | 63 | 31 | 59** | 41** | # | # | # | # | # |
| 2 | Bathinda | 57 | 29 | # | # | # | # | # | # | # |
| 3 | Ferozepur | 63 | 25 | 50** | 50** | # | # | # | # | # |
| 4 | Gurdaspur | 79 | 47 | # | # | # | # | # | # | # |
| 5 | Ludhiana | 77 | 47 | 60** | 40** | # | # | # | # | # |
| 6 | Rupnagar | 94 | 38 | # | # | # | # | # | # | # |
| 7 | Rural Average | 74 | 37 | 59 | 41 | 1 | 21 | # | 1 | 2 |
| 8 | Urban Average | 33 | 34 | 52 | 48 | # | # | # | # | # |
| 9 | State Average | NA | NA | 57 | 43 | 1 | 17 | # | 1 | 1 |

*f. Child Care System*

| *Sl. No.* | *Units* | *Access of Anganwadis within 1 km.* | *Usage of Anganwadis* |
|---|---|---|---|
| 1 | Amritsar | 75 | 0** |
| 2 | Bathinda | 86 | 17** |
| 3 | Ferozepur | 50 | 6** |
| 4 | Gurdaspur | 71 | 8** |
| 5 | Ludhiana | 88 | 39** |
| 6 | Rupnagar | 61 | # |
| 7 | Rural Average | 70 | 15 |

## III.17: Rajasthan

### a. Drinking Water

| Sl. No. | Units | Use of Public Protected Source | Use of Private Protected Source | Public Protected Source within 100 Metres | Breakdown of Public Taps within 3 Months | Breakdown of Public Handpumps within 3 Months | Households Involved in Maintenance | Willingness to Pay More | Full Satisfaction with Public Drinking Water Facilities: Piped Supply: Adequacy of Supply | Piped Supply: Quality of Water | Other Protected Public Source: Adequacy of Supply | Other Protected Public Source: Quality of Water |
|---|---|---|---|---|---|---|---|---|---|---|---|---|
| 1 | Jaipur | 65 | 8 | 48 | # | 48* | 27* | 79 | 24* | 29** | 13* | 25* |
| 2 | Jaisalmer | 73 | 0 | 26 | 39* | # | 19* | 37 | # | # | 3* | 8* |
| 3 | Bharatpur | 16 | 14 | 12 | # | # | # | 73 | # | # | # | # |
| 4 | Bhilwara | 80 | 2 | 51 | # | 73 | 85 | 87 | # | # | 2 | 23 |
| 5 | Alwar | 54 | 8 | 41 | # | 69** | 8** | 75 | 16** | 35** | 4** | 12** |
| 6 | Kota | 85 | 9 | 67 | # | 46* | 33 | 71 | 9** | 43** | 22 | 53 |
| 7 | Pali | 68 | 3 | 45 | 54** | # | 41* | 51 | 7** | 41** | 3* | 9* |
| 8 | Sikar | 80 | 4 | 74 | # | # | 58 | 68 | 4* | 7* | 0** | 9** |
| 9 | Dungarpur | 96 | 0 | 57 | # | 64 | 81 | 78 | # | # | 3 | 43 |
| 10 | Rural Average | 68 | 5 | 47 | 47 | 58 | 50 | 70 | 9 | 31 | 7 | 28 |
| 11 | Urban Average | 92 | 2 | 81 | # | 67 | 55 | 85 | 9 | 16 | 4 | 28 |
| 12 | State Average | 75 | 5 | 56 | 45 | 60 | 51 | 75 | 9 | 23 | 6 | 28 |

## b. Health Care

| Sl. No. | Units | Health Facility within 1 km. | Dependence for Minor Ailments | | Dependence for Major Ailments | | Presence in Government Health Facilities of | | Paid for Medical Services Availed (Out-Patients) | Full Satisfaction of Out-Patients with Behaviour of | |
|---|---|---|---|---|---|---|---|---|---|---|---|
| | | | Govt. Facility | Pvt. Hospitals | Govt. Facility | Pvt. Hospitals | Doctors | Paramedics | | Doctors | Paramedics |
| 1 | Jaipur | 40 | 67 | 2 | 84 | 7 | 56 | 61 | 28 | 6 | 5 |
| 2 | Jaisalmer | 58 | 98 | 0 | 99 | 0 | 33* | 77* | 11* | 3* | 3* |
| 3 | Bharatpur | 53 | 52 | 14 | 76 | 9 | 50* | 58* | 34* | 9* | 8* |
| 4 | Bhilwara | 47 | 90 | 1 | 94 | 3 | 69* | 76* | 71* | 5* | 2* |
| 5 | Alwar | 47 | 72 | 7 | 92 | 6 | 65 | 71 | 26 | 9 | 11 |
| 6 | Kota | 40 | 74 | 9 | 87 | 10 | 64* | 77* | 28* | 16* | 22* |
| 7 | Pali | 50 | 89 | 2 | 93 | 1 | 45 | 75 | 6 | 3 | 4 |
| 8 | Sikar | 65 | 83 | 3 | 83 | 10 | 77* | 77* | 6* | 0* | 0* |
| 9 | Dungarpur | 77 | 98 | 2 | 96 | 4 | 57 | 84 | 91 | 1 | 2 |
| 10 | Rural Average | 52 | 79 | 5 | 89 | 6 | 57 | 73 | 35 | 6 | 6 |
| 11 | Urban Average | 65 | 60 | 5 | 81 | 14 | 64 | 71 | 28 | 3 | 3 |
| 12 | State Average | NA | 74 | 5 | 87 | 8 | 59 | 73 | 33 | 5 | 5 |

## c. Road Transport

| Sl. No. | Units | Access to Cement/Tarred Road | Availability of | | | Usage of Transport Facility | | Full Satisfaction With | | |
|---|---|---|---|---|---|---|---|---|---|---|
| | | | Bus Stops | Public Bus | Private Bus | Public Bus | Private Bus | Punctuality of Govt. Buses | Frequency of Govt. Buses | Behaviour of Bus Conductors |
| 1 | Jaipur | 44 | 48 | 61 | 91 | 7 | 76 | # | # | # |
| 2 | Jaisalmer | 58 | 50 | 25 | 81 | 13 | 68 | # | # | # |
| 3 | Bharatpur | 53 | 24 | 57 | 56 | 23 | 30 | 8** | 5** | 5** |
| 4 | Bhilwara | 24 | 18 | 41 | 91 | 7 | 82 | # | # | # |
| 5 | Alwar | 35 | 65 | 54 | 75 | 25 | 49 | 8** | 8** | 8** |
| 6 | Kota | 30 | 20 | 36 | 52 | 26 | 33 | 36** | 38** | 36** |
| 7 | Pali | 56 | 63 | 52 | 83 | 20 | 67 | 0** | 0** | 0** |
| 8 | Sikar | 47 | 41 | 55 | 67 | 32 | 43 | 0** | 0** | 0** |
| 9 | Dungarpur | 41 | 18 | 62 | 66 | 31 | 25 | 20** | 24** | 24** |
| 10 | Rural Average | 42 | 38 | 46 | 75 | 21 | 52 | 11 | 12 | 12 |
| 11 | Urban Average | NA | NA | 66 | 80 | 42 | 4 | 7 | 7 | 7 |
| 12 | State Average | NA | NA | NA | NA | 26 | 39 | 9 | 10 | 10 |

## d. Public Distribution System

| Sl. No. | Units | PDS Outlet within 1 km. | Households Possessing Own Ration Card | Use of PDS by Card Owners At Least Once in 2 Months | Reliability of PDS Facilities | | Extent of Full Satisfaction With | | |
|---|---|---|---|---|---|---|---|---|---|
| | | | | | Regular Availability of Staple Foodgrain | Price Always Displayed | Quantity of Supplies | Quality of Supplies | Fairness of Shopkeeper |
| 1 | Jaipur | 56 | 100 | 70 | 0 | 46 | 5 | 5 | 5 |
| 2 | Jaisalmer | 67 | 97 | 90 | 8 | 12 | 4 | 4 | 2 |
| 3 | Bharatpur | 59 | 100 | 93 | 0 | 29 | 6 | 4 | 7 |
| 4 | Bhilwara | 29 | 100 | 92 | 10 | 67 | 5 | 2 | 1 |
| 5 | Alwar | 35 | 99 | 96 | 1 | 43 | 4 | 4 | 5 |
| 6 | Kota | 35 | 98 | 88 | 1 | 26 | 12 | 8 | 2 |
| 7 | Pali | 50 | 88 | 64 | 1 | 35 | 7 | 6 | 0 |
| 8 | Sikar | 53 | 96 | 66 | 2 | 19 | 0 | 2 | 4 |
| 9 | Dungarpur | 29 | 99 | 96 | 35 | 67 | 7 | 6 | 5 |
| 10 | Rural Average | 46 | 97 | 84 | 7 | 40 | 6 | 5 | 4 |
| 11 | Urban Average | 90 | 97 | 81 | 4 | 60 | 10 | 10 | 10 |
| 12 | State Average | NA | 97 | 83 | 6 | 45 | 7 | 6 | 5 |

## e. Primary School

| Sl. No. | Units | Access to a Primary Education Facility | | Dependence for Primary Education Facility | | Full Satisfaction with Behaviour of Teachers in Govt./Aided School | Awareness of Mid-Day Meal Scheme | Utilise Mid-Day Meal (Among Aware) | Extent of Full Satisfaction With | |
|---|---|---|---|---|---|---|---|---|---|---|
| | | Govt. School | Pvt. School | Govt. School | Pvt. School | | | | Quality of School Building | Quality of Toilet |
| 1 | Jaipur | 88 | 53 | 65** | 35** | # | # | # | # | # |
| 2 | Jaisalmer | 86 | 7 | 93** | 7** | # | # | # | # | # |
| 3 | Bharatpur | 78 | 50 | 69** | 31** | 13** | 54** | # | 13** | 3** |
| 4 | Bhilwara | 82 | 18 | 85* | 15* | 2** | 83** | 97** | 0** | 0** |
| 5 | Alwar | 88 | 53 | 77** | 33** | # | # | # | # | # |
| 6 | Kota | 76 | 47 | 62** | 38** | # | # | # | # | # |
| 7 | Pali | 94 | 18 | 90** | 10** | 5** | 29** | # | 3** | 0** |
| 8 | Sikar | 100 | 59 | 88** | 12** | 7 | 5** | # | 2** | 5** |
| 9 | Dungarpur | 82 | 18 | 91** | 9** | 6** | 75** | # | 13** | 3** |
| 10 | Rural Average | 85 | 36 | 80 | 20 | 8 | 40 | 89 | 7 | 3 |
| 11 | Urban Average | 51 | 36 | 59 | 41 | 0* | 48* | # | 1* | 0* |
| 12 | State Average | NA | NA | 75 | 25 | 6 | 42 | 86 | 6 | 2 |

## f. Child Care System

| Sl. No. | Units | Access of Anganwadis within 1 km. | Usage of Anganwadis |
|---|---|---|---|
| 1 | Jaipur | 72 | 15** |
| 2 | Jaisalmer | 92 | 35** |
| 3 | Bharatpur | 88 | 23* |
| 4 | Bhilwara | 82 | 34* |
| 5 | Alwar | 88 | 18** |
| 6 | Kota | 70 | 11** |
| 7 | Pali | 63 | 36** |
| 8 | Sikar | 53 | # |
| 9 | Dungarpur | 82 | 31* |
| 10 | Rural Average | 76 | 26 |

## III.18: Sikkim

*a. Drinking Water*

| Sl. No. | Units | Use of Public Protected Source | Use of Private Protected Source | Use of Unprotected Source | Public Protected Source within 100 metres | Full Satisfaction with Public Drinking Water Facilities — Piped Supply | |
|---|---|---|---|---|---|---|---|
| | | | | | | Adequacy of Supply | Quality of Water |
| 1 | East District | 85 | 2 | 14 | 85 | 24 | 24 |
| 2 | North District | 86 | 1 | 13 | 86 | 14 | 22 |
| 3 | Rural Average | 85 | 2 | 13 | 85 | 20 | 23 |
| 4 | Urban Average | 100 | 0 | 1 | 100 | 12 | 28 |
| 5 | State Average | 90 | 1 | 9 | 90 | 17 | 25 |

## *b. Health Care*

| *Sl. No* | *Units* | *Health Facility within 1 km* | *Dependence for Minor Ailments* | | *Dependence for Major Ailments* | | *Presence in Government Health Facilities of* | | *Paid for Medical Services Availed (Out-Patients)* | *Full Satisfaction of Out-Patients with Behaviour of* | |
|---|---|---|---|---|---|---|---|---|---|---|---|
| | | | *Govt. Facility* | *Pvt. Hospitals* | *Govt. Facility* | *Pvt. Hospitals* | *Doctors* | *Paramedics* | | *Doctors* | *Paramedics* |
| 1 | East District | 94 | 83 | 3 | 96 | 1 | 90* | 94* | 15* | 56* | 56* |
| 2 | North District | 100 | 100 | 0 | 100 | 0 | 61 | 98 | 1 | 1 | 1 |
| 3 | Rural Average | 97 | 93 | 1 | 98 | 0 | 72 | 96 | 6 | 21 | 21 |
| 4 | Urban Average | 45 | 89 | 2 | 95 | 3 | 84 | 89 | 14 | 18 | 6 |
| 5 | State Average | NA | 92 | 2 | 97 | 1 | 77 | 94 | 9 | 20 | 16 |

## *e. Road Transport*

| *Sl. No.* | *Units* | *Access to Cement/ Tarred Road* | *Availability of* | | | *Usage of Transport Facility* | | *Full Satisfaction With* | | |
|---|---|---|---|---|---|---|---|---|---|---|
| | | | *Bus Stops* | *Public Bus* | *Private Bus* | *Public Bus* | *Private Bus* | *Punctuality of Govt. Buses* | *Frequency of Govt. Buses* | *Behaviour of Bus Conductors* |
| 1 | East District | 13 | 56 | 94 | 100 | 38 | 16 | 27* | 28* | 26* |
| 2 | North District | 46 | 8 | 39 | 8 | 47 | 7 | 0 | 0 | 0 |
| 3 | Rural Average | 28 | 35 | 69 | 59 | 42 | 12 | 15 | 15 | 14 |
| 4 | Urban Average | NA | NA | 51 | 62 | 36 | 18 | 9 | 7 | 6 |
| 5 | State Average | NA | NA | NA | NA | 40 | 14 | 13 | 13 | 12 |

## *d. Public Distribution System*

| *Sl. No.* | *Units* | *PDS Outlet within 1 km.* | *Households Possessing Own Ration Card* | *Use of PDS by Card Owners At Least Once in 2 Months* | *Reliability of PDS Facilities* | | *Extent of Full Satisfaction With* | | |
|---|---|---|---|---|---|---|---|---|---|
| | | | | | *Regular Availability of Staple Foodgrain* | *Price Always Displayed* | *Quantity of Supplies* | *Quality of Supplies* | *Fairness of Shopkeeper* |
| 1 | East District | 94 | 82 | 82 | 38 | 50 | 28 | 26 | 22 |
| 2 | North District | 92 | 86 | 86 | 47 | 98 | 2 | 3 | 7 |
| 3 | Rural Average | 93 | 84 | 84 | 42 | 70 | 17 | 16 | 16 |
| 4 | Urban Average | 98 | 78 | 79 | 18 | 85 | 11 | 9 | 10 |
| 5 | State Average | NA | 82 | 82 | 34 | 75 | 15 | 14 | 14 |

## *e. Primary School*

| Sl. No. | Units | Access to a Primary Education Facility | | Dependence for Primary Education Facility | | Full Satisfaction with Behaviour of Teachers in Govt./Aided School | Awareness of Mid-Day Meal Scheme | Utilise Mid-Day Meal (Among Aware) | Extent of Full Satisfaction With | |
|---|---|---|---|---|---|---|---|---|---|---|
| | | Govt. School | Pvt. School | Govt. School | Pvt. School | | | | Quality of School Building | Quality of Toilet |
| 1 | East District | 31 | 6 | # | # | # | # | # | # | # |
| 2 | North District | 77 | 8 | # | # | # | # | # | # | # |
| 3 | Rural Average | 52 | 7 | 84** | 16** | 16** | 77** | 36** | 19** | 14** |
| 4 | Urban Average | 17 | 39 | 33** | 67** | # | # | # | # | # |
| 5 | State Average | NA | NA | 63* | 37* | 16** | 60** | 34** | 17** | 12** |

## *f. Anganwadi*

| Sl. No. | Units | Access of Anganwadis within 1 km. | Usage of Anganwadis |
|---|---|---|---|
| 1 | East District | 94 | # |
| 2 | North District | 31 | # |
| 3 | Rural Average | 66 | # |

## III.19: Tamil Nadu

### *a. Drinking Water*

| Sl. No. | Units | Use of Public Protected Source | Use of Private Protected Source | Public Protected Source within 100 Metres | Breakdown of Public Taps within 3 Months | Household Involved in Maintenance | Willingness to Pay More | Full Satisfaction with Public Drinking Water Facilities | | | |
|---|---|---|---|---|---|---|---|---|---|---|---|
| | | | | | | | | Piped Supply | | Other Protected Public Sources | |
| | | | | | | | | Adequacy of Supply | Quality of Water | Adequacy of Supply | Quality of Water |
| 1 | Chidambaram | 94 | 1 | 88 | 44 | 1 | 29 | # | # | 11 | 30 |
| 2 | Dharmapuri | 80 | 4 | 67 | 63* | 20 | 24 | # | # | 28 | 84 |
| 3 | Madurai | 97 | 1 | 94 | 37 | 22 | 14 | # | # | 29 | 29 |
| 4 | North Arcot | 95 | 2 | 88 | 50 | 7 | 10 | # | # | 22 | 28 |
| 5 | Periyar | 91 | 4 | 81 | 72 | 39 | 16 | # | # | 40 | 43 |
| 6 | Pudukkottai | 71 | 2 | 63 | 30 | 4 | 48 | # | # | 46 | 54 |
| 7 | Salem | 92 | 1 | 89 | 40 | 29 | 19 | # | # | 81 | 82 |
| 8 | Tiruchirappalli | 97 | 1 | 80 | 34 | 5 | 27 | 60** | 61** | 60 | 69 |
| 9 | Rural Average | 90 | 2 | 81 | 46 | 16 | 23 | 54 | 59 | 38 | 50 |
| 10 | Urban Average | 90 | 2 | 89 | 18 | 25 | 7 | 51 | 60 | 55 | 65 |
| 11 | State Average | 90 | 2 | 83 | 40 | 17 | 18 | 52 | 60 | 41 | 53 |

## *b. Health Care*

| Sl. No. | Units | Health Facility Within 1 km. | Dependence for Minor Ailments | | Dependence for Major Ailments | | Presence in Government Health Facilities of | | Paid for Medical Services Availed (Out-Patients) | Full Satisfaction of Out-Patients With Behaviour of | |
|---|---|---|---|---|---|---|---|---|---|---|---|
| | | | Govt. Facility | Pvt. Hospitals | Govt. Facility | Pvt. Hospitals | Doctors | Paramedics | | Doctors | Paramedics |
| 1 | Chidambaram | 41 | 52 | 35 | 58 | 38 | 66* | 98* | 1* | 0* | 0* |
| 2 | Dharmapuri | 25 | 61 | 39 | 63 | 36 | 73 | 80 | 16 | 45 | 44 |
| 3 | Madurai | 65 | 59 | 5 | 64 | 35 | 79 | 97 | 8 | 11 | 25 |
| 4 | North Arcot | 57 | 68 | 19 | 67 | 30 | 74 | 97 | 8 | 20 | 10 |
| 5 | Periyar | 47 | 64 | 16 | 62 | 34 | 68 | 79 | 8 | 17 | 18 |
| 6 | Pudukkottai | 18 | 58 | 26 | 76 | 21 | 66 | 90 | 7 | 26 | 25 |
| 7 | Salem | 69 | 69 | 20 | 75 | 21 | 70 | 87 | 7 | 54 | 54 |
| 8 | Tiruchirappalli | 17 | 54 | 31 | 40 | 51 | 61 | 91 | 3 | 32 | 32 |
| 9 | Rural Average | 44 | 60 | 24 | 64 | 33 | 70 | 90 | 8 | 25 | 26 |
| 10 | Urban Average | 42 | 35 | 27 | 50 | 39 | 74 | 90 | 12 | 44 | 43 |
| 11 | State Average | NA | 53 | 24 | 60 | 33 | 71 | 90 | 9 | 29 | 29 |

## *c. Road Transport*

| Sl. No. | Units | Access to Cement/Tarred Road | Availability of | | | Usage of Transport Facility | | Full Satisfaction With | | |
|---|---|---|---|---|---|---|---|---|---|---|
| | | | Bus Stops | Public Bus | Private Bus | Public Bus | Private Bus | Punctuality of Govt. Buses | Frequency of Govt. Buses | Behaviour of Bus Conductors |
| 1 | Chidambaram | 71 | 69 | 74 | 40 | 65 | 9 | 0 | 1 | 1 |
| 2 | Dharmapuri | 25 | 50 | 94 | 94 | 79 | 20 | 39 | 38 | 40 |
| 3 | Madurai | 100 | 94 | 90 | 77 | 72 | 15 | 23 | 23 | 30 |
| 4 | North Arcot | 43 | 64 | 78 | 93 | 58 | 25 | 5* | 6* | 7* |
| 5 | Periyar | 75 | 94 | 94 | 88 | 85 | 8 | 30 | 30 | 33 |
| 6 | Pudukkottai | 71 | 71 | 82 | 77 | 82 | 13 | 15 | 13 | 17 |
| 7 | Salem | 56 | 75 | 94 | 75 | 84 | 12 | 59 | 59 | 59 |
| 8 | Tiruchirappalli | 25 | 67 | 90 | 92 | 55 | 46 | 13 | 11 | 21 |
| 9 | Rural Average | 58 | 74 | 88 | 84 | 73 | 18 | 25 | 25 | 28 |
| 10 | Urban Average | NA | NA | 98 | 95 | 75 | 16 | 58 | 58 | 60 |
| 11 | State Average | NA | NA | NA | NA | 73 | 17 | 34 | 34 | 37 |

## *d. Public Distribution System*

| Sl. No. | Units | PDS Outlet within 1 km. | Households Possessing Own Ration Card | Use of PDS by Card Owners At Least Once in 2 Months | Reliability of PDS Facilities | | Extent of Full Satisfaction With | | |
|---|---|---|---|---|---|---|---|---|---|
| | | | | | Regular Availability of Staple Foodgrain | Price Always Displayed | Quantity of Supplies | Quality of Supplies | Fairness of Shopkeeper |
| 1 | Chidambaram | 87 | 79 | 74 | 96 | 63 | 0 | 0 | 0 |
| 2 | Dharmapuri | 63 | 93 | 92 | 63 | 88 | 11 | 8 | 10 |
| 3 | Madurai | 63 | 87 | 88 | 76 | 86 | 24 | 24 | 23 |
| 4 | North Arcot | 100 | 85 | 88 | 80 | 67 | 4 | 4 | 6 |
| 5 | Periyar | 100 | 95 | 93 | 53 | 58 | 30 | 23 | 30 |
| 6 | Pudukkottai | 81 | 90 | 81 | 81 | 50 | 7 | 7 | 15 |
| 7 | Salem | 82 | 88 | 87 | 79 | 92 | 48 | 44 | 54 |
| 8 | Tiruchirappalli | 94 | 94 | 93 | 76 | 66 | 32 | 20 | 33 |
| 9 | Rural Average | 88 | 89 | 87 | 75 | 70 | 20 | 17 | 22 |
| 10 | Urban Average | 88 | 94 | 94 | 69 | 71 | 28 | 25 | 30 |
| 11 | State Average | NA | 90 | 89 | 73 | 71 | 22 | 19 | 24 |

## e. Primary School

| Sl. No. | Units | Access to a Primary Education Facility | | Dependence for Primary Education Facility | | Full Satisfaction with Behaviour of Teachers in Govt./Aided School | Awareness of Mid-Day Meal Scheme | Utilise Mid-Day Meal (Among Aware) | Extent of Full Satisfaction With | |
|---|---|---|---|---|---|---|---|---|---|---|
| | | Govt. School | Pvt. School | Govt. School | Pvt. School | | | | Quality of School Building | Quality of Toilet |
| 1 | Chidambaram | 67 | 33 | 58 | 42 | # | # | # | # | # |
| 2 | Dharmapuri | 75 | 6 | 97 | 4 | 44** | 100** | 100** | 11** | 4** |
| 3 | Madurai | 88 | 12 | 92 | 8 | 29** | 98** | 100** | 24** | 20** |
| 4 | North Arcot | 50 | 0 | 74 | 26 | # | # | # | # | # |
| 5 | Periyar | 63 | 19 | 93 | 7 | 40** | 91** | 100** | 36** | 22** |
| 6 | Pudukkottai | 59 | 18 | 85 | 15 | 16** | # | # | 3** | 0** |
| 7 | Salem | 88 | 0 | 98 | 2 | 67** | 100** | 100** | 69** | 23** |
| 8 | Tiruchirappalli | 75 | 8 | 90 | 11 | # | # | # | # | # |
| 9 | Rural Average | 71 | 8 | 87 | 13 | 36 | 95 | 100 | 27 | 13 |
| 10 | Urban Average | 67 | 17 | 81 | 19 | 44 | 94 | 100 | 36 | 30 |
| 11 | State Average | NA | NA | 86 | 15 | 38 | 95 | 100 | 30 | 18 |

### *f. Child Care System*

| *Sl. No.* | *Units* | *Access of Anganwadis within 1 km.* | *Usage of Anganwadis* |
|---|---|---|---|
| 1 | Chidambaram | 88 | 21** |
| 2 | Dharmapuri | 63 | 46** |
| 3 | Madurai | 88 | 31** |
| 4 | North Arcot | 14 | 52** |
| 5 | Periyar | 63 | # |
| 6 | Pudukkottai | 82 | 36** |
| 7 | Salem | 88 | 18** |
| 8 | Tiruchirappalli | 100 | 30** |
| 9 | Rural Average | 82 | 33 |

## III.20: Tripura

### *a. Drinking Water*

| Sl. No. | Units | Use of Public Protected Source | Use of Private Protected Source | Public Protected Source within 100 Metres | Breakdown of Public Handpumps within 3 Months | Breakdown of Public taps within 3 Months | Households Involved in Maintenance | Willingness to Pay More | Full Satisfaction with Public Drinking Water Facilities | | | |
|---|---|---|---|---|---|---|---|---|---|---|---|---|
| | | | | | | | | | Piped Water | | Other Protected Public Sources | |
| | | | | | | | | | Adequacy Supply | Quality Water | Adequacy Supply | Quality Water |
| 1 | North Tripura | 61 | 57 | 40 | 55** | 32** | 27 | 35 | # | # | 2 | 5 |
| 2 | West Tripura | 57 | 24 | 42 | # | 47** | 8 | 38 | # | # | 0 | 2 |
| 3 | Rural Average | 60 | 22 | 41 | 39* | 40* | 19 | 36 | 0** | 0** | 1 | 3 |
| 4 | Urban Average | 71 | 30 | 68 | # | 58** | 2** | 55 | 10* | 11 | 0** | 0** |
| 5 | State Average | 63 | 25 | 49 | 37* | 46 | 16 | 36 | 7 | 8 | 1 | 3 |

### *b. Health Care*

| Sl. No. | Units | Health Facility Within 1 km. | Dependence for Minor Ailments | | Dependence for Major Ailments | | Presence in Government Health Facilities of | | Paid for Medical Services Availed (Out-Patients) | Full Satisfaction of Out-Patients With Behaviour of | |
|---|---|---|---|---|---|---|---|---|---|---|---|
| | | | Govt. Facility | Pvt. Hospitals | Govt. Facility | Pvt. Hospitals | Doctors | Paramedicos | | Doctors | Paramedicos |
| 1 | North Tripura | 39 | 72* | 1* | 77* | 3* | 19** | 27** | 9** | 0** | 0** |
| 2 | West Tripura | 69 | 89* | 1* | 97* | 3* | 47* | 59* | 15* | 2* | 2* |
| 3 | Rural Average | 53 | 80 | 1 | 86* | 3* | 34 | 44 | 12 | 1 | 1 |
| 4 | Urban Average | 34 | 19* | 14* | 44* | 30* | # | # | # | # | # |
| 5 | State Average | NA | 59 | 6 | 72 | 13 | 39 | 47 | 12 | 1 | 1 |

## *c. Road Transport*

| *Sl. No.* | *Units* | *Access to Cement/Tarred Road* | *Availability of* | | | *Usage of Transport Facility* | | *Full Satisfaction With* | | |
|---|---|---|---|---|---|---|---|---|---|---|
| | | | *Bus Stops* | *Public Bus* | *Private Bus* | *Public Bus* | *Private Bus* | *Punctuality of Govt. Buses* | *Frequency of Govt. Buses* | *Behaviour of Bus Conductors* |
| 1 | North Tripura | 0 | 33 | 11 | 11 | 6 | 0 | # | # | # |
| 2 | West Tripura | 6 | 31 | 20 | 5 | 8 | 1 | # | # | # |
| 3 | Rural Average | 3 | 32 | 15 | 8 | 7 | 1 | # | 6** | 0** |
| 4 | Urban Average | NA | NA | 39 | 27 | 0 | 2 | - | - | - |
| 5 | State Average | NA | NA | NA | NA | 5 | 1 | 0** | 6** | 0** |

### *d. Public Distribution System*

| Sl. No. | Units | PDS Outlet within 1 km. | Households Possessing Own Ration Card | Use of PDS by Card Owners At Least Once in 2 Months | Reliability of PDS Facilities | | Extent of Full Satisfaction With | | |
|---|---|---|---|---|---|---|---|---|---|
| | | | | | Regular Availability of Staple Foodgrain | Price Always Displayed | Quantity of Supplies | Quality of Supplies | Fairness of Shopkeeper |
| 1 | North Tripura | 17 | 37 | 33 | 4* | 27* | 0* | 1* | 3* |
| 2 | West Tripura | 81 | 82 | 71 | 9 | 19 | 22 | 20 | 1 |
| 3 | Rural Average | 47 | 59 | 52 | 7 | 21 | 15 | 14 | 2 |
| 4 | Urban Average | 97 | 78 | 43 | 17* | 43* | 20* | 20* | 0* |
| 5 | State Average | NA | 65 | 50 | 10 | 27 | 16 | 16 | 1 |

## e. Primary School

| Sl. No. | Units | Access to a Primary Education Facility | | Dependence for Primary Education Facility | | Full Satisfaction with Behaviour of Teachers in Govt./Aided School | Awareness of Mid-Day Meal Scheme | Utilise Mid-Day Meal (Among Aware) | Extent of Full Satisfaction With | |
|---|---|---|---|---|---|---|---|---|---|---|
| | | Govt. School | Pvt. School | Govt. School | Pvt. School | | | | Quality of School Building | Quality of Toilet |
| 1 | North Tripura | 44 | 0 | 97** | 3** | 0** | 27** | # | 0** | 0** |
| 2 | West Tripura | 40 | 5 | 98** | 2** | 0** | 8** | # | 0** | 0** |
| 3 | Rural Average | 41 | 3 | 98* | 2* | 0* | 16* | # | 0* | 0* |
| 4 | Urban Average | 24 | 11 | 80** | 20** | 3** | 0** | # | 3** | 0** |
| 5 | State Average | NA | NA | 91 | 9 | 1 | 11 | # | 1 | 0 |

## f. Child Care System

| Sl. No. | Units | Access of Anganwadis within 1 km. | Usage of Anganwadis |
|---|---|---|---|
| 1 | North Tripura | 78 | # |
| 2 | West Tripura | 81 | # |
| 3 | Rural Average | 79 | 9** |

## III.21: Uttar Pradesh

### *a. Drinking Water*

| Sl. No. | Units | Use of Public Protected Source | Use of Private Protected Source | Public Protected Source within 100 Metres | Breakdown of Public Handpumps within 3 Months | Households Involved in Maintenance | Willingness to Pay More | Full Satisfaction with Public Drinking Water Facilities — Other Protected Sources: Adequacy of Supply | Full Satisfaction with Public Drinking Water Facilities — Other Protected Sources: Quality of Water |
|---|---|---|---|---|---|---|---|---|---|
| 1 | Aligarh | 44 | 54 | 41 | 18* | 62* | 65 | 69* | 71* |
| 2 | Bahraich | 33 | 55 | 32 | 20* | 53* | 36 | 75* | 73* |
| 3 | Ballia | 28 | 69 | 28 | # | # | 42 | # | # |
| 4 | Bareilly | 20 | 78 | 17 | # | # | 23 | # | # |
| 5 | Basti | 24 | 67 | 21 | # | # | 24 | # | # |
| 6 | Etah | 39 | 53 | 37 | 15* | 74* | 65 | 65* | 63* |
| 7 | Hardoi | 37 | 39 | 33 | 16* | 50* | 65 | 48* | 56* |
| 8 | Jalaun | 57 | 30 | 51 | 38* | 45* | 45 | 32* | 33* |
| 9 | Jhansi | 51 | 18 | 40 | 28* | 41* | 48 | 40* | 41* |
| 10 | Mirzapur | 54 | 18 | 50 | 13* | 11 | 68 | 33 | 44 |
| 11 | Pratapgarh | 37 | 37 | 32 | 10* | 5* | 46 | 20* | 23* |
| 12 | Rae Bareli | 46 | 25 | 43 | 8* | 7* | 51 | 35* | 36* |
| 13 | Saharanpur | 22 | 75 | 21 | # | # | 53 | # | # |
| 14 | Siddharthnagar | 24 | 61 | 24 | 4** | 59** | 65 | 80** | 83** |
| 15 | Rural Average | 37 | 49 | 33 | 16 | 40 | 76 | 48 | 52 |
| 16 | Urban Average | 52 | 45 | 50 | 12 | 39 | 59 | 54 | 55 |
| 17 | State Average | 39 | 49 | 36 | 16 | 40 | 63 | 49 | 54 |

## b. Health Care

| Sl. No. | Units | Health Facility Within 1 km. | Dependence for Minor Ailments | | Dependence for Major Ailments | | Presence in Government Health Facilities of | | Paid for Medical Services Availed (Out-Patients) | Full Satisfaction of Out-Patients With Behaviour of | |
|---|---|---|---|---|---|---|---|---|---|---|---|
| | | | Govt. Facility | Pvt. Hospitals | Govt. Facility | Pvt. Hospitals | Doctors | Paramedics | | Doctors | Paramedics |
| 1 | Aligarh | 18 | 10 | 5 | 30 | 26 | 76** | 9** | 39** | 39** | 49** |
| 2 | Bahraich | 18 | 8 | 4 | 41 | 57 | # | # | # | # | # |
| 3 | Ballia | 25 | 47 | 2 | 82 | 17 | 60 | 64 | 7 | 8 | 9 |
| 4 | Bareilly | 41 | 27 | 4 | 28 | 36 | 60* | 87* | 19* | 6* | 8* |
| 5 | Basti | 35 | 35 | 5 | 35 | 25 | 91* | 74* | 22* | 23* | 20* |
| 6 | Etah | 41 | 4 | 5 | 10 | 74 | # | # | # | # | # |
| 7 | Hardoi | 33 | 37 | 4 | 34 | 34 | 75 | 74 | 21 | 16 | 16 |
| 8 | Jalaun | 47 | 38 | 14 | 59 | 17 | 54** | 59** | 9** | 29** | 27** |
| 9 | Jhansi | 33 | 19 | 7 | 54 | 16 | 56** | 68** | 22** | 24** | 28** |
| 10 | Mirzapur | 29 | 20 | 2 | 58 | 33 | 90** | 79** | 13** | 6** | 8** |
| 11 | Pratapgarh | 39 | 3 | 3 | 63 | 32 | # | # | # | # | # |
| 12 | Rae Bareli | 53 | 9 | 1 | 69 | 28 | 85** | 85** | 10** | 10** | 0** |
| 13 | Saharanpur | 47 | 9 | 11 | 17 | 46 | # | # | # | # | # |
| 14 | Siddharthnagar | 14 | 23 | 5 | 35 | 26 | 87** | 84** | 13** | 0** | 0** |
| 15 | Rural Average | 34 | 21 | 5 | 42 | 34 | 72 | 76 | 17 | 16 | 17 |
| 16 | Urban Average | 23 | 11 | 2 | 37 | 47 | 73 | 78 | 12 | 29 | 24 |
| 17 | State Average | NA | 19 | 4 | 41 | 37 | 72 | 76 | 16 | 18 | 18 |

### *c. Road Transport*

| Sl. No. | Units | Access to Cement/Tarred Road | Availability of | | | Usage of Transport Facility | | Full Satisfaction With | | |
|---|---|---|---|---|---|---|---|---|---|---|
| | | | Bus Stops | Public Bus | Private Bus | Public Bus | Private Bus | Punctuality of Govt. Buses | Frequency of Govt. Buses | Behaviour of Bus Conductors |
| 1 | Aligarh | 46 | 18 | 18 | 47 | 2 | 56 | # | # | # |
| 2 | Bahraich | 25 | 12 | 17 | 39 | 2 | 33 | # | # | # |
| 3 | Ballia | 0 | 31 | 39 | 89 | 4 | 13 | # | # | # |
| 4 | Bareilly | 73 | 24 | 14 | 24 | 7 | 63 | # | # | # |
| 5 | Basti | 64 | 12 | 22 | 50 | 9 | 34 | # | # | # |
| 6 | Etah | 39 | 6 | 24 | 53 | 5 | 23 | # | # | # |
| 7 | Hardoi | 50 | 22 | 12 | 24 | 2 | 51 | # | # | # |
| 8 | Jalaun | 38 | 35 | 29 | 59 | 9 | 75 | # | # | # |
| 9 | Jhansi | 33 | 33 | 13 | 44 | 7 | 66 | # | # | # |
| 10 | Mirzapur | 33 | 14 | 26 | 74 | 4 | 13 | # | # | # |
| 11 | Pratapgarh | 0 | 17 | 26 | 58 | 7 | 14 | # | # | # |
| 12 | Rae Bareli | 0 | 12 | 55 | 50 | 4 | 4 | # | # | # |
| 13 | Saharanpur | 50 | 26 | 20 | 50 | 8 | 68 | # | # | # |
| 14 | Siddharthnagar | 70 | 21 | 29 | 41 | 20 | 11 | 3** | 3** | 5** |
| 15 | Rural Average | 44 | 20 | 25 | 50 | 6 | 37 | 18 | 19 | 19 |
| 16 | Urban Average | NA | NA | 62 | 78 | 19 | 19 | 46 | 46 | 39 |
| 17 | State Average | NA | NA | NA | NA | 8 | 34 | 28 | 29 | 26 |

## *d. Public Distribution System*

| Sl. No. | Units | PDS Outlet within 1 km. | Households Possessing Own Ration Card | Use of PDS by Card Owners At Least Once in 2 Months | Reliability of PDS Facilities | | Extent of Full Satisfaction With | | |
|---|---|---|---|---|---|---|---|---|---|
| | | | | | Regular Availability of Staple Foodgrain | Price Always Displayed | Quantity of Supplies | Quality of Supplies | Fairness of Shopkeeper |
| 1 | Aligarh | 29 | 97 | 87 | 2 | 12 | 26 | 25 | 27 |
| 2 | Bahraich | 29 | 87 | 86 | 2 | 22 | 34 | 48 | 29 |
| 3 | Ballia | 25 | 86 | 87 | 0 | 25 | 8 | 11 | 6 |
| 4 | Bareilly | 53 | 92 | 75 | 0 | 13 | 3 | 4 | 10 |
| 5 | Basti | 41 | 71 | 70 | 3 | 12 | 14 | 14 | 11 |
| 6 | Etah | 77 | 78 | 71 | 0 | 8 | 12 | 20 | 21 |
| 7 | Hardoi | 33 | 66 | 52 | 0 | 12 | 4 | 5 | 11 |
| 8 | Jalaun | 41 | 97 | 92 | 1 | 41 | 16 | 17 | 16 |
| 9 | Jhansi | 44 | 96 | 91 | 4 | 24 | 22 | 18 | 25 |
| 10 | Mirzapur | 57 | 90 | 85 | 1 | 31 | 7 | 9 | 4 |
| 11 | Pratapgarh | 56 | 91 | 90 | 1 | 15 | 6 | 10 | 5 |
| 12 | Rae Bareli | 18 | 91 | 91 | 0 | 22 | 5 | 6 | 8 |
| 13 | Saharanpur | 53 | 96 | 89 | 3 | 20 | 7 | 5 | 13 |
| 14 | Siddharthnagar | 50 | 70 | 70 | 0 | 10 | 6 | 4 | 3 |
| 15 | Rural Average | 43 | 86 | 80 | 1 | 19 | 12 | 14 | 14 |
| 16 | Urban Average | 78 | 79 | 63 | 0 | 30 | 16 | 19 | 16 |
| 17 | State Average | NA | 86 | 78 | 1 | 21 | 13 | 15 | 14 |

## e. Primary School

| Sl. No. | Units | Access to a Primary Education Facility | | Dependence for Primary Education Facility | | Full Satisfaction with Behaviour of Teachers in Govt./Aided School | Awareness of Mid-Day Meal Scheme | Utilise Mid-Day Meal (Among Aware) | Extent of Full Satisfaction With | |
|---|---|---|---|---|---|---|---|---|---|---|
| | | Govt. School | Pvt. School | Govt. School | Pvt. School | | | | Quality of School Building | Quality of Toilet |
| 1 | Aligarh | 77 | 47 | 57* | 43* | 10** | 45** | # | # | # |
| 2 | Bahraich | 61 | 17 | 90** | 10** | 45** | 61** | # | # | # |
| 3 | Ballia | 83 | 39 | 66** | 34** | 14** | 59** | # | # | # |
| 4 | Bareilly | 86 | 57 | 71* | 29* | 5* | 92* | 67** | 3* | 2* |
| 5 | Basti | 89 | 50 | 60* | 40* | 28** | 98** | 28** | # | # |
| 6 | Etah | 94 | 47 | 78* | 22* | 21* | 31* | # | 19* | 5* |
| 7 | Hardoi | 88 | 53 | 80* | 20* | 10* | 96* | 70* | 10* | 0* |
| 8 | Jalaun | 88 | 59 | 84* | 16* | 21** | 36** | # | # | # |
| 9 | Jhansi | 88 | 25 | 88** | 12** | 22** | 55** | 60** | # | # |
| 10 | Mirzapur | 68 | 32 | 73** | 27** | 3** | 56** | # | # | # |
| 11 | Pratapgarh | 74 | 26 | 77* | 23* | 2** | 66** | 61** | # | # |
| 12 | Rae Bareli | 70 | 45 | 72* | 28* | 5** | 86** | 82** | # | # |
| 13 | Saharanpur | 95 | 80 | 57** | 43** | 34** | 60** | # | # | # |
| 14 | Siddharthnagar | 82 | 41 | 85* | 15* | 10* | 92* | 19** | 11* | 8* |
| 15 | Rural Average | 82 | 45 | 74 | 26 | 15 | 68 | 58 | 18 | 8 |
| 16 | Urban Average | 40 | 43 | 47 | 53 | 7* | 43* | # | 12* | 5* |
| 17 | State Average | NA | NA | 71 | 29 | 15 | 67 | 57 | 18 | 8 |

## *f. Child Care System*

| *Sl. No.* | *Units* | *Access of Anganwadis within 1 km.* | *Usage of Anganwadis* |
|---|---|---|---|
| 1 | Aligarh | 65 | 18* |
| 2 | Bahraich | 29 | # |
| 3 | Ballia | 25 | # |
| 4 | Bareilly | 24 | 11** |
| 5 | Basti | 65 | 17* |
| 6 | Etah | 6 | # |
| 7 | Hardoi | 61 | 38 |
| 8 | Jalaun | 59 | 13** |
| 9 | Jhansi | 56 | 23* |
| 10 | Mirzapur | 21 | # |
| 11 | Pratapgarh | 22 | 10** |
| 12 | Rae Bareli | 41 | 12* |
| 13 | Saharanpur | 58 | 26* |
| 14 | Siddharthnagar | 50 | 8** |
| 15 | Rural Average | 42 | 19 |

## III.22: West Bengal

### *a. Drinking Water*

| Sl. No. | Units | Use of Public Protected Source | Use of Private Protected Source | Public Protected Source within 100 Metres | Breakdown of Public Handpumps within 3 Months | Breakdown of Public Taps within 3 Months | Households Involved in Maintenance | Willingness to Pay More | Full Satisfaction with Public Drinking Water Facilities | | | |
|---|---|---|---|---|---|---|---|---|---|---|---|---|
| | | | | | | | | | Piped Water | | Other Protected Public Sources | |
| | | | | | | | | | Adequacy Supply | Quality Water | Adequacy Supply | Quality Water |
| 1 | Bardhaman | 85 | 15 | 55 | 18 | # | 3 | 21 | # | # | 40 | 33 |
| 2 | Jalpaiguri | 57 | 18 | 53 | 14 | # | 0* | 16* | # | # | 10* | 11* |
| 3 | Malda | 71 | 23 | 48 | 19 | # | 8 | 24 | # | # | 0 | 0 |
| 4 | Midnapur | 97 | 3 | 64 | 26 | # | 1 | 15 | # | # | 19 | 14 |
| 5 | South 24 Paraganas | 97 | 3 | 54 | 23 | # | 8 | 16 | # | # | 29 | 36 |
| 6 | West Dinajpur | 74 | 24 | 62 | 15 | # | 0 | 19 | # | # | 25 | 36 |
| 7 | Rural Average | 80 | 14 | 56 | 20 | 2* | 4 | 18 | # | # | 22 | 23 |
| 8 | Urban Average | 81 | 8 | 71 | 13 | 10 | 4 | 25 | 14* | 15* | 32 | 35 |
| 9 | State Average | 81 | 12 | 61 | 20 | 8 | 4 | 21 | 14* | 15* | 25 | 27 |

## b. Health Care

| Sl. No. | Units | Health Facility Within 1 km. | Dependence for Minor Ailments | | Dependence for Major Ailments | | Presence in Government Health Facilities of | | Paid for Medical Services Availed (Out-Patients) | Full Satisfaction of Out-Patients with Behaviour of | |
|---|---|---|---|---|---|---|---|---|---|---|---|
| | | | Govt. Facility | Pvt. Hospitals | Govt. Facility | Pvt. Hospitals | Doctors | Paramedics | | Doctors | Paramedics |
| 1 | Bardhaman | 25 | 65 | 0 | 91 | 0 | 67** | 76** | 14** | 3** | 5** |
| 2 | Jalpaiguri | 50 | 56 | 9 | 84 | 13 | 38* | 54* | 10* | 14* | 5* |
| 3 | Malda | 29 | 28 | 1 | 90 | 6 | 85* | 86* | 0* | 11* | 0* |
| 4 | Midnapur | 47 | 69 | 0 | 98 | 1 | 69** | 75** | 6** | 2** | 4** |
| 5 | South 24 Paraganas | 31 | 64 | 0 | 94 | 3 | 61* | 81* | 6* | 10* | 1* |
| 6 | West Dinajpur | 18 | 43 | 1 | 96 | 1 | 29** | 80** | 0** | 23** | 0** |
| 7 | Rural Average | 33 | 54 | 2 | 92 | 4 | 60 | 75 | 6 | 10 | 3 |
| 8 | Urban Average | 57 | 35 | 7 | 79 | 11 | 72 | 83 | 18 | 14 | 4 |
| 9 | State Average | NA | 47 | 3 | 88 | 6 | 63 | 77 | 9 | 11 | 3 |

## *c. Road Transport*

| Sl. No. | Units | Access to Cement/Tarred Road | Availability of | | | Usage of Transport Facility | | Full Satisfaction with | | |
|---|---|---|---|---|---|---|---|---|---|---|
| | | | Bus Stops | Public Bus | Private Bus | Public Bus | Private Bus | Punctuality of Govt. Buses | Frequency of Govt. Buses | Behaviour of Bus Conductors |
| 1 | Bardhaman | 6 | 44 | 31 | 56 | 1 | 39 | # | # | # |
| 2 | Jalpaiguri | 19 | 31 | 31 | 31 | 0 | 32 | # | # | # |
| 3 | Malda | 6 | 12 | 0 | 6 | 2 | 28 | # | # | # |
| 4 | Midnapur | 18 | 24 | 6 | 35 | 1 | 32 | # | # | # |
| 5 | South 24 Paraganas | 38 | 38 | 19 | 38 | 13 | 33 | # | # | # |
| 6 | West Dinajpur | 6 | 18 | 6 | 6 | 3 | 30 | # | # | # |
| 7 | Rural Average | 15 | 27 | 15 | 28 | 3 | 32 | # | # | # |
| 8 | Urban Average | NA | NA | 45 | 50 | 13 | 36 | 23* | 26* | 20* |
| 9 | State Average | NA | NA | NA | NA | 7 | 33 | 25* | 28* | 27* |

## d. Public Distribution System

| Sl. No. | Units | PDS Outlet within 1 km. | Households Possessing Own Ration Card | Use of PDS by Card Owners At Least Once in 2 Months | Reliability of PDS Facilities | | Extent of Full Satisfaction With | | |
|---|---|---|---|---|---|---|---|---|---|
| | | | | | Regular Availability of Staple Foodgrain | Price Always Displayed | Quantity of Supplies | Quality of Supplies | Fairness of Shopkeeper |
| 1 | Bardhaman | 63 | 96 | 94 | 19 | 54 | 3 | 3 | 1 |
| 2 | Jalpaiguri | 44 | 87 | 84 | 14 | 59 | 0 | 1 | 1 |
| 3 | Malda | 35 | 97 | 94 | 3 | 66 | 0 | 0 | 0 |
| 4 | Midnapur | 53 | 96 | 95 | 10 | 56 | 5 | 1 | 7 |
| 5 | South 24 Paraganas | 44 | 99 | 97 | 8 | 52 | 4 | 3 | 0 |
| 6 | West Dinajpur | 29 | 98 | 98 | 3 | 48 | 1 | 1 | 1 |
| 7 | Rural Average | 44 | 96 | 94 | 9 | 56 | 2 | 2 | 2 |
| 8 | Urban Average | 96 | 89 | 69 | 8 | 57 | 2 | 1 | 4 |
| 9 | State Average | NA | 94 | 85 | 9 | 56 | 2 | 1 | 2 |

## e. Primary School

| Sl. No. | Units | Access to a Primary Education Facility | | Dependence for Primary Education Facility | | Full Satisfaction with Behaviour of Teachers in Govt./Aided School | Awareness of Mid-Day Meal Scheme | Utilise Mid-Day Meal (Among Aware) | Extent of Full Satisfaction With | |
|---|---|---|---|---|---|---|---|---|---|---|
| | | Govt. School | Pvt. School | Govt. School | Pvt. School | | | | Quality of School Building | Quality of Toilet |
| 1 | Bardhaman | 38 | 0 | 88** | 12** | # | # | # | # | # |
| 2 | Jalpaiguri | 63 | 0 | 98** | 2** | 4** | 100** | 80** | 0** | 0** |
| 3 | Malda | 65 | 6 | 95** | 5** | 3** | 74** | # | 0** | 0** |
| 4 | Midnapur | 77 | 6 | 98** | 2** | 17** | 98** | 87** | 13** | 4** |
| 5 | South 24 Paraganas | 56 | 6 | 93** | 7** | 50** | 82** | # | 35** | 3** |
| 6 | West Dinajpur | 59 | 0 | 100** | 0** | 28** | 95** | 97** | 13** | 0** |
| 7 | Rural Average | 60 | 3 | 98 | 2 | 18 | 92 | 88 | 12 | 3 |
| 8 | Urban Average | 41 | 4 | 81 | 19 | 31* | 81* | 83* | 24* | 12* |
| 9 | State Average | NA | NA | 94 | 6 | 21 | 90 | 87 | 14 | 4 |

## *f. Child Care System*

| *Sl. No.* | *Units* | *Access of Anganwadis within 1 km.* | *Usage of Anganwadis* |
|---|---|---|---|
| 1 | Bardhaman | 94 | 6** |
| 2 | Jalpaiguri | 44 | # |
| 3 | Malda | 71 | # |
| 4 | Midnapur | 59 | # |
| 5 | South 24 Paraganas | 81 | 15** |
| 6 | West Dinajpur | 82 | 7** |
| 7 | Rural Average | 72 | 15 |

# Index

**W**